Education and the social construction of 'race'

Does the education system help or hinder the fight against racism? The Swann Report (1985) is to date the most important report in the field of education for a multicultural society in Britain. *Education and the Social Construction of 'Race'* provides a careful and constructive critique of this report and of recent sociological research into racial and ethnic relations. This includes a critique of Michael Banton's recently elaborated 'rational choice' theory of 'racial' and ethnic relations.

The author undertakes a searching philosophical and sociological analysis of multicultural and antiracist education. He shows how the education system itself can reinforce racist assumptions and behaviour in society, but also argues that through educational and social reconstructing it can promote constructive cross-cultural relations.

Peter Figueroa is a Jamaican settled in Britain. He is a Senior Lecturer in Education at the University of Southampton. He has lectured and carried out research since 1968 in colleges and universities around the world, and has had many previous publications on this topic.

Education and the social construction of 'race'

Peter Figueroa

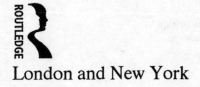

ROUTLEDGE

London and New York

First published in 1991
by Routledge
11 New Fetter Lane, London EC4P 4EE

Simultaneously published in the USA and Canada by
Routledge
a division of Routledge, Chapman and Hall Inc.
29 West 35th Street, New York, NY 10001

Typeset by NWL Editorial Services, Langport, Somerset
Printed and bound in Great Britain by
Biddles Ltd, Guildford and King's Lynn

British Library Cataloguing in Publication Data
Figueroa, Peter *1936–*
    Education and the social construction of 'race'.
    1. Great Britain. Multicultural education
    I. Title
    370.115

    ISBN 0–415–00914–6

Library of Congress Cataloging in Publication Data
Figueroa, Peter M.E.
    Education and the social construction of 'race'/Peter
    Figueroa.
    Includes bibliographical references and index.
    ISBN 0–415–00914–6
    1. Discrimination in education—Great Britain.
    2. Racism—Great Britain. 3. Educational
    equalization—Great Britain. I. Title.
    LC212.3.G7F54 1991
    370.19'342 —dc20   90–48746
                                                              CIP

For Carol, Emma and James

Contents

Tables

Acknowledgements

I would like to thank all those, individuals and institutions, who have helped to make this book possible. Above all, my warm thanks are due to my wife and my two lovely children, Emma and James. I would also like to thank the student-teachers, teachers, pupils and examiners without whose generous co-operation our research would not have been possible. I am grateful, too, to all the research assistants and efficient secretaries. The manuscript, and indeed not least my handwriting, presented the wordprocessing operators with a demanding and arduous task: very many thanks are due to them. Many thanks, too, to the publishers' readers who made helpful comments on my manuscript.

Some of the materials in this book have appeared in earlier versions in various publications, and I am grateful to the different publishers and copyright holders for permission to use them here. They have all been re-edited, in some cases very substantially. Several of them have also been expanded. The published papers are: 'Student-teachers' images of ethnic minorities: a British case study', originally published in *International Perspectives on Education and Society*, vol. 1, edited by Abraham Yogev and Sally Tomlinson, Greenwich, CT: JAI Press Inc, 1989; 'L'educazione multietnica', originally published in *Vita e pensiero*, LXXII (2): 135–52, 1989; 'Beyond bargaining in British "race" relations', originally published in *Canberra Anthropology*, 10(1): 86–95, 1987; 'Teachers' and pupils' racist and ethnocentric frames of reference: a case study', jointly written by myself and L.T. Swart, originally published in *New Community*, XIII(1): 40–51, 1986, the copyright of which is held by the Commission for Racial Equality; 'Ethnocentrism in examinations for the Certificate of Secondary Education in England: the case of History', originally published in *Educational Research Then and Now*, conference papers collected by the Australian Association for Research in Education, 103–6, 1985; 'Educational inequality of children of Caribbean background in Britain', originally published in *Dependence and Interdependence in Education – International Perspectives*, edited by K. Watson, London: Croom Helm, 1984; 'Minority pupil progress', originally published in *Education and Cultural Pluralism*, edited by M. Craft, London: Falmer Press, 1984; and 'Race relations and cultural differences: some ideas on a racial frame of reference', originally published in *Race Relations and Cultural Differences*, edited by G.K. Verma and C. Bagley, London: Croom Helm, 1984.

I am also grateful to the Australian National University for a visiting fellowship, 1984–86, which permitted me to do early work on some of the relevant materials, and which paid my expenses to present papers on some of these materials at various conferences in Australia. I must also thank the Istituto Siciliano per l'Educazione, la Formazione, l'Orientamento e la Ricerca for an invitation to travel from Australia to present the original version of a paper entitled, 'Cosa è l'educazione multietnica? – riflessioni filosofiche e sociologiche', at an international conference on *Regioni d'Europa – Frontiere Educative*, organized by them in Catania, Sicily, in 1986, under the dynamic leadership of Professoressa Maria Teresa Moscato of the University of Catania. I would also like to thank the British Council, Sydney, Australia, for a grant which made it possible for me to fly from Canberra to give the original version of a paper entitled, 'The phenomena of "race" and ethnic group: beyond rational choice', at the National Research Conference of the Australian Institute of Multicultural Affairs, Melbourne University, 1986.

Finally, I would gratefully like to acknowledge two grants from the Commission for Racial Equality and one small grant from the Southern Regional Examinations Board (SREB), which made possible the research reported in Chapters 6, 7, and 8, and in the section in Chapter 9 on '*The Townview case study* (1980–83)'. I am particularly grateful to the SREB for supporting us in looking critically at their syllabuses and examination papers. I would also like to express my thanks to my colleague who co-directed this SREB project with me, Roger J.L. Murphy, who has since moved to a Chair at Nottingham University.

Introduction

I'M NOT PREJUDICED, BUT ...

It was the year 1964. The first post-war anti-immigration law (the Commonwealth Immigrants Act 1962) had only recently been passed. The first, weak, anti-discrimination law (the Race Relations Act 1965) was not yet in force. A non-English student was making a phone call in a red telephone booth in north London. Twenty-eight years old, he had recently arrived from continental Europe. There he had done a first degree in Philosophy at the Pontifical Urban University in Rome, where there were students from forty or more countries from around the world. Then he had done research in the phenomenological philosophy of Maurice Merleau-Ponty at the University of Louvain in Belgium, and had gone on to Paris to attend Merleau-Ponty's lectures. He had also taught English to German children in two grammar-type schools in West Berlin and in Bielefeld.

In 1955 he had sailed across the Atlantic on the Reina del Pacífico, a steamship crowded with migrants. But he had only been in-transit in the 'mother country' on his way through London and Paris to Rome. Now he had come on an overseas Leverhulme entrance studentship to do a conversion course in Sociology, and then a doctorate, at the London School of Economics and Political Science (LSE), and he needed 'digs'.

'Hello, I'm just ringing to enquire about the flatlet ...'
'Where are you from?'
'Jamaica.'

I could imagine the image that came into her mind.

'I'm not prejudiced, but we have people from Australia, South Africa, Germany, Sweden ... so you may not ...'
'Listen, I've lived and worked and studied in Italy, Belgium, France, Germany ... and I speak the languages. So if you don't mind, could I just come and see the room?'

When I got there the landlady took care to introduce me to an Italian young lady who, as it happened, was just coming out of a room near to the one I was interested in. We exchanged a few pleasantries in Italian. I took the room.

Some months later some tension developed. between the landlady and myself. Late one afternoon when I got back from LSE a lanky Swedish girl who was helping the landlady ran up to me with a letter. I was touched at her concern, and thanked her warmly. When I opened the letter it was a terse note from a solicitor giving me notice – without any reasons – to vacate within one week. I rang the Jamaica High Commission, but was told: 'There's nothing that can be done. It happens to us all the time'. This incident and the ones which follow can be accounted for with the help of my concept of the racist frame of reference which is discussed in Chapter 2 below. The incident also illustrates power relations. Frames of reference and power relations operate conjointly and interactively.

The hunt for accommodation was on again. I rang about a 'bed-sitter' in Belsize Park. The woman asked where I was from.

'Jamaica.'
'I'm not prejudiced, but at my age I could not cope with the tensions.'
'Listen, I've lived and worked and studied in different parts of Europe ... '

I got the room. The landlady was an elderly unmarried woman, one of the first female graduates of LSE. We became good friends, and I stayed there for three years, moving only to go and live in Haringey while I was doing the follow-up door-to-door interviews of West Indian and other school-leavers for my doctoral research.

MY EARLY 'RACE' RELATIONS RESEARCH

This research (Figueroa 1968, Figueroa and McNeal 1969, Figueroa 1974, Figueroa 1976) was funded by the Institute of Race Relations as part of the Survey of Race Relations (see Rose *et al.* 1969). The purpose of my study (Figueroa 1974: 2) was to investigate the prospects of West Indian school-leavers in Britain, and the extent to which British racism was an important factor accounting for these prospects. I started preliminary library work and field-work for this study, in particular the development of research instruments, in 1965/6. The preliminary field-work took place in a secondary school and in youth clubs in the Paddington area.

With the help of statistics of 'immigrants' in schools made available informally and confidentially by an HMI, I selected fourteen schools for study in, and bordering on, Islington and Lambeth. I then wrote to the ILEA for the necessary permission. More than a month later the response came back in the negative: it was not 'at all a suitable time to conduct research in London schools into questions of employment of West Indian school-leavers, a matter which ... the Youth Employment Service of the Authority is constantly watching'. In a separate letter commenting on my draft questionnaire I was told: 'asking questions in schools, specifically about racial topics, may serve to create racial problems where they did not previously exist'. Objections were also raised to asking questions about pupils' home circumstances and even religion. When I made the politic changes, and pursued the matter, the following response came back, 5 months after the initial application:

> We are in a transition period as far as immigrant young people are concerned. Employers have had very few young people so far who have had most of their education in this country and their attitudes tend to be affected by their impressions of earlier employees who were recruited just after they arrived here ... it would not be wise ... to take part in a survey at a time which may not be typical of the future, or to do anything that might prejudice employers' attitudes.

This suggests that the ILEA had something to hide, that they were inclined to 'blame the victim', and that they were unable to see that the employers' attitudes had much deeper roots than their experience with one set of employees, or than the asking of a question designed to investigate stereotypes. Indeed those attitudes and the reactions to such a question would have been 'framed' by deeper-seated assumptions and relations. In the event the study finally took place, starting in July 1966, in ten schools in Haringey, which was outside the area controlled by the ILEA. The field-work was completed in 1967 with the interviewing of a matched sample of 'White' and 'Caribbean' pupils after they had left school.

Shortly after all the field-work had been finished I took a supply job teaching French and German to 'O' and 'A' level pupils at the Stationers' Company's School in Haringey. This had been a boys' grammar school and had recently been amalgamated with the upper part of a boys' secondary modern school, one of the schools I had studied, to form a comprehensive school. Most of the 'immigrants' continued to be housed on what had been the secondary modern school's site. My teaching took place in the old grammar school, where facilities were superior.

This was about the time of Enoch Powell's highly controversial and bloodstained speeches on 'immigration'. One day, as I sat minding my business at a desk in the staff room, I overheard some of the teachers lamenting about the new 'rubbishy intake'. One of the older teachers then said that he agreed with Enoch Powell – except that he did not go far enough: the gas chambers were what was needed. I could as well not have been there. Wrongly, no doubt, I kept quiet.

The main findings of my study of school-leavers were (Figueroa 1974: 2, 3 and 400–1) that the West Indians experienced worse prospects than the Whites, even though the Whites came from deprived backgrounds similar to those of the West Indians. I concluded (Figueroa 1974: 3) that a 'complex, multi-dimensional situation seems to exist, in which one of the important factors accounting for the depressed prospects of the West Indian school-leavers is, apparently, British racism'. In fact, I found, first, that most of the respondents, especially the White school-leavers, 'alleged that "immigrants" were discriminated against', and, second, that the White respondents seemed to share a racist 'frame of reference regarding West Indians, and "immigrants" generally' (Figueroa 1974: 2 – see also 409–10).

My concept of racist frames of reference (see Chapter 2 below) informed, and further developed out of, this research into West Indian school-leavers. My concept of ethnicist frames of reference (Chapters 2 and 3) was a logical later development. I found Blumer's work (1939, 1953, 1955, 1958 and 1961) particularly germane to my way of thinking. However, I got the term 'frame of reference' from Richmond (1954: 3–7, 19, 60–1, 150–2 and 169), although I developed it differently. It had also been used by others, in particular by social psychologists such as Newcomb and Charters (1952). I originally defined it (Figueroa 1974: 34–9) as a lived, largely taken-for-granted world view, or ideology, which has social and structural consequences (and supports), and which consists of four closely interrelated dimensions: the evaluative, the cognitive, the affective and the conative. It was not an individual phenomenon, but a group one. It was in such terms that I saw racism, and I indicated that the combating of racism must include working along all four dimensions (Figueroa 1974: 418–19). This stress, not only on the shared cognitive dimension, but also on the affective dimension and on shared values, as well as on the shared behavioural or conative dimension, pre-dates the work of Jeffcoate (1976, 1979a, 1979b), of Cohen and Manion (1983) and of Lynch (1986, 1987).

When my thesis was ready, I sent a copy to the Institute of Race Relations, which by then had had its 'palace revolution' (Sivanandan 1974). Sivanandan, the new Director, wrote back saying the situation had changed, and the issue was now 'the State's . . . pre-occupation . . .

with the "muggers" . . . the Black youths who refuse to work, because the work is "shit-work"'. Here was an example, from the Left, of dichotomous thinking – as though 'the State's . . . pre-occupation . . . with the "muggers"' and racism (understood in a sense which highlighted the ideological in terms of group frames of reference) were mutually exclusive and unrelated.

From this early research and these earlier experiences, on the basis of my academic concerns and my concerns as a Jamaican settled in Britain, my interest in 'race' and ethnic relations and in multicultural and antiracist education grew. This interest has been strengthened now that I have two children both born in England, one in 1982 and the other in 1986, and both of part West Indian background, but with a White English mother. I now realize that in Britain such children cannot usually take their identities for granted in the same way that White English children can. For instance, one day when my daughter was about 4 or 5 years old and we were living in West Sussex, she was playing out at the front with two little White girls a little older than herself. I went to get her for lunch and just caught the tail-end of their conversation. One of the other girls was saying '. . . . but you can't be English, 'cos you're Black'. I tried to explain that the English are constituted of all sorts, and some are Black.

THE PRESENT VOLUME

The collection of papers which I have brought together in this book indicates my interest, addresses some of my main concerns, and develops some of my key ideas, in these fields of 'race' and ethnic relations and of multicultural and antiracist education. Although these papers were not originally written as parts of a single volume, they do represent a unity of concern and a unity of thought. They have been extensively edited, rewritten, modified and updated for this book.

'Race' as a social construction

The theme of the book has three major aspects. The first is that 'race' is a social construction (see especially Chapter 2). In 'race' relations one is concerned not just with individual prejudice, nor merely with labelling, but with assumptions, and ways of seeing, interrelating and interacting that are shared within the 'in-group'.

That 'race' is a social construction implies two things. On the one hand 'race', as distinct merely from, for example, skin colour, has no biological or scientific validity. Rather, it is part of a group myth or of a distorted world view shared by a particular group, or built into a particular social system. In a sense, therefore, it is 'ideological' – but with at least two provisos. The first is that the ideological, in the broadest sense, is not understood as detached from (whether as subservient to or determinant of) actual material relations, and that ideology is not understood simply as discourse (see Giddens 1979: 183) and discourse is not understood as merely subjective or as lost in the realm of 'the dogmatic mystification of post-hermeneutic skepticism' (Dillon 1988: 176). Even distorted discourse relates to 'modes of lived existence': is formed by them and informs them. The second proviso is that, modifying Giddens' understanding of ideology (Giddens 1979: 188), we allow that the ideological in the strict sense refers to the mobilization uncritically by *any* group of 'structures of signification' to legitimate its sectional interests. However, such mobilization has particular import- ance where the group concerned is hegemonic, and the interests in question are inequitable *vis-à-vis* the dominated group. Furthermore, it is not the case that ideology is simply a secondary phenomenon serving to sustain forms of domination. The two are mutually interdependent.

On the other hand, but closely related to the above, 'race' has 'material' reality in so far as actual social relations, status and the distribution of resources and power are articulated along lines ideo- logically defined as 'racial'. In other words, 'races' may be real groups (and not simply some group's categories); but they are based on *social* processes rather than on 'biological' or 'natural' factors or forces.

Similar statements may be made regarding 'ethnicity'. The major difference from 'race', however, is that the factor assumed as determinant is not drawn from the world of natural discourse – as is, for instance, 'colour', physical characteristic or phenotype – but from that of the discourse of culture (see Chapter 3). This makes ethnicism both more and less 'ideological' than racism. It is more ideological in so far as culture, unlike phenotype, is squarely of the order of human, purposive creation and has values and concepts at its core. But it is also less ideological in so far as culture by its very nature is inherently of social significance, whereas phenotype is not, and only gains social significance through an ideological transformation. However, in 'ethnicity', culture also undergoes an ideological transformation.

Schooling and the construction and 'deconstruction' of 'race'

The second major aspect of this book's theme is that 'race', racism and ethnicism can be sustained and even constructed or 'reconstructed' through schooling and more widely within the education system (see

Chapters 3 and 6–9). This can occur through the failure of the school to raise awareness about, and to challenge, racism and ethnicism. It can also come about through messages actually and positively transmitted, whether these are only indirect and covert or more direct and overt, and whether they occur in the classroom, through the assessment procedures, through the physical features of the 'plant', through the school's patterns of relations, or whatever. It can, moreover, come about through the procedures, modes of organization, practices and interrelations – not just as messages or symbolic systems, but as actual modes of lived experience, of selection, allocation, etc.

The third major aspect of this book's theme, remaining perhaps mainly at the level of a sub-text, is that the education system, and the individual school can play and should play an important part in combating racism and inequality, and in furthering the commitment to and mobilization of a range of basic social values such as equality, freedom, solidarity if not fraternity, pluralism and openness (see, especially, the latter parts of Chapters 3, 6, 8 and 9, as well as Chapters 4 and 5). Just as school processes can contribute directly or indirectly to the social construction of 'race', of racist and ethnicist frames of reference, of racist and ethnicist structures and relations, so too can they help to 'deconstruct' them – that is, to uncover their underlying assumptions, values and affects, and their driving forces, as well as to dismantle them and replace them with more equitable values, assumptions, relations and structures.

Organization of the book

Some of the chapters which follow discuss relevant theoretical issues (Chapters 1–5). Others present data which illustrate the 'ideological' and 'material' relations and processes in Britain, especially within the education system (Chapters 6–9).

Chapter 1 provides a sharp critique of Banton's 'rational choice' theory of 'racial' and ethnic relations. Chapter 2 develops an essay towards a different way of understanding. It gives central importance to the notion of frames of reference.

Chapter 3 examines the notion and rationale of multicultural and antiracist education. In it I discuss both sociological and philosophical issues, and develop my own view on the matter. On this background, Chapter 4 provides a critical discussion of the Swann Report (DES 1985a).

Chapter 5 raises some general issues about the project of changing attitudes or of transforming frames of reference. This is done with special reference to teachers. Chapters 6–8 report on empirical work in which I have been involved: Chapter 6 on the perceptions student-teachers have of Black people and of education for a multicultural society; Chapter 7 on 'race' and ethnic relations in one school, and in particular on the racist, ethnicist and ethnocentric frames of reference that teachers and especially pupils there seemed to hold; and Chapter 8 on the question of bias in school-leaving examinations.

Finally, Chapter 9 examines the literature on 'achievement' and 'underachievement'. It takes the view, in conclusion, that the situation would be better understood (and could then be better addressed) by focusing on the concept of educational inequality – and by asking how best equality (that is equity) *and* quality (including openness and richness) could be promoted.

Peter Figueroa
Southampton

1 Beyond rational choice

BANTON'S 'RATIONAL CHOICE' THEORY

One of the weaknesses in many of the debates in Britain during the post-war period about minority ethnic pupils in the British school system, and about multicultural and antiracist education has been insufficient attention to important underlying philosophical issues and theoretical issues of a sociological nature. Michael Banton, a senior British sociologist, is one of the few sociologists in Britain to have focused on issues of 'race' relations throughout most of this post-war period (for example, Banton 1955, 1959, 1967, 1977, 1983a, 1985a and 1987); but he has only given passing attention to educational issues (for example Banton 1983b). Although a dialogue with his views on 'racial' and ethnic relations is not a main purpose of this book, these views, at least in his more recent publications, provide an excellent and distinguished example of a dominant way of thinking in many quarters today – one which is very different from the philosophical and theoretical approaches which underpin the views I develop in this book. It seems, therefore, a useful starting point to discuss briefly and critically Banton's recent and influential 'rational choice' theory of 'racial' and ethnic relations (see, for example, Banton 1983a, 1985a and 1987) – especially since he has claimed that one of the ways in which this theory has merits over other theories is that it has clear implications for social policy and practice (Banton 1983a: 389).

According to Banton's 'rational choice' theory (Banton 1983a, 1985a and 1987), 'racial and ethnic relations' are not a special kind of social relations (for example, Banton 1985a: 135). 'Physical and cultural differences do not of themselves create groups or categories' (Banton 1983a: 105). Race and ethnicity are not natural or fixed categories. It is only when physical and cultural differences 'are given cultural significance and used by humans for their own purposes that social forms result' (Banton 1983a: 105). It is when they are used to allocate roles that groups or categories arise.

Thus 'racial and ethnic relations' need, according to Banton, to be seen within a general theory of social relations. For Banton the best such theory is the 'rational choice' or exchange theory of social relations. The starting point for this is 'a view of social action as the allocation of scarce means to competing ends' (Banton 1987: 122). The first assumption of the theory is that of optimization, namely that 'individuals act to obtain maximum net advantage' (Banton 1987: 122) – that is, to increase their own benefits and to reduce their costs. But they live in a world of scarcity. They are thus in competition with each other. However, as they differ, having differing tastes and resources, they bargain and exchange goods and services with each other, in pursuit of their own advantage (Banton 1983a: 136; 1985a: 121). In other words, they act 'rationally' (see Banton 1983a: 108) – or, if they do not, one must ask: at what cost? The important point is that 'rational choice' theory looks at all behaviour in terms of 'rationality' (Banton 1983a: 108). Banton concedes that all behaviour may not be 'rational'; but he nevertheless clearly seems to think that 'rationality' is the basic distinguishing feature of human behaviour, and that the criterion of 'rationality' may be applied to all behaviour.

The second assumption is that past action constrains present choice (and present action future choice). One implication of this second assumption is that the resources available to a person constrain that person's options: those who command more resources have more alternatives. According to Banton another implication is that under normal circumstances 'changes will result in greater rationalization of social relations, reducing inconsistencies and resolving conflicts in the social pattern' (Banton 1987: 122), for individuals will always be seeking the 'best buy'.

Furthermore, this 'rational choice' theory relies upon the principle of prescriptive altruism. This is 'a rule requiring recognition of binding mutual interdependence and a willingness to forego selfish gratification' (Banton 1987: 124). This is necessary since: 'Humans can develop their potential only if they are brought up in social groups' (Banton 1987: 124).

Another basic principle underlying the theory is that of group alignment. Individuals band together to achieve their ends, through collective action (Banton 1985a: 13; 1987: 124). Or they 'follow a strategy that assumes others will engage in such action ... Social groups result from ... the goal-seeking actions of individuals' (Banton 1987: 124). In fact, social groups are only coalitions, and individuals can weaken, strengthen or cross group boundaries. Relationships between different parties (individuals or groups) 'are maintained only as long as they are rewarding to the parties' (Banton 1983a: 403).

Banton seeks with his 'rational choice' theory to account only for aggregate behaviour, not for individual acts (Banton 1983: 108–9; 1987: 139). This does not mean that the group is the unit of analysis, but that the concern is with overall patterns, which are the outcome of individual variations. The approach is one of methodological individualism, which accepts that groups 'are constituted from individual behaviour and are subject to continual change as individuals respond to changes in their circumstances' (Banton 1987: 140). The starting point is individual behaviour, but recognition is given to the constraints on it and to 'the way in which individuals are organised in collectivities' (Banton 1987: 140).

Social relations generally are treated as though they are a form of market relations. Banton recognizes, however, that, if uncontrolled, the 'free market' is ultimately socially destructive – for each individual would be fighting just for himself or herself. Banton (1983a: front fly-leaf) therefore refers to Meade (1973: 52) with approval, quoting him as follows: 'the ideal society would be one in which each citizen developed a real split personality, acting selfishly in the market place and altruistically at the ballot box'. One needs on the one hand 'economically efficient' selfishness, and on the other an ethical search for justice and a rule of voting to choose between conflicting views.

The central argument in Banton's (1983a: 12) theory is that 'competition is the critical process shaping patterns of racial and ethnic relations'. Within the framework of this theory Banton sets out five characteristics of 'racial' and ethnic relations, and indicates five overlapping theories corresponding to these. The five characteristics are the definition of 'racial' and ethnic groups by *boundaries*, in terms of *identification signs*, *perceived social location*, *existence in historical time*, and *differential values*.

Thus, there is first of all the theory of *boundaries* according to which physical and cultural differences are used to create groups and categories, with ethnic groups resulting from inclusive processes and 'racial' categories from exclusive ones. When groups encounter, individuals identify with their own group, since that is where the rewards lie. The boundaries are affected by 'the form and intensity ' of competition' (Banton 1983a: 104; 1987: 126) which takes place when groups interact. Boundaries tend to dissolve when people compete as individuals. Such competition is called bargaining (Banton 1985a: 13). But elsewhere Banton (for example, 1985a: 124) refers to bargaining between groups. When people compete as groups, boundaries tend to harden and the possibilities of inter-group 'harmony' are reduced (Banton 1983a: 136; 1985a: 13). 'The essence of group competition is monopoly' (Banton 1983a: 123).

It is not the ethnic or 'racial' content of the identity that is important, but how the group processes (and especially the processes of inclusion and exclusion) work. As already indicated it is not the physical or necessarily the cultural differences as such that are important, but the social significance they are given and how they are used to allocate roles.

Banton also seems to imply that there is a 'race' relations cycle. In 'the earlier phases' of the encounter between 'groups' there is group competition. Subsequently, comes 'racial' ideology as a rationalization (Banton 1983a: 206). Then in later phases, group competition yields place to individual competition – and to the dissolving of boundaries (see Banton 1983a: 208).

According to the theory of *signs*, relations between groups vary with 'the characteristic that is the basis for group formation' (Banton 1987: 127). It is typical of groups based on 'race' that membership is involuntary and is transmitted in families. Also the same features have different 'sign value' in different societies, it being 'human societies which rather arbitrarily draw distinctions and use them to create or reinforce social discontinuities' (Banton 1987: 128).

The theory of *categories* deals with 'discontinuities in the assessment of status' as between groups (Banton 1987). There can either be a two-category system or a multi-category system. In the former the general assumption that one side can only gain at the loss of the other helps to maintain the categories. 'The solidarity of one group evokes the solidarity of the other so that conflicts easily escalate' (Banton 1987: 128). The categories in multi-category systems are mostly based upon occupational monopolies. Further: 'While the weaker groups may enter into coalitions to advance their political interests it may not be possible to maintain them for long' (Banton 1987: 129).

The theory of *group power* (Banton 1987: 129) 'is concerned with the terms on which members of groups exchange goods and services, and with the way power affects the implicit bargaining about price'. Banton refers to power as 'the securing of submission or compliance' (Banton 1987: 129) and he speaks of 'the superior party' exercising power 'in order to obtain a service' (Banton 1987: 129). The things that power derives from 'can all be considered as resources' (Banton 1987: 130). This includes both natural and human resources. Resources can remain unharnessed, or they can be mobilized. An individual will join in group mobilization 'only when he expects the benefits of his participation to exceed the costs' (Banton 1987: 136, where he cites Hechter *et al.* 1982).

Finally, in the theory of *discrimination*, Banton (1987: 132–3) holds that: 'The intensity and form of competition in a market influence the amount of discrimination that is possible and can reduce or increase any motivation to discriminate. In a competitive market the incidence of discrimination should decline.' But Banton (1987: 133) also holds that 'buyers' and 'sellers' avoid risky decisions which may result in costly mistakes. Furthermore, he (Banton 1987: 134) states that: 'People generalize from information available to them, often despite its being insufficient, and this can set up a self-fulfilling prophecy.'

Banton (1987: 135) insists that discriminatory behaviour may be rational behaviour. Thus he cites the example of an employer who discriminates against a particular group because of a *belief* that the members of that group will be bad employees. Banton maintains that such an employer has acted rationally 'judged by the conventional criteria of business reality', even if not from the standpoint of society.

He does grant that: 'Racial discrimination can be seen as a public bad' from the point of view of society as a whole (Banton 1987: 135). 'Racial harmony' will then be the public good to be sought. It is, however, difficult to define positively. Hence 'it is better to define racial harmony as an absence of discrimination and other features which embitter social relations or may come to do so' (Banton 1987: 135). He does imply that among such undesirable 'pollutants' is 'grossly unfair relations' even if they 'may for a time appear harmonious' (Banton 1987: 135).

CRITIQUE OF BANTON'S THEORY

First of all the name, 'rational choice' theory, is at the least misleading. In attempting to justify the name and clarify the theory, Banton (1985c: 590) indicates that he preferred 'rational choice' over 'social exchange' because 'exchange is only one part of the domain of choice'. At the same time he (1985c: 590) asserts that it is not a theory of choices, but rather 'a theory of boundaries'. Subsequently Banton (1987: 122) has stated that the name 'rational choice theory', is used 'to indicate that this theory is a member of a family of theories which start from a view of social action as the allocation of scarce means to competing ends'. He (1987: 123) also says that: 'The rationality . . . in question is not a property of some actions rather than others, but a criterion for studying the pattern of behaviour over time.'

But since the words 'rational' and 'rationality' already have folk and technical meanings, it is confusing to use them in yet some other way. Furthermore, why use the word 'choice' if the theory is not a theory of choices? And why apply the criterion of 'rational choice' to certain patterns of actions if we know they do not actually involve rational choice?

However, the problem is not just one of names, but also of substance. Banton *is* concerned with choice and *does* make assumptions about rationality. Thus he (1985c: 591) concedes that he 'did not sufficiently specify the mechanisms by which individual choices can generate social patterns', and he clearly considers that group boundaries are affected by individual choices.

More centrally, Banton uses 'rational' in a narrow sense with two aspects: self-interest and instrumentality. Instrumentality, of course, corresponds to the notion of the allocation of scarce means to competing ends. But self-interest goes beyond this and narrows down this principle considerably, since the ends of actions are not necessarily in the interest of the actor, nor necessarily perceived by the actor as so being: they may, for instance, be in someone else's interest, and may be perceived as such. One may genuinely and without regard to one's own self-interest be motivated by other-interest or group interest. For example, many parents in their day-to-day lives put the interest of their offspring above their own. Even the sociobiologists' attempt to account for this in terms of the promotion of one's own genes would require a notion of species-interest or ancestor-interest rather than pure self-interest.

However, even action based on other-interest or group-interest can be 'rational' in the sense of being based on instrumental calculations. It is perfectly possible to be concerned with the economic allocation of scarce resources to ends which are not self-interested. Means–ends calculative maximization of self-interest is but a sub-set of the means–ends calculative maximization of ends.

There are actually two closely interrelated sets of issues here: that of self-interest versus other-interest (or of egotism versus altruism), and the more general one of the relations of the individual and the social. Banton recognizes that there is a problem, but his theoretical solutions are not satisfactory.

One approach which he takes is to endorse, as we have seen, Meade's view that the good citizen requires a split personality (Banton 1983a: front fly-leaf). As a sociological or economic theory, or as a social philosophy, this is untenable, and illustrates the inherent contradictions of dichotomous thinking. How is supposedly economically efficient selfishness to hold together with the ethical search for justice?

The ethical search for justice implies taking every person, including all others, as an end in themselves rather than as a means. This is ultimately what equality means. That concept will be further explored in

Chapter 3. But in economically efficient selfishness – or 'rationality' in the narrow sense given to it in 'rational choice' theory – the supreme end and value is oneself; and everything else and all other persons are reduced to means to that end.

Rational choice theory with its basic principle of economically efficient selfishness implies at base all-out war of everyone with everyone else. The principles on which it claims society is based would lead to the disintegration of society. Rather than the anti-egalitarian, closed and inherently conflictural principle of one's own advantage above everything else, what is needed, as I shall argue in Chapter 3, are egalitarianism and openness. One can just as rationally work towards these goals as towards self-interest, and it is only by taking them as basic values that one can consistently expect constructive interrelations between individuals and groups.

More recently Banton (1987: 123–4) has approached the 'problems' of self-interest versus other-interest and of the individual versus the social by adopting the principles of 'prescriptive altruism' and of 'group alignment', as we have seen. But, as stated, these do not overcome the basic contradictions of the dichotomous thinking. They are clearly secondary to the prime assumption that social action is driven by the principle of the maximization of one's own net advantage. The account offered of the generation of the principle of prescriptive altruism in the mother–child relationship is a purely contingent and empirical one; whereas the assumption of optimization is stated as an inherent and necessary one. Similarly, the principle of group alignment is offered merely as a matter of convenience, secondary to the assumption of optimization, and, indeed, merely as a means by which individuals can attain their ends.

Thus, in the utilitarian conception, the social would seem to be secondary to the individual, reducible to the individual, merely a contingent coming together of individuals each in pursuit of their own maximum net advantage. But the social is neither simply the sum of individual action, nor is it something contingently added on. The human person is inherently social. Human beings necessarily become what they are in interaction with others. They always appear in a given socio-cultural situation, and their access to reality is always through a pre-given culture, which is of course social in origin, in its functions, and in so far as it is shared. (Yet each individual makes this culture his or her own, selectively, and modulates or modifies it – though in interaction with others.) Even the so-called basic wants or needs of the human person are inevitably culturally mediated – as can be seen, for instance, in diet and in the beliefs, taboos and practices that surround food, raw or cooked. It is not possible to attribute priority either to the individual or to the social, and neither can one be reduced to the other. This theme will be further developed in Chapter 2.

Banton's 'rational choice' theory is narrow, not only in the sense that it limits its criterion of rationality to self-interested instrumentality (omitting non self-interested instrumentality), but also in so far as it neither directly addresses non-instrumental rationality nor non-rational behaviour. Rationality is not just a matter of self-interest nor of instrumentality, but also of value orientation, value-consistency, and correctness with reference to certain criteria – such as the rules of logic and of empirical knowledge.

Furthermore, Banton's 'rational choice' theory is also narrow in so far as it largely neglects the bases on which even self-interested calculative behaviour takes place. All action and choice – instrumental or not, reflective or 'spontaneous', rational or non-rational – take place within the context of values, symbolic systems, beliefs and assumptions, all of which in effect positively define the possibilities and set the limits. This is central to any theory of 'race' and ethnic relations, and I refer to it under the notion of frames of reference. I shall develop this notion in Chapter 2.

Such frames of reference, shared by the members of a group, can help explain behavioural and social patterns, whereas the notion that people choose to maximize their own advantage cannot of itself explain such patterns – unless, that is, we know what people consider to be in their advantage. Indeed, although Banton states that it is not the content of the ethnic group identity that is important, he notes (1983a: 361) that 'rational choice' theory cannot predict behaviour without information about people's specific values and preferences. He (1983a: 403) also points out that social control is not just about rewards and punishment, as might be implied by a theory of motivation based on the pursuit of self-interest and on means–ends calculations, but is also about values. Indeed, I would add that, in choice and action, questions of social acceptability and of ethical correctness may often be overriding considerations. People often act on the basis of values apprehended as absolutes. Banton (1985b: 537) does recognize this in a later publication, but still remains puzzled, for instance, by 'the appeal of nationalism' over the past two centuries. Banton (1983a: 115) accepts as a limitation of his theory that it 'cannot explain the initial values which the groups bring to the encounter'.

A further point is that action may also be 'non-rational' in the sense that it may – adapting Weber's typology – be guided by tradition, habit, affect, the influence of a charismatic figure or some other authority.

Indeed, conflicts in self-interest, as for instance between short-term and long-term self-interest, are often resolved or bypassed by action based not only on values perceived as absolute, but also on taken-for-granted social norms, perceived social pressures, traditions, authority, affect or habit. Moreover, even action based on self-interest may be 'blind' – and in that sense not rational at all. It may in particular be based on affect, rather than on information and calculation.

Furthermore, action may be manipulated or coerced. One may be in a position of such powerlessness that one has virtually no choice at all, or at least that one's alternatives are severely limited. Smith (1985: 486) castigates Banton for formulating a general theory of 'race' and ethnic relations 'as if they are always and everywhere freely created by the rational choice of all parties involved'. As Smith (1985: 495–7) points out, power differentials and their operation are central to understanding group action and interaction – particularly in 'race' and ethnic relations.

Banton does, as we have seen, confront the issue of power in a later publication (1987: 129–132) where he puts forward a 'rational choice' theory of group power. This is formulated in terms of how power, which is seen as deriving from a variety of resources, affects bargaining and the price in any exchange. However, the metaphor of exchange is not adequate to cover all human relations. What does it mean to speak of exchange or bargaining in the case of coercion or where choice is virtually nil – as is the case with ascriptive boundaries such as racist ones? How can situations of genocide be described as exchange or bargaining? How can crude exploitation, driving people off their lands, robbing them of their rights or property be termed exchange or bargaining, or spoken of as 'the superior party' obtaining 'a service' (Banton 1987: 129)? (In passing, the ambiguity of 'superior' is interesting.)

As Smith (1985: 490) points out, Banton himself (1983a: 81) states that 'people compete with one another only by observing recognized rules of conduct'. What 'recognized rules of conduct' does shooting people for sport, or gassing men, women and children, or simply confiscating people's property, or excluding them from certain positions or educational opportunities, adhere to? At best, any behavioural rules that could be formulated in such situations would be racist rules and would probably not be recognized by the victims, who would not be party to an exchange or bargaining. What would be important here would be those racist rules, the racist frames of reference within which these rules operate and the racist distribution of power.

Situations of conflict do not fit very well into the model of competition and bargaining. Banton himself (1985a: 15) has distinguished between competition and conflict. Where basic rights are in question – as often in 'race' relations – one has a situation of conflict: people do not bargain about what they perceive as their basic or inalienable rights. In such situations the conflict may erupt into physical violence: a riot, for instance, is not an example of a situation of competition or bargaining.

Finally, Banton (1987: 136–7) seems basically persuaded by the 'rational choice' theory as elaborated by Hechter *et al.* (1982). However, although it may seem logical that rational action *ought* to be determined by the factors these authors identify (expected public good, private reward, estimated probability of success, private punishment and the cost of injury and their likelihood), human action does not in fact typically proceed in this way, nor is anything gained by analysing it as though it did. Such an assumption cannot be tested. One could always assert retrospectively that, in view of the outcome, there must have been a particular balance of expected rewards and an estimated probability of success, etc.

To summarize the argument so far, social action is not only, nor even overwhelmingly, 'determined' by the pursuit of one's own individual advantage or by (explicit or implicit) means–ends calculations, or calculations of probabilities; and it is therefore unsatisfactory to judge all action from that point of view. A theory of 'race and ethnic relations' must take account of all types of action, 'rational' and 'non-rational', instrumental and non-instrumental, coerced and free, competitive and conflictual, bargaining and non-bargaining, and must integrate the notions of power, equality and inequality into its scheme.

Furthermore, such a theory must also take account of what is specific to 'race' and ethnic relations – namely phenomena such as 'race' and ethnic group, racism and ethnicism, and the processes of mutual racist or ethnicist social definition and of racist or ethnicist social structuring. Remarkable as it may seem, Banton's theory hardly does this, so much does he insist on the notion that 'race' and ethnic relations are not a special kind of social relations. One can agree with him (Banton 1983b: 6) that 'race' and ethnic relations do not rest 'objectively' on any biological basis, and yet maintain that they have distinctive characteristics as social relations. As we have seen, Banton states that people utilize physical and cultural differences in pursuing advantage through competition and bargaining. However, he fails to specify satisfactorily the conditions under which this happens, or why the boundaries are drawn where they are drawn, and using the criteria that are used rather than others.

He even fails to make it consistently clear whether for him

boundaries along phenotypical and cultural lines pre-exist the competition. One of his main propositions is that 'racial' groups (or rather categories) are formed through social processes, and in particular through processes of exclusion. He states (Banton 1983a: 77 – my italics) that: 'The long-run "problem" of "race" relations is that of explaining how groups identified by such signs [phenotopical features] come to be *created* . . . maintained, and . . . dissolved.' He also stresses (Banton, 1985c: 590) that his theory is a theory of boundaries. One might therefore properly expect it to deal, among other things, with the rise of boundaries. Yet he indicates (Banton 1985b: 546 – my italics) that his theory '*starts* with racial boundaries because unless at least one group has a racial boundary there can be no racial relations'.

Moreover, this position seems to imply that, in practice at least, Banton tends to see a 'racial' boundary as an objective pre-given reality, rather than as one arising through social processes of definition, allocation and interaction (not only inter-group but, above all, intra-group). It is true that Banton (1983a: 8) has argued that 'race' is a 'second-order abstraction'. People perceive not 'race' but phenotypical differences, which are then ordered into '"racial" classifications'. In other words 'race' is a construct, a category. But Banton seems to tend to slip from treating 'race' as a second-order abstraction, or as a category, to treating it as a first-order, observable phenomenon or group. Thus, he uses 'race' and 'racial' freely, as though these refer unproblematically to actual groups, rather than in the first place to particular cultural or ideological categories or constructs.

By contrast he avoids the notion of 'racism'. Yet 'race' has no scientific validity (see Hiernaux *et al.* 1965), only assuming social significance in a system of thought and social relations which is racist. Rex (1985: 560) has charged that Banton 'does not regard racism and racial discrimination as a problem'.

An example of what a 'rational choice' model of society implies is to be seen in Banton's application of his theory to the question of how the British could have decimated the Australian Aborigines as if they were not human. Banton states that 'the simplest answer':

> is that when men are subject to little social restraint they will pursue what they consider their interest without scruple, and will later seek to justify it . . . In the first half of the nineteenth century they asserted that the native peoples were savages and cannibals beyond the reach of reason; in the latter half of that century they made increasing use of ideas of racial inferiority.
>
> (Banton 1983a: 121)

Besides, different attitudes towards competition as between the invaders and the Aborigines facilitated misunderstanding and conflict. Aboriginal culture stressed sharing, while 'the whites ... were strongly oriented towards maximizing their incomes' (Banton 1983a: 122).

First of all, Banton's point that Aboriginal and British cultures were differently oriented towards competition could suggest that the overriding importance his theory gives to competition and self-interest is perhaps a construct of a particular culture rather than a universal sociological phenomenon. Further, the strong orientation of the British invaders 'towards maximizing their incomes' (Banton 1983a: 122) could suggest that the genocide was a result of British greed rather than of 'rational' self-interest, unless greed is equated with 'rationality'.

As Smith (1985: 491) forcefully puts it, the 'failure of RCT ['rational choice' theory] to handle vicious race relations is evident from Banton's effort to present the slaughter of aborigines in Australia and North America as effects of rational decisions by whites to optimize their net advantages on a group basis'. And Smith points out that 'natives' were sometimes shot simply for sport.

In any case, it is not clear from the theory why, if self-interest is the motive-force of human behaviour, one should feel the need to justify one's action in any other terms. In fact, it is unsatisfactory to think that the early British in Australia were just a collection of individuals 'subject to little social restraint'. The genocide was not the act of isolated individuals, but of people who belonged to communities. There were hunting parties, protection of the Whites by the military, and support of the Whites by the media (see, for example, Yarwood and Knowling 1982; and Ryan 1981). White people still largely carried the world view, the values, assumptions, images, norms and social-control mechanisms that they had brought from Britain.

Besides, Banton supplies little documentary evidence to support the view that the 'racial ideology' was simply a rationalization after the event. He fails to note that racist assumptions were implicit in the earliest images the British held of the Aborigines, even though it may be true that explicit ideas of 'racial' inferiority became commoner in the second half of the nineteenth century. Even people like Cook and Banks stressed from the outset the 'blackness' – and, along with this, the difference, nakedness and 'savagery' – of the Aborigines, while seeing themselves by contrast as civilized and fully human (see, for example, Yarwood and Knowling 1982). In fact the long-standing inhabitants of Australia were, and still are, extremely diverse peoples, and they had their own complex, highly developed world views. But the settlers overpowered them, constructing them as 'the Aborigines'.

BEYOND BARGAINING

Banton (1983a and 1985a) also makes more extensive applications of his theory, including a discussion of the 'race relations industry' in Britain and why, according to him (1985a: 121), its output 'seemed so disappointing in relation to the input into it'. The main thrust of Banton's argument in discussing this last question is that both the 'majority–minority relations and the policy process can . . . be seen in terms of bargaining' (Banton 1985a: 121). Both 'majority' members (whom Banton equates with the 'English') and 'minority' members pursue objectives and make, or refuse, deals. Banton suggests that the 'majority', the 'West Indians', the Sikhs, etc., constitute interest groups; that is, each of these 'groups' makes up a society of individuals banded together in pursuit basically of individual advantage. These groups are in competition with each other, and 'race relations' in Britain constitutes a bargaining situation. Banton also points to hostility and exclusion between the groups, and to a process of polarization – especially as fostered, according to him, by some ethnic minorities (Banton 1985a: 56–62, 103–8, 114–16). The ability of the different group members to pursue their objectives, to compete and bargain, depends on the resources they command. One task of public policy is to expedite the bargaining and, by preventing exploitation, to regulate it.

Fundamental to Banton's argument seems to be that the 'race relations' bargaining situation in Britain had been characterized by uncertainty, which had rendered the process of bargaining difficult. This supposed uncertainty was a function of the myth of return, and especially of a supposed lack of commitment by the 'immigrants' to British society and customs. The unfavourable characterization in terms of physical characteristics of the 'immigrants' by majority members (Banton 1985a: 127), and calls for 're-patriation', had likewise contributed to uncertainty. The confusion was increased by people in favour of 'multi-cultural education' advocating unclear solutions of 'cultural pluralism' (Banton 1985a: 129).

This argument is open to many of the critical points already made. The avoidance of the concept of racism is noticeable. Even Banton's (1985a: 30–46) discussion of the use of phenotypical characteristics as signs in classifying people, or in judging their 'respectability' and the social status which was their 'entitlement' (Banton 1985a: 33), is carried out within the context of it being only reasonable for people to make such calculations in situations of competition. The story that Banton (1985a: 37) puts forward of the development supposedly in the late 1950s of 'a dark colour' as a 'sign of an illegitimate competitor for scarce resources valued by the native working class' is highly dubious as a historical statement. It is an oversimplified and distorted story to fit his theory. As we shall see in the following chapter, there was in Britain not just a 'heritage of ideas about race' (Banton 1985a: 38), but also a long-standing negative stereotypical view of people of Black African background. This pre-dated and helped account for the view of 'immigrants' as 'illegitimate competitors' rather than the other way round.

Banton (1985a: 35) refers to the 1958 anti-Black riot in Notting Hill saying that 'coloured immigrant' competition for housing was regarded as one of its underlying causes. However, 'down with blacks' and 'kill the niggers' were slogans used during those riots (Walvin 1973). Is this the way one approaches 'competitors'? In any case, those riots were not the first anti-Black riots in Britain. There were also disturbances in 1919, for instance, when Black people and their property were attacked.

It seems to me that Banton has also overstated the incidence and importance of uncertainty in British 'race relations'. He provides little evidence to support his claims. It could, on the contrary, be maintained that many of the White British were quite certain in perceiving and relating to the ethnic minority people concerned as having low status and being 'obviously' different. More importantly, Banton seems constantly to have an 'immigrant' perspective in mind. But a large proportion of the minority ethnic members are in fact born in Britain and have no uncertainty about belonging to Britain. Also not only they, but the immigrants too, have always been certain about wanting fair treatment.

Banton also provides little evidence to support his claims of the incidence or importance of the supposed lack of commitment to Britain by 'immigrants'. Besides, what exactly does commitment to Britain mean? And commitment to which Britain? The commitment of the White British themselves should not simply be taken for granted. Furthermore, it is perfectly possible to have double or multiple group membership and commitment in a more complex social reality than Banton seems to envisage.

Banton tends to slip into treating categories, often rather stereotyped categories, as groups. For instance the 'majority', the 'Asians' and the 'West Indians' are social constructions largely relating to and serving social inequality. The 'majority' is highly and complexly differentiated, socially, culturally, ideologically and in terms of power. So are the 'Asians'. Similarly, the 'West Indians' encompass power, social class and cultural (including religious, linguistic and ideological) diversity, and include immigrants as well as British born.

Banton seems to give more importance and attention to cultural difference and to processes of cultural change and maintenance than to issues of power, social class and social stratification, or of racist and similar ideological frames of reference. He holds that cultural change is comparable to changes in consumer behaviour, and results from a balance between costs and benefits. Assimilation results from 'individual calculations of the benefits and costs of different courses of action in a context of changing preferences' (Banton 1985a: 49).

For 'immigrants', 'cultural change . . . can . . . be seen as the response of individuals to two sets of incentives', relating respectively to 'the sending society' and to 'the receiving society' (Banton 1985a: 53). The 'incentives' that impelled 'Asian immigrants' towards change were the 'close constraints' of their culture, and monetary rewards in British society. Against these were their strong attachment to their culture and certain features of 'English culture' which they found repellent. For 'West Indians', incentives to change were poverty in the West Indies and prospective monetary rewards in Britain. Against these was 'White prejudice'. Banton asserts, without any attempt at substantiation, that West Indian culture was 'less complex' (Banton, 1985a: 51) than Asian culture, and so its 'pull' was less strong.

Against this it could be maintained that West Indian cultures are misunderstood because they are both similar to, but different from, British cultures. Above all, they have low status in Britain. The situation could be described as 'bi-diacultural'. More accurately, it is characterized by the interrelation of 'Creole' and metropolitan cultures. The cultural interrelations are complex, and the status and power differentials are crucial. Furthermore, in so far as Caribbean Creole cultures and British metropolitan cultures are similar and bear many 'family' resemblances, it would not be surprising that West Indian cultures did not seem to have a strong 'pull' *vis-à-vis* British cultures. In any case, it is misleading to compare single-religion groups like the Sikhs or Muslims, or even Hindus, with 'West Indians' (as Banton 1985a: 51–61 does) because of the great diversity of the peoples from the numerous Caribbean countries.

Banton claims that 'West Indian' collective action 'suddenly appeared a possibility in the mid–1960s when the Black consciousness movement spread from the United States' (Banton 1985a: 61). Actually, there was such collective action long before the 1960s – see, for example, Fryer (1984: 293) and Ethnic Minorities Unit, GLC (1986: 48). Besides, Black consciousness had roots in the West Indies, especially Jamaica, where the term 'Black' has long since been in use – see, for example, Edwards 1967. There was also an attempt, Banton says, 'to create a maximal constituency' (Banton 1985a: 61) by referring to all 'non-Whites' as 'Black'. This 'polarizing' tactic failed because of powerlessness and the divisions among the 'non-Whites', and even within the 'Caribbeans'.

I would argue that the assertion of distinctive identities is not of itself 'polarizing'. Differences can be compatible: they can be complementary, or dynamically integrated – or perhaps just mutually stimulating. Banton seems to assume, without any question, that the aim of policy should be the promotion of 'racial harmony' (for example, Banton 1985a: vii, ix–x, 69–72, 126 and 129–131), apparently taking it for granted that the main 'problem' is 'hostility', and that differences in political views and, more widely, ethnic differences – in particular differences in the processes of negotiation – tend of themselves to lead to group competition, conflict and hostility. However, I would maintain – and nothing Banton says demonstrates the contrary – that it is perfectly possible for ethnically different 'groups' to interact constructively and creatively without submerging their differences. The richness and complexity of social life relate to the interaction of difference, not to its submergence. Even bargaining relies on difference in 'wants ... goods ... and ... bargaining units' (Banton 1985a: 13), and trading relations – which are bargaining relations – take place perfectly well across cultural boundaries. Besides, as we have seen, not all social relations are bargaining relations, and not all social relations can usefully be thought of as involving, even implicitly, mean–ends – or, less still, self-interested – calculations. Indeed, the notion of hostility suggests that one might act on the basis of pure affect.

The 'problem' between 'Blacks' and 'Whites' in Britain is not simply 'hostility' or 'rejection' (although these exist) but has more to do with assumptions, perceptions, stereotypes – in brief frames of reference – linked with inequality. As we shall see in the following chapter, these frames of reference are often unstated, defining the 'in-groups' and 'out-groups' in relation to each other, in terms of their supposed differential characteristics and relative status. Thus, there can be subordination, unfairness, equivocation or discrimination – *de facto* if not intentional – even though there is no hostility.

The basic concern should be much more with equality or social justice and with constructive interaction than simply with 'harmony' – in the sense of holding the same opinions and values or following the same practices (see Banton 1985a: x and 131). In the sparse references that Banton makes to equality, he suggests that there can be 'harmony' without equality (Banton 1985a: ix–x and 13). Thus slaves may be 'content with their condition' (Banton 1985a: x), and 'New

Commonwealth immigrants . . . accommodated themselves to the interests of the white majority . . . [with] little evidence of racial disharmony' (Banton 1985a: x). But the fact is that slaves have often revolted, and some Black people in Britain have ended up rioting in the 1980s. There is also much evidence of 'racial disharmony' in Britain in the 1940s and 1950s, and indeed much earlier – such as Blacks being attacked by Whites (see, for example, Figueroa 1982: 32; Walvin 1973: 206, 209–10, 211, 213; Little 1948; Glass and Pollins 1960; Hiro 1971; and Fryer 1984: 227ff and 298ff). In addition, there is evidence of inequitable treatment and massive discrimination in the 1960s, 1970s and 1980s (see, for example, Daniel 1968; Smith 1977; Brown 1984; and Brown and Gay 1985).

It was Roy Jenkins (1966), then Home Secretary, who introduced the legislation which, according to Banton, recognized 'racial harmony' as a 'public good'. Yet the goal for Jenkins was not the submergence of difference, but integration defined 'not as a flattening process of assimilation but as *equal opportunity*, accompanied by *cultural diversity*, in an atmosphere of mutual tolerance' (see Banton 1985a: 71 – my italics). For the different ethnic 'groups' and 'sub-groups' to interact constructively, and without feeling threatened, not only must commonalities be recognized. Differences must also be accepted and taken into account as differences. If one 'group' or the other unilaterally insists on consensus, there is likely, paradoxically perhaps, to be conflict.

After developing the notions of racism and ethnicism and especially of racist and ethnicist frames of reference in the following chapter, I shall take up the issues of pluralism and especially of multicultural education in Chapter 3.

2 Racist frames of reference

SOCIAL RELATIONS

'Race' relations are social relations. Hence a theory of 'race' relations must ultimately be placed within a wider theory of social relations. However, 'race' relations have distinctive features which differentiate them from other social relations, though at one level they share some of this with a 'family' of social relations which include, for example, 'ethnic', 'gender' and 'age' relations. The distinctiveness of 'race' relations do not rest on phenotypical differences as such, which do not, as Banton (1983: 135) says, of themselves create groups – nor determine intergroup relations.

To my mind the major differentiating characteristics of 'race' relations are to be found in what I call racist frames of reference (Figueroa 1974, 1984a, 1986). The main purposes of this chapter are to set out the notion of a racist frame of reference and to indicate its importance in understanding 'race' relations in Britain. It is not, however, my purpose to develop here a full blown theory of 'race' and ethnic relations, nor less still, a comprehensive theory of social relations. Those would require separate works. Nevertheless, I shall briefly attempt to place the central notion of a racist frame of reference in the necessary wider context.

The conception of the social which underlies my view of 'race' relations is one which assumes a dynamic holding together, an intrinsic, mutually defining and mutually realizing inter-relationship, of aspects that are commonly considered dualistically and atomistically, such as: subject and object, culture and structure, the spiritual and the material, superstructure and infrastructure, *langue* and *parole*, ego and alter, the individual and the social.

It is typical of social reality, as distinct from the natural world, that people 'construct' over time, in and through interaction with each other – and within the constraints of the given (cultural, social and natural) –

their reality. The model of efficient causality, which may usefully be applied to the natural world, is thus of very limited service in considering the social world. To say this, however, is not to espouse an atomistic model in regard to the social world, which is characterized by what may be termed an 'internal causality'. People determine to act in various motivated ways. They have intentions. They interpret reality (their own situations and the actions of others) and they act and react accordingly, in view of their intentions – and given the actual possibilities – in effect choosing in and through interaction this or that possible alternative. As a result, their interpretations and intentions may be reinforced, or modified, and will further inform action.

The social can thus be seen as the dynamic interacting of intentional, meaning-'giving' 'individuals', mutually defining, sustaining and taking account of each other. And it can be seen as being, inseparably, the patterns and regularities, the reciprocal positioning, the structures, that may be thought of as informing that interacting. These patterns, these structures are intrinsic to the interacting, and also both result from and constrain it.

As argued in Chapter 1, neither the social nor the individual can be accorded priority one over the other. The individual is not just a 'rational chooser'; neither just a calculating machine, a computer, nor just a consumer, a bundle of wants and needs that have to be fulfilled, a self-seeker. He or she is a physical, bodily, conscious, questioning, reflexive, other-oriented being, constantly – if tacitly – 'taking account' of his or her situation, of himself or herself, and of others. 'Taking account' includes processes of awareness, interpretation and making adjustments. Networks of actors are interlocked in these processes. The social is this interacting, its medium, its resultant, their structures. Each actor only *is* and becomes what he or she is in and through interaction with others, and in mutual interdependence with them. Each person becomes themselves, and gains self-awareness only through and with others. Yet each person's taking account of the other is always on the background of himself or herself.

Always my action at some level involves awareness and definition of myself, of others, of my situation, of the action itself, etc. Besides, directly or indirectly, the action always relates to others, directly or indirectly taking them into account, at the very least in so far as they have inscribed their presence in the space or location of the action. I inhabit a world that I and others have 'reworked' and are constantly 'reworking' (see Merleau-Ponty 1964). My every vehicle of action and interpretation is learned from others or through direct or indirect interaction with them; is forged, modified, sustained and passed on in and through interaction. Furthermore, as Blumer (1969: 12–15) following Mead (1934) has argued (see also Strauss 1956), has argued, each individual is also inherently 'social' in the sense that in their very make-up they imply 'self-interaction'. The social consists of and results from individual action, but the individual is inherently social.

A central aspect of social being, of 'being with and through others', is culture. My every action is made possible, *and* constrained, by my culture. In broad terms culture refers to characteristic constellations of conceptual constructs, symbolic systems, beliefs, values, and behavioural patterns shared by a group or set of groups, differentiating it from other groups or sets of groups, thus defining identity. This identity may be both 'objective' and 'subjective' in the sense that groups may differ in cultural characteristics such as the languages they speak or the religious beliefs they hold, but also among their cultural differences will be their awareness and definition of themselves as different from others. Each group within a set will share in varying ways and degrees one or more features with other groups in the same set. However, each group will also, to a greater or lesser extent, have some feature, or variations in features, which differentiate it from other groups. Similarly individuals within each group will 'participate' differentially in the group culture, depending on that individual's own social interrelating, social position, social history and experiences.

This culture is not a set of abstract values, symbols or meanings. Rather it is the meanings, symbols and values embodied in everyday social living and interaction. The patterns of social relations which constitute the social structure is the culture in operation. The ways in which people interact and interrelate are expressions of their beliefs, perceptions, expectations.

Actions always have a figure–ground structure so that the focus of the action – this act of discrimination, for example – stands out against a set of assumptions, a dominant image, which at the moment is unstated and untargeted (see Merleau-Ponty 1945 on the figure–ground structure of perception). This set of assumptions, this 'image', animates and constrains the action, informs it, orientates it and circumscribes it, gives it meaning, directedness and definition, serves as the basis on which 'at least tacitly, the actual ways of acting are selected' (Figueroa 1974: 35) – on which the course of action is 'determined' and unfolds. Such a set of assumptions, such an image, I refer to as a frame of reference. Such frames of reference guide and inform social action, and are themselves socially generated, learned, sustained and modified.

A voluntaristic model of society is implied in this view of the social, as I have indicated elsewhere (Figueroa 1974: 35). According to this

(Figueroa 1974: 35), 'social actions and interactions are best understood as being relatively free. Hence they cannot . . . be understood simply as being caused either by external, material forces, or by psychic forces, such as "blind prejudice".' Rather, one may consider that 'implicitly at least, choices are constantly being made' out of 'a range of various possible ways of acting' (Figueroa 1974: 35). However, the freedom involved here is a limited freedom, situated biographically, historically, socially and culturally. My options are options mediated by my culture, which for me is in a sense a given that I learn in and through interaction with others, but which is also produced and modified, which is realized in and by such interaction – to which I am a party. My alternatives are created, opened up *and* constrained in and by my relations to and with others.

Furthermore, to speak of choice is not to imply only means–ends calculations, nor less still only a self-interested motivation. People act in many different ways, not only to maximize their net advantage. They also act in the following ways: to an end for someone else's advantage, or for the group's advantage, or for a cause; on the basis of some value, rule or accepted norm; out of love or attraction or interest or fascination; from anger or under the force of some other passion; on the basis of attitudes; from fashion, or under social pressure; out of habit; from tradition; under the influence of another person.

Some actors and some groups are able – by virtue of asymmetrical relationships, or because they are less constrained, or because they have greater control over resources – to hold more steadfastly to, or to impose more effectively, their definitions, their intentions, their values, their frames of reference, their culture, or the patterns or structures they wish. Power includes power to define the situation, to define others, to define oneself, to generate, maintain, modify and diffuse the frames of reference. Power is not just control over the means of production. For what matters is the control of the means of production of what is scarce and *valued*. Hence what also matters is control of supply and, more fundamentally, of values. But what is valued is largely a function of culture, of group definition, as can be seen for instance in fashion – and in 'race' relations.

RACISM

The phenomena which we significantly continue to refer to as 'race relations' or as 'race and ethnic relations' are, in my view, typical social phenomena which cannot be adequately comprehended within the bounds of an efficient casual model. Instead, an adequate understanding of 'race relations' needs to include the notion of 'race' as a social construction or reality. In a similar though not identical way 'ethnic relations' needs to include the notion of 'ethnic group' as a social construction. Central to these social constructions, according to the present view, are certain largely taken-for-granted understandings – which are shared by the in-group members, are closely associated with group identity, and provide as it were a basic 'backdrop' to perception, knowledge, judgement and action. These are what I refer to as the 'racist frame of reference' and the 'ethnicist frame of reference'. These operate at the level of culture and are central to an understanding of racism – and ethnicism.

However, besides the cultural level or dimension of racism (and ethnicism) one may also distinguish analytically the individual, the interpersonal, the institutional and the structural levels or dimensions. These are all closely interrelated and do not occur separately. At the cultural level I understand racism, as already indicated, as the operation of a shared racist frame of reference. It is this which specifically differentiates 'race' relations from other forms of social relations. Similarly 'ethnicism' is the operation of an ethnicist frame of reference. Hence at this level 'race' relations may be thought of as crucially involving an ideology, or world view, comprising assumptions and values that are taken for granted and largely unverbalized or unthematized, that are buried deep in the culture. In a largely parallel way 'ethnic' relations involve a taken-for-granted set of assumptions and values. In the one case 'race' is taken as the organizing concept, and what are taken as 'natural' or inherent characteristics serve as differentiating or typical signs or symbols. In the other case 'ethnic' group or 'ethnicity' is taken as the organizing concept, and certain cultural or historical characteristics, real or supposed, serve as differentiating or typical signs or symbols.

I shall expand somewhat on the related notions of 'ethnic group', 'ethnicity', 'ethnicisim' and the 'ethnicist' frame of reference in the following chapter. Here I shall first of all consider the other 'levels' or dimensions of racism, and then develop in more detail the central notion of the racist frame of reference and look at the British situation in a historical perspective.

At the individual level of racism there is prejudice in the broad sense of a prejudgement or overgeneralization held by an individual. In particular, racism is sometimes equated with prejudice – understood as virulent hostility due to individual, psychological problems – and is then contrasted with 'racial' tolerance. However this is too narrow a meaning of prejudice and (more so) of racism. The notion of 'racial' tolerence can be ambiguous and may itself feed on racist thinking. It is possible for a person to be tolerant and free of prejudice and yet still to be racist in his or her thinking or behaviour. Such a person may, for instance, be paternalistic in behaviour, or their thinking might be characterized by stereotypes. Thus, for example, a teacher who stereotypes all 'West Indians' (including youngsters born in Britain) as 'by nature' good at games, art and music (but inherently bad at mathematics, language and academic subjects generally) is racist in his or her thinking, however well-disposed such a teacher may be towards 'West Indians'.

Besides, such prejudice and stereotypes are usually a function of a group frame of reference, and have a social aetiology and a social orientation. Racism is not just a matter of an individual's beliefs or prejudices, but has to do with the way a group (at least implicitly) defines itself in counter-distinction to what it defines as 'out groups', and the way these 'groups' relate to each other.

Banton (1959: 30–31; 1967: 8, 298) is also critical of prejudice – in this narrow individual sense of virulent hostility – if it is understood as 'irrational'. However, one problem with his early critique of prejudice in 'race' relations is that:

> it is misleading to imply simply that prejudice is 'irrational'. The be-
> lief system on which a person acts may be objectively false, ill-
> founded or misapplied, but so long as this person is convinced
> (however irrationally) of this belief system and that it is being appro-
> priately applied, certain role expectations and actions may follow
> quite rationally from it.
>
> (Figueroa 1974: 33)

Even behaviour which is partially rational may be socially counterproductive and ethically undesirable. As already argued in Chapter 1, 'rationality' – in the sense of instrumentality and more so in the narrower sense of the maximization of self-interest – does not itself provide an adequate criterion of social action.

At the interpersonal level of racism are interactions, communication, and interrelations – on the basis of, within the terms of, or according to (and conversely generating and sustaining) a racist frame of reference. Such interactions, communication and interrelations may either be with in-group members or with those construed as belonging to the out-group 'race'. In the former case, they will be with in-group members in so far as they are specifically differentiated from 'out-group members'; or else the point of reference of the interaction or commu-nication will be the 'out-group race' as construed. For example, certain forms of behaviour or relations will be seen as more appropriate with in-group than out-group members. Thus it has been found that friendship patterns among pupils often follow 'ethnic' group boundaries (see, for instance, Figueroa 1974 and Davey 1987).

At the institutional level of racism is the way the society *de facto* – or even by design – disadvantages certain 'groups' by working on the basis of the assumptions drawn from, or influenced by, a racist frame of reference, and built into the organization, rules or processes of the society. The institutionalization might be formal or unintended, it might be society-wide or might apply only in particular spheres or within particular institutions (such as the school), or it might be some combination of more than one of these. An example of society-wide, formal institutionalized racism would be racist laws. An example of a more limited and unintentional form of institutionalized racism would be reading books in junior schools which omitted any reference to, or any illustrations of, Black people. The negative, if subtle, effect of this might be all the more direct on Black pupils taught from such books.

Finally, at the structural level of racism is the way society is articulated or structured, vertically or horizontally, by so-called 'race' – in other words, along racist lines, or boundaries, in accord with a racist ideology or racist frame of reference. Important here is the differential distribution along such boundaries of resources, rewards, status and power. For example, as we shall see in Chapter 9 in respect of education, and briefly in Chapter 3 in other respects, 'Asians' and 'West Indians' are disproportionately badly placed on a range of social indicators. However, several factors – such as social class, cultural difference, sexism, ethnicism, and racism – intersect in complex ways so that sub-groups (e.g. East African 'Asians', Bangladeshi, Sikh girls) within these broad categories are differentially placed. The notion, for instance, that 'West Indians' constitute an 'underclass' (see for example, Rex and Tomlinson 1979) is at the least a distortion. Not only are there middle class 'West Indians' in Britain, but racism is experienced by them as well as by working class 'West Indians'. Besides, the concept of 'underclass' seems theoretically unsound, as the 'underclass' must itself be part of the class system. In this respect the concept of insider–outsider (Glass 1964) is more satisfactory. There are parallels and interactions – material and ideological – between social structuring by 'race' and by class, but one cannot be reduced to the other.

Central, then, in so-called 'race relations' is the racist frame of reference. It is embodied in, gives rise to, maintains, reproduces, justifies, and is produced, sustained and reproduced by social relations, social practices, social institutions and social structures – especially structures of inequality, subordination, exploitation or oppression. The ideological and the material, the cultural and the structural are inseparable from each other; in other words, are different sides of the same phenomenon. 'Race' is essentially a construct – ideologically and materially – of racist thinking, racist relations and racist systems.

The popular debate about racism which followed the publication of the Interim Report of the Committee of Inquiry into the Education of Children from Ethnic Minority Groups (DES 1981) – the Rampton Report – illustrates well the importance of developing a concept like racist frames of reference. The Rampton Report (DES 1981: 12) itself defines racism as 'a set of attitudes and behaviour towards people of another race which is based on the belief that races are distinct and can be graded as "superior" or "inferior"'. The first point here is that this quote could suggest with the words 'towards people of another race' that the Committee itself believes that there are distinct 'races'. Secondly, 'attitudes and behaviour' could suggest a focus on an individual-psychological level. Thirdly, the main point in the Rampton Report's definition is that the racist considers his or her own 'race' as 'superior'. This, however, like constructing racism merely in terms of 'tolerance–intolerance', is too narrow a definition. What matters is in effect constructing 'race' in the group consciousness and in practice as a general determining factor at all.

Banton (1967: 8) has insisted that the term 'racism' should be taken to mean the (nineteenth century) 'scientific' *doctrine* 'that a man's behaviour is determined by stable inherited characters deriving from separate racial stocks having distinctive attributes and usually considered to stand to one another in relations of superiority to inferiority'. As I have argued, however (Figueroa 1974: 34), this fails to take account of 'tacit, implied beliefs, attitudes and orientations . . . Shared beliefs, values and attitudes can be . . . so deeply embedded that the interacting members are not – or . . . are only peripherally – aware of them, even though they act in accordance with them.'

More recently, by a sleight of terminological usage, Banton (1987: ix) has virtually dispensed with the notion of racism altogether by stating that: 'Racial typology was a better name for the body of doctrine than scientific racism' since its 'central concept was not race but type'. However, it would seem that actually the central concept was '*racial*' type. This no doubt involved both 'scientific' and everyday assumptions about the centrality, significance and reality of 'race', and remains an outstanding form of racist thinking.

What I am suggesting is that even if prejudice in some narrow individualistic sense (rigid and hostile rejection, intolerance or even feelings of superiority), or in the sense of a formal or explicit doctrine, is apparently of little widespread importance, nevertheless racism as a shared racist frame of reference, involving 'race' (and, inseparably, 'race relations') as a social construction, may be of basic significance.

CONSTRUCTION OF REALITY

There are two central aspects to the notion of the construction of social reality. The first is that people act on the basis of how they see the situation, in other words on the basis of their 'definition of the situation'. What matters is not just what objectively is the case, but what people believe to be the case. Cooley's dictum that 'if men define social situations as real, they are real in their consequences' has become a sociological axiom. This axiom does not in my view entail that material forces are of no consequence for human behaviour and for social reality. Nor does it mean that the consequences which follow from people's definitions will necessarily be in *accord* with those definitions. Even in ambiguous social reality it is metaphorically possible to walk into a brick wall. One's definition of the situation may be in conflict with that of other parties to the situation, and one may soon realize in such a case that the outcome of one's actions was not what one would have expected from one's definition of the situation – especially where the other parties to the situation hold more power than one does. Nevertheless – and this is basically what is being stated as the first aspect of the notion of the construction of reality – each actor's definition of the situation will inform the situation for him or her and affect his or her action (and may thereby help to shape the situation for others and influence their action – in terms of their own 'definition', which may itself be influenced). The actor is not simply acted on by the situation (nor, however, are his powers of definition of the situation absolute).

The second aspect is that the actor is always in a situation which is not just of his or her making, but is the net result of interaction with and among others (as also of forces of the natural world). Social reality is constructed in and through interaction within the parameters of the given – in view of shared and contested perceptions, beliefs, interpretations, values, norms, intentions and affects. The actor's powers of definition are typically exercised in interaction with others. Furthermore, the joint construction of social reality does not just mean an interpretation or symbolic definition of that reality, but an operant or enactive producing or accomplishing of it, even if that largely occurs through 'symbolic interaction'. It is the very networking that is the social reality and that constructs the social reality. Social reality is jointly – if unequally – constructed by those who are situated in it. As Blumer

(1969: 10) says: 'Both . . . joint activity and individual conduct are formed *in* and *through* this ongoing process'.

RACIST FRAMES OF REFERENCE

In defining the situation, actors bring to bear on it any previous knowledge or experience (including feelings, judgement or action) which may seem relevant to it. It is 'maps' of such 'knowledge' or 'experience', which serve to orientate the actor, that I refer to as frames of reference. They are part of our interpretational system. These frames of reference are not to be taken in an individualistic or subjectivist sense. They are not just abstract, ideational operations. They are inherent to social interaction – in and through which they are constructed. They are shared with other members of the in-group, are socially learned, and fulfil important social functions.

The myths and assumptions that serve in the modern world (and, in particular, in Britain) in defining and structuring particular situations in terms of 'race' are the racist frames of reference. They provide an important definition of boundaries along which power is distributed – and in terms of which relations are patterned and social interactions, along with the inherent and basically *inexplicit* 'interpretive process', are accomplished. Such a racist frame of reference, broadly speaking, is a socially constructed and socially reproduced and learned way of orienting with and towards others and the world, involving ultimately tacit assumptions, such as: there do actually exist objectively different 'races'; these share 'by nature' (or genetically or inherently) certain common characteristics, including (or closely linked with) certain social characteristics; the different 'races' are mutually exclusive if not hierarchically ordered; each person belongs to one (and only one) such 'race', thereby possessing certain physical and cultural characteristics and typically occupying a certain social location.

'Race' is generated in and through a racist frame of reference and in and through particular social relations. Like education (Young 1971), sex (Ardener 1978) and childhood (Holland 1980), it is a social construction. This is not to try and deny the existence of different-looking populations, any more than one denies that the physics syllabus in schools tells us something about natural phenomena, or that there are anatomical differences associated with reproduction, or that age and maturity differences exist. However, cultures differ, for instance, in the roles, status and image they assign to women and children. People, through interaction and the mutually interpretive process this involves, categorize, highlight and make sense of the given in particular ways, and establish order through particular patterns of relations. What matters is not just actual differences (in appearance for instance), but the way these are related to and invested with meaning and importance through interaction. What is significant are the patterns of relations that are established, the lines along which they are drawn, and the myths and assumptions that go along with, and inform, these relations and boundaries. 'Race' refers both to the network of largely unspoken, taken-for-granted assumptions, myths, etc, and to the actual constellation of relationships and the patterned distribution of power which give rise to and express it, and which it informs, justifies, generates and sustains.

A racist frame of reference does not refer just to a set of beliefs. The assumptions and myths are not to be understood just cognitively. I have argued elsewhere (Figueroa 1974: 36–8) that there are four main closely interrelated aspects: the cognitive, the evaluative, the affective and the conative. Apart from the given conceptual framework, the symbols and beliefs, are the existing evaluations, the patterns of affective orientation, the behavioural norms and tendencies and the already given patterns of actions and interactions, the existing social relations – and these all go to 'define' or provide the 'lived' frame in terms of which any new action, perception, judgement, thought, knowledge, feeling or experience is situated, given meaning and value, and realized. This 'definition', however, usually takes place implicitly, rather than being a consciously reflective operation. The racist frame of reference is rooted essentially at the level of subsidiary awareness or the taken-for-granted, at the level of hidden structures or even of the social 'deep structures' (see Merleau-Ponty 1945 on *le cogito tacite*; and Polanyi 1958 on the related notion of subsidiary awareness).

Racist (and ethnicist) frames of reference are developed, realized, embodied, enacted and maintained through concrete processes of interaction and interrelation. Like a language they are themselves produced in and through interaction, yet are always given, being learned through a process of reproduction, so that they are actively taken up and modified in practice. They are generated and learned both through inter-'group' interaction and communication (or non-communication) and especially through intra-group interaction and communication. They are generated and learned through the very patterns of interactions and relations. However, adapting Blumer's view (1961: 225–6), the 'big event', 'public figures of prominence' and 'strong interest groups' play particularly important roles in determining and diffusing the racist frames of reference. Some of the concrete processes through which racist (or ethnicist) self-definition and other-definition and in-group and out-group differentiation take place, which they give rise to and which gives rise to them, are for instance: naming (see Jordan 1984: 281) and name-calling (see Figueroa 1985); unequal educational placement or treatment; public statements such as discriminating advertisements, or certain pronouncements by politicians or other distinguished figures; reports and discussions in the media; the enactment and administration of discriminatory laws, or the discriminatory administration of the law; and various other acts of discrimination.

'Race' and 'ethnic group' are social constructions, not only in the sense that they are correlates of the racist and ethnicist frames of reference, but also in so far as they are the product of social interaction. 'Race' and 'ethnic group', the frames of reference and the concrete forms of social interaction are interdependent.

One example of such processes is to be found in the criminalization of Black British youths – by which, revealingly enough, is usually understood young males of West Indian background. This has been a complex process over a period of time. On the one hand it has involved social forces like poor educational opportunities, high unemployment, decayed inner city environments, resulting in *some* frustrated or alienated 'Black youths' turning to crime. On the other hand it has simultaneously involved racist or ethnicist frames of reference, and in particular, for instance, the stereotyping of 'Black youths' in general as deviants or criminals. Besides, mutual suspicion between the Black youths and the police has contributed to the process. This mutual suspicion is itself a function of: (1) the very different social locations of these two 'groups'; (2) cultural differences and misunderstandings; and (3) especially, ethnicist or racist frames of reference. These processes have led to riots and have been reinforced by them.

Another example of some of the processes of self- and other-identification and differentiation can be found in a study by Jordan (1984). She found that Australian Aboriginal identity varied across different settings (city, country town and tradition-oriented site), and in each case was somehow appropriate to the particular setting. Identity was generated in relation to certain 'reality definers' in the community, and in reaction against or in contrast with the 'white world'. Identity was formed partly through experience in school.

Yet another example of the interaction of frames of reference, concrete processes and structures can be found in Martin's (1978) study of the construction of knowledge concerning 'the migrant presence' in Australia. She showed how the definers and the definitions changed, and what roles these definers and definitions played in the determining of social policy and in social practice. She also instanced the interaction between concrete factors and 'ideological' features similar to frames of reference. She showed, for example, the way in which 'social knowledge' operates to attach meaning to research findings in the field of 'migrant health' (Martin 1978: 162). She also pointed out that little was learned from the early experiences of the presence of 'migrant' children in the school system because of 'the lack of any theoretical structure' (Martin 1978: 133) – and, presumably, because of the operation of 'social knowledge' only. On the other hand, a range of factors – such as demographic factors and funding – also affected the definitions (Martin 1978: 120 and 123). More fundamentally, the degree of participation in the construction of knowledge related to the different positions of different groups in the hierarchical and non-hierarchical structure of the society. Besides, the acknowledgement of 'the experiences of only the favoured few . . . as legitimate sources of social knowledge' (Martin 1978: 213) was often justified by negative evaluations of 'the explanatory framework' of the migrants.

FUNCTIONS OF RACIST FRAMES OF REFERENCE

Racist frames of reference serve several functions. First, in a broad sense, is the interpretive function. A racist frame of reference permits the categorization, managing and ordering of the experienced world, and provides a simple, stable explanation of various social phenomena. It thus also provides a simple basis for action, incorporating as it does a view of the world that is both a way of accounting and a value position.

It contributes significantly to the 'definition' of group identity and self-identity (see Husband 1979, whose analyses fit well with these ideas). It is thus of central importance, for it concerns 'a crucial aspect of the determination and co-ordination of social action and interaction, namely the very way in which groups, their membership and their relative social location are defined, symbolised, judged and treated' (Figueroa 1974: 36). The racist frame of reference helps to stake out and maintain hard boundaries and closedness. It thus divides and separates while providing the underpinning to what Blumer (1961: 221, 217) has called a 'sense of group position', which for him 'is a general kind of orientation . . . a sense of where the two racial groups *belong* . . . a norm and imperative' – not just a set of feelings.

Thus, by the same token as it distinguishes, separates, draws firm boundaries and closes off, the racist frame of reference provides those who share it with a rallying point for group loyalty and cohesion. Contrary to what Banton seems to hold, the inclusive and exclusive processes of group definition and formation are interdependent. The racist frame of reference can help to bridge the worlds of a majority, or at least of certain sectors of a socially divided nation, and to maintain a certain 'national' unity against 'outsiders'. These 'outsiders', however, are often also 'insiders', being often citizens, residents, workers, or just part of the society's economic system, and serving to fulfil certain functions – for example, integrative functions – for that society and system. The racist frame of reference papers over the cracks in what Ruth Glass (1964) has called the 'parent' society by 'constructing' a scapegoat.

Finally, and closely related to the above, the racist frame of reference provides a rationale for the existing order of institutionalized racism, and a simple justification for 'racially' exploitative social practices and arrangements. It thus performs a systems maintenance function, and so serves the interests of the privileged classes, of those who hold power. It serves to produce and reproduce inequality, thus enhancing the freedom of some and limiting that of others.

However, the order of institutionalized racism – in which 'Black' people are typically in a low social location – itself leads to and supports a racist frame of reference. There tends to be, in brief, a circular and mutually reinforcing relationship between a (*de facto*) racist power structure and the racist frame of reference. The racist frame of reference springs from, expresses, is embodied in, and (supports or underpins) certain forms of social relations – that is, the power structure of institutionalized racism. So, although the term 'race' has little objective validity as a socio-biological reality, 'races' as actually 'constructed' through social interaction constitute important structural features of a stratified (or divisive) social system, and are characterized by differential access to power.

RACIST FRAMES OF REFERENCE IN BRITAIN

There is quite a lot of evidence suggestive of a racist frame of reference in Britain. For example, much of the data in the now classic survey of 'race relations' in Britain (Rose *et al.* 1969: 567, 569, 570, 587) suggest – despite Rose *et al*'s own conclusions (1969: 675) – that racism as a negative or narrow way of seeing, without any hostility necessarily implied, was a widespread phenomenon. A careful re-analysis of these survey data by Bagley (1970) supports my interpretation (see Figueroa 1974: 412–14).

Similarly, in a study of West Indian, British and Cypriot school-leavers, I found (Figueroa 1974 and 1976) that: the British respondents had negative stereotypes especially of West Indians; the West Indians had on the whole a positive group self-image, though not one as completely favourable as the group self-image held by the British; rather than patterns of friendly interaction between these groups, the data pointed to 'negative or rejecting patterns of action on the part of the British *vis-à-vis* the West Indians' (Figueroa 1976: 231); there were some limited data 'implying negative or rejecting affects or "feelings" on the part of the British regarding "immigrants"' (Figueroa 1974: 376); several statements by respondents indicated racist thinking and a linked negative evaluation, but did not suggest that virulent hostility was a particularly salient phenomenon.

Brittan (1976) has reported findings suggesting widespread and negative (or narrow stereotyping) of West Indian pupils by school teachers; and Bagley and Verma (1975) have reported results showing marked 'racism' and stereotypes among pupils. Husband's research (1979) is particularly suggestive of how Black people have been symbolized as 'immigrants' (rather than, for example, as settlers) and have been seen as a 'threat', the implicit assumption being that they and their ways are undesirable. The much publicized statement by Margaret Thatcher, a 'public figure of prominence', that 'this country might be rather swamped by people with a different culture' takes on its full meaning and impact only if the unspoken assumption is made – not just that those people's cultures are *different* but that they are not equally as desirable or valid as one's own (see also Barry 1988: 96). Similarly, if Black people as such are particularly seen as a threat in housing, jobs, etc, this is because they are not accepted as having equal rights. They are clearly no more a 'threat' than any other competitors on the housing or employment market. Moreover, along with these assumptions, judgements, evaluations and stereotypes is the commonly known, and sometimes exaggerated fact (see Rose *et al.* 1969) that on almost any social index (employment, accommodation, education) Black people have tended to be overrepresented at the lower end of the scale (see, for example, Daniel 1968, Smith 1977, Brown 1984 and Brown and Gay 1985).

There is a good deal of historical evidence supporting not only the view of the longstanding existence of a racist frame of reference in Britain, but also its intimate link with racist social structures, and the role of the 'big event', 'public figures of prominence' and 'strong interest groups' in its generation and diffusion. Despite Banton's (for example 1983a: 33–4, 76–7) repeated strictures about 'presentism' – that is, 'the tendency to interpret other historical periods in the terms of the concepts, values and understanding of the present time' – there seem to be structural similarities across the centuries in British racist frames of reference. As Walvin (1973: 173, 215) says, for example, 'From eighteenth-century plantocratic caricatures, to Carlyle and Trollope, through *The Times* of the 1860s to the more "scientific" apologists for racialism late in the century, common images of the Negro were passed on', and, 'the events of the postwar years . . . form a continuation of the well-established history of black people in this country, rather than being a new story'. Of course, beliefs, concepts and ways of under-standing and accounting for changed over the centuries. Nevertheless, similarities might include: categorization and stereotyping in terms of 'characteristics' seen as inherent; 'in-group'/'out-group' differentiation in such terms; and notions of 'in-group' superiority.

Little (1948), in putting forward his 'colour–class hypothesis' largely on the basis of historical evidence, was perhaps the first scholar in the post-war period to stress the importance of beliefs associating 'colour' with low status, and to suggest that in Britain 'coloured' people are considered inferior and not very desirable socially as a result of the British colonial past and especially of the slave trade.

In fact, at least from the sixteenth century if not much earlier, there already existed in Britain, partly on the basis of adventurers' accounts (Walvin 1973), a negative or subordinating orientation towards 'Black' people. (See also Fryer 1984: 6–7 and 135–44.) Walvin (1973) quotes a sixteenth-century writer, Eden, who refers to Africans as 'Moores, Moorens, or Negroes, a people of beastly lyvynge, without a god, law, religion or commonwealth' – all of which was, of course, false. Walvin (1973: 160) also quotes as follows from a 1788 number of the *Gentleman's Magazine*, 'perhaps the most popular and influential periodical of the day': 'The Negro is possessed by passions not only strong but ungovernable; . . . a temper extremely irascible; a disposition insolent . . . As to [most of the] fine feelings of the soul, the Negro . . . is nearly deprived of them'.

Indeed, it is clear that the 'media' then – as now – played an important part in the formation and development of 'public opinion'. In the eighteenth century graphic cartoonists frequently made Negroes a target, reducing them to grotesque shapes (Walvin 1973: 159). There was also a mass of books, tracts, newspaper and magazine articles comprising a literary caricature of the Negro, especially 'during and immediately after the campaign for abolition and emancipation' (Walvin 1973: 159). This was indeed a 'big event', and the powerful interest group of the plantocracy was mainly responsible for these writings. The *Encyclopaedia Britannica* of 1810, likewise quoted by Walvin (1973), characterized the Negro as 'this unhappy race . . .

strangers to every sentiment of compassion . . . an awful example of the corruption of man left to himself'. Carlyle (1853) in his polemics also depicts a stereotype of the Negro as crude, lazy and depraved (see also Fryer 1984: 146–65).

Another 'big event' stirring up public debate and stoking the popular imagination in Britain was the Jamaica revolt of 1865, Governor Eyre's butchery of those involved and the political *cause célèbre* which Eyre's case became. As Walvin (1973: 172) says: 'Eyre found enormous support for his legalized savagery, notably from Ruskin, Tennyson, Kingsley, Dickens and Carlyle' – all 'public figures of prominence'. Walvin (1973: 161) also highlights the 1882 invasion of Egypt saying: 'The need to justify and explain the new empire . . . led to a far-ranging debate about the Negro and other non-white peoples'. So thoroughly was this period saturated with racist thinking that the debate took place not only at the popular level and the level of polemic, but also at the academic and 'scholarly' level. This was the age of 'scientific racism and social darwinism' (see, for example, Bolt 1971 and Fryer 1984: 165–81).

Not only was there this generally 'superior' and negative orientation towards Black people, they were often actually largely located in the lowest strata in the social system, both within Britain and in the Empire. However, by the nineteenth century Black people in Britain were to be found in 'all walks of life' (Walvin 1973: 72). Besides, the structural relationship of Britain (the 'mother country') to the rest of the Empire was essentially similar to that which existed, and exists, between White and Black people within Britain. As Rex and Tomlinson (1979) have argued, present-day British society, and especially 'race-relations' in Britain today, cannot be understood without an understanding of Empire. Great Britain and the colonies formed one complex economic, political, and social system, with the mother country as the 'overlord', with the 'Whites' in the dominant positions, and with Black slaves, 'coolies' and other 'natives' as the exploited groups. The frames of references which developed were an expression of this relationship, helping to produce, justify and perpetuate it, and have themselves developed as part of the British cultural tradition. They are embedded in the particular social structure and are part and parcel of the society's culture. At a popular level this can be seen in the continued use of the golliwog as an object of affection even today. This provides a stereotype of 'Negroes' which corresponds for example to many of Carlyle's (1853) disdainful and 'inferior' views: 'a pretty kind of man', 'grinning', an 'affectionate kind of creature' – childish, simple, and not very cerebral, nor really of the mature, adult world, but subordinate.

RACIST FRAMES OF REFERENCE, SOCIO-CULTURAL CONSEQUENCES AND CHANGE

Some of the theories put forward in Britain in recent years to account for the oppressed position of 'Black' people, especially those of West Indian background, in the education system and in society in general, can actually be understood within this tradition. It may be significant, for instance, that the greatest aspiration Rex and Tomlinson (1979) seemed able to hold out for the 'Black' people in Britain was that they should become integrated into the *working class*.

Notions of linguistic or cultural deficiency on the part of Black people fit into the traditional British racist frame of reference. For instance, the Department of Education and Science (DES 1971) seemed to assume that 'non-English speaking immigrant children' suffered from 'the restricted code' of the 'culturally deprived' and are thus hindered from developing 'certain kinds of thinking'. In other words, the dubious assumptions are made here that: there is a correlation between linguistic code and cognitive ability; and standard English permits higher levels of thought than the 'immigrant' languages. Difference tends to be equated with deficiency.

Cultural difference – such as linguistic differences, differences in patterns of child-rearing, differences in habits of dress and food, differences in family and religious patterns, and differences in values – can lead to misunderstanding and conflicts, and can help to account for 'race' relations. But such differences *need* not lead to conflicts and difficulties. Sharp and Green (1975) have argued that parents can 'work' the school system even when their values differ from those of the teachers. Besides, cultural differences could also be turned to positive advantage in 'race' relations – for instance, in the multicultural classroom. Culture contact can be a source of positive social change. What seems to be more important than cultural difference is the orientation towards such difference: the extent to which the differences are seen as oppositional, and are exaggerated – or even 'fabricated'. What is also important is a mismatch between the way each group sees itself, is seen, and sees each other – each having a different perspective and different interests. It may be difficult for these groups, given their different locations, different perspectives and the way they interrelate (especially the extent to which this interrelationship may be oppositional), to identify such mismatch. This may help to feed racist frames of reference, making it more difficult for these to be modified or discarded.

These racist frames of reference are part and parcel of the institutionalized, and often oppositional, separateness of the 'White' and 'Black' social worlds, closely linked as these frames of reference are to group identity, cohesion and distinctiveness, and to the interaction between the groups. Especially in an oppositional relationship each group may try to develop its own strategies for control – given its situation and its definition of that situation – so as to sustain its construction of reality and accomplish what it sees as its interests. The strategies of the different groups would be rather different: for example, on the one hand, the dominant racist frame of reference, discrimination, legal exclusion from the society or its citizenship, 'law and order' enforcement, and the differential distribution of knowledge; and, on the other hand, protest, disruptive behaviour, non-conformity, acceptance of a frame of reference and of a group identity exalting Blackness and cultural distinctiveness, rejection of the education system, an attempt to set up one's own, or even an attempt 'to play' the existing system. This institutionalized and oppositional separateness and these opposing strategies for control may make the welding of common experience and structures rather difficult.

However, such a situation of 'race' relations, being dynamic, may also be quite unstable. There is an in-built tension between the dominant and subordinated groups because of their differing structural positions. This tends to result in their having different and probably conflicting constructions of reality. Even oppressed groups actively interpret their situation, give it meaning, and build as far as possible a positive group identity. Maureen Stone (1981) is one of the Black British social scientists in effect to assert this. However, the exploited, oppressed or subordinated group may be likely to take over the general 'race' orientation of the frame of reference of the dominant group while rejecting essential particularities of the dominant frame of reference – and thus rejecting its own subordination. For instance, 'Black is beautiful' (but oppressed and unfairly treated) involves a frame of reference, which (at least on the face of it) takes phenotypical charac- teristics as key social (or political) criteria or identifiers. However, this frame of reference is different from (and may tend to be a mirror image of) the dominant group's. A group constructing its reality in anti-dominant terms such as these, and not having many avenues of power, is likely to seek to assert itself in various non-conformist, non- cooperative, protest or even violent forms – such as in Britain in the 1980s. Although this can result in reinforcing the dominant group's racist frame of reference – and can lead to greater conflict and confrontation – it can also lead to positive change. It can, for instance, result in people becoming more clearly aware of the social realities of their situation, and of the interdependence of the different 'groups'. It can also lead people to discuss the issues, and to question and modify their assumptions, strategies and tactics.

CONCLUSION

The idea which I have sought to develop in this chapter is that of 'race' as a social construction in terms of a taken-for-granted racist frame of reference, which is shared by the members of the 'in-group', but not necessarily, or perhaps only partially, with the members of the 'out-group'. The ideas explored have implications for the study of 'race relations' and for policy and action, both in general terms and specifically in the field of education. It is not adequate to focus simply either on 'racial harmony' or on 'costs' and 'rewards'. It is also essential to be concerned with frames of reference and with the 'material' processes and structures – which are 'dialectically' related to the frames of reference.

3 What is multicultural and antiracist education?

Philosophical and sociological reflections

MULTICULTURAL EDUCATION AND ITS CRITICS

My aim in this chapter is to contribute to a critical philosophical and sociological discussion of the nature of multicultural and antiracist education. It is useful to start by considering some of the criticisms of 'multicultural education' and related concepts. Banks, (1981: 52) writing in the context of the United States of America, has stressed that 'culture is the root of multicultural'. But culture has a very wide meaning, referring to all the 'human made components of society' (Banks 1981: 52). Hence, multicultural education itself has a very 'generic focus' (Banks 1981: 52). As such it 'can make a substantial contribution to the liberal education of students', promoting 'respect and equity for a wide range of cultural groups' such as females, Black people, the Amish, White southerners and Appalachian Whites (Banks 1981: 52). The danger, however, is that the specific problems of certain 'ethnic and racial groups' will probably be overlooked (Banks 1981: 53). It is unsatisfactory simply to lump together the problems of very different groups. Multicultural education is 'a comprehensive but inadequate concept' (Banks 1981: 181). It provides an escape, through a focus on culture, from the more controversial but real and very important issues of 'race'. It simply assumes that the problems are primarily cultural (Banks 1981: 184–5).

Banks' arguments have much force. Culture is a very broad concept, too broad by itself for our purposes. I would suggest that in Britain, as indeed in many other societies, the important factor is not just actual cultural difference but, as with 'race', much more how those differences are evaluated, interpreted, accounted for, used to explain social realities, and related to. Indeed, social significance is sometimes given even to trivial or imaginary cultural differences, as it is to trivial physical differences. As in the case of racism, such interpretive processes are central to what I term 'ethnicism'. Processes of distortion and stereo-typing play an important part in such interpretive work.

Another very wide concept that is sometimes used is that of education for a 'plural' society. In this usage when 'plural' is taken to mean 'culturally plural', the same criticisms also apply as apply to 'multi-cultural education'. But 'plural' can have an even wider connotation than culture, and so can be even more ambiguous.

Banks puts forward the concept of 'multiethnic education' as being more specific and so more satisfactory than 'multicultural education' (Banks 1981: 55). It focuses on 'ethnic' groups within society – not on any and all sub-cultural groups. It is also concerned with prejudice, dis-crimination ánd 'racial' group experience, since these characterize the experience of 'ethnic groups'. One must focus, Banks says, not only on the cultural differences, but also on 'racial differences and racial hostility' (Banks 1981: 181).

However, Banks also stresses that this – in particular, the accepting of specific ethnic allegiances – must take place within the 'overarching and shared American values and ideals' (Banks 1981: 216), which, he maintains (perhaps somewhat wishfully) are drawn from all ethnic groups in the USA (Banks 1981: 217). He also holds that education should foster not only ethnic and national identifications but also a global one.

Again, I would agree with much of this. One of my main criticisms, however, is that there is perhaps too ready an acceptance of the notion of an 'overarching' and shared set of values and ideals. Banks says, for instance, that 'individuals can have ethnic allegiances and charac-teristics . . . as long as their ethnic values and behaviors do not violate or contradict American democractic values and ideals' (Banks 1981: 216). This could in effect imply that the ethnic minorities must conform in the essentials, and may differ only in secondary matters.

Still, Banks is right in saying that the issue of 'race' is of central importance – provided, however, that 'race' is understood as a social construction, since, as Hiernaux *et al.* (1965) have shown, it has little scientific validity. In other words, it is racism and inequality – along lines construed as 'racial' – that are critical.

Mullard (1982), referring to Britain, but following a different line of argument, also points to the importance of racism. His criticisms are of what he terms 'multiracial education'. He distinguishes three phases in its development in Britain. These were, in order, assimilationist, integrationist and cultural pluralist. But all three stemmed from the same 'social imperative – to maintain as far as possible the dominant structure of institutions, values and beliefs' (Mullard 1982: 121). All three 'meant the . . . integrating of alien black groups . . . into a society dedicated to the preservation of social inequality' (Mullard 1982: 130).

Not only did all three phases focus exclusively on 'culture' to the exclusion of issues of racism: they were all themselves racist. In practice 'multiracial education' has operated as 'an instrument of control . . . of the subordination rather than the freedom of blacks' (Mullard 1982: 131). In effect it teaches 'black pupils . . . that they will always remain second-class citizens' (Mullard 1982: 131). This argument leads to a rejection of 'multiracial' or 'multicultural' education, and to a call for 'antiracist education' instead.

It is true that education in Britain, even when it is supposed to have been 'multicultural' or 'multiracial' has not done very well by many minority ethnic peoples, especially those of West Indian, Bangladeshi and Turkish Cypriot backgrounds, as well as the long-established community of the 'Liverpool Blacks' (see DES 1985a). But this does not necessarily mean that 'multicultural' education as such is at fault. It may rather be that it has either not been thought through with sufficient care and thoroughness, and/or has not been adequately put into practice. Or it may be that many different things have gone under the name of 'multicultural' or 'multiracial' education.

Roberts and Clifton (1982) develop yet another line of argument. They put forward a criticism of the Canadian policy of multi-culturalism. In effect they reject ethnic pluralism, such as that espoused by Banks, and give great value to consensus. They do not specifically consider education. However, an argument against 'multicultural education' follows implicitly from their position. It could be formulated somewhat as follows. Either 'multicultural education' is divisive or is only concerned with 'symbolic ethnicity' (Roberts and Clifton 1982). In the first case it is simply to be rejected. In the second it is not an appropriate item for the expenditure of public funds.

To understand this argument fully it is necessary to consider here their general criticism of Canadian multiculturalism, even though this may involve some anticipation of my general argument. Roberts and Clifton (1982: 88) state that multiculturalism is merely an ideology, a set of 'ill-founded beliefs . . . uncritically held by those whose interests are furthered by such justifications'. Their central argument is that a sociological understanding of society requires that a clear distinction be drawn between culture and social structure. Adding their own emphases, they define culture in Kornhauser's (1978) words as 'the *shared meanings* by which people give order, expression, and value to common experiences'. Again quoting Kornhauser (1978), they define structure as 'the stabilization of cooperative efforts to achieve goals, by means of the differentiation of a social unit according to positions characterized by a set of activities, resources, and links to other positions and collectivities'.

They then maintain with Gordon (1964) that 'cultural assimilation can occur without structural assimilation', but 'structural assimilation without cultural assimilation is much less likely' (Roberts and Clifton 1982: 89). But, they add, most ethnic groups in Canada are not able to maintain the necessary 'standards of structural tightness' (Roberts and Clifton 1982: 89–90). They 'lack the structural resources to transmit their cultural heritage' (Roberts and Clifton 1982: 88). It is thus impossible 'to preserve a truly multicultural mosaic in Canada' (Roberts and Clifton 1982: 89–90). Only 'symbolic ethnicity' persists. This is important only as a purely voluntary 'part of an individual's psychological profile' (Roberts and Clifton 1982: 91).

Clearly, this argument implies that multicultural education does not rest on a firm conceptual basis. Genuine cultural diversity tends to disappear within the unifying structure of Canadian society. Thus, 'multicultural education' could only be concerned with 'symbolic ethnicity', a purely personal matter that ought not to be the object of public policy.

On the other hand, to genuinely encourage cultural diversity is to threaten 'institutional commonality' (Roberts and Clifton 1982: 91) and to create 'the potential for civil discord' (Roberts and Clifton, 1982: 91). The underlying notion is that genuine cultural pluralism necessarily requires structural pluralism – and that that is disintegrative, centrifugal, leading to fragmentation and break-up.

First of all, the empirical data Roberts and Clifton cite on Canada are not convincing. More fundamentally, however, their view rests on an oversimplified position that gives consensus priority over all other values. Besides, it seems to be assumed that 'structural integration' is an all-or-nothing phenomenon – and, similarly, that people cannot share in more than one culture. Above all it seems to be assumed that the only unity a complex social order can have is via an overarching culture and a common set of shared institutions.

However, I can see no reason why different units, groups or sub-systems within a society should not each have at least some distinctive cultural features and some social institutions of its own – a complex society consists of several such units, groups or sub-systems each with some distinctive cultural and institutional features. Besides, individuals belong to more than one such unit, group or sub-system. An individual in Canada, for example, may be a trade-unionist, a Roman Catholic, a teacher, a young woman and Anglo-Irish. An individual in

Britain may be a manual worker, a Sikh, an immigrant, a male, a father, an active amateur musician and a royalist. Just as one may be bilingual, so may one be bicultural – at least within certain limits.

It seems to me therefore that 'multicultural' education can be about much more than 'symbolic ethnicity'. It can foster cultural difference, equality between different cultural (or 'ethnic') 'groups', and openness across such 'groups' – that is, understanding and acceptance of cultural (or 'ethnic') difference, and also constructive interaction and even solidarity, across such difference. Thereby, far from being divisive, 'multicultural' education can help underpin a rich and complex social order.

Depending on how it is understood, and on actual practice, it can also be antiracist. It is sometimes said that multiculturalism and antiracism are at opposite ends of a continuum (see, for example, Brandt 1986: 114). This metaphor, however, is oversimple and distorting. Admittedly, *prima facie* multiculturalism does not *necessarily* imply antiracism; nor, *pace* the Institute of Race Relations (1982a: iv), does antiracism *prima facie necessarily* imply multiculturalism. Multiculturalism as between, for example, Finns and Spaniards in Australia does not necessarily imply antiracism. Nor does antiracism between middle class Black and White people in the USA necessarily imply multiculturalism. But neither is there any inherent opposition between multicultural and antiracist education.

The conception and practice of education that are needed depend both on the values held and on the actual social realities. My contention is that Britain is both culturally diverse *and* racist – like many other countries, with variations – while nevertheless being liberal and containing important antiracist forces. Moreover, the cultural diversity and the racism are closely linked and interact. Hence, as I shall argue, education in Britain needs to be both multicultural and antiracist. But what is needed is not a bit of multiculturalism plus a bit of antiracism, not a 'moderate' stance in the middle of some imagined continuum; but a 'radical', thorough-going, well-thought-out, coherent education that is through and through multicultural and antiracist.

There are, however, as with 'multicultural education', varying views of 'antiracist' education (see, for example: Twitchin and Demuth 1985; Institute of Race Relations 1982a; ALTARF 1984; Mullard 1982; Sivanandan 1985; Gaine 1987; Brandt 1986; Rex 1987a; Carter and Williams 1987; Hatcher 1987; Oldman 1987; Troyna 1987).

One could perhaps identify two main sets of approaches: those which seek amelioration within the existing educational and social systems, and those which assume that real change can come only if the existing systems are completely overthrown. The first set would include such approaches as: attitude change; raising of awareness, sometimes in the specific form of racism awareness training deriving from Katz (1978); punishing racist behaviour, such as name-calling; deracializing the existing curriculum; and explicit antiracist political education. Some of these approaches, such as the last one, could also be pertinent to the second set depending on its theoretical context, its intention and the actual manner of its implementation.

The second set *de facto* consists of approaches mainly with a Marxist underpinning. These include: teaching, with the intention of furthering the cause of radical social transformation, about the existence of racist exploitation and showing its roots as being within the capitalist system, springing especially from the transatlantic slave system and from the economic and social relations of Empire; a 'radical reappraisal of all aspects of education to ensure that they are ideologically consistent with the imperatives of antiracist principles' (Troyna 1987: 6); 'dismantling the institutional structure and prevailing ethos in education which ensures and legitimates the *existence* of the hierarchy' (Troyna 1987: 6).

Marxist thinkers such as Sivanandan (1982: 162ff; 1985) have attacked approaches such as those in the first set as deficient in their theoretical analysis since they often focus on attitudes and concepts, and fail to see, according to Sivanandan, that the act precedes the word, and that in the capitalist system the economic factor is dominant and determines social relations. As Carter and Williams (1987: 174) put it, those specifically in the Katz tradition, despite their talk of racism being prejudice *plus power*, have merely 'a personalized view of power and an understanding of racism which sets it aside from economic relations'. It is not just individuals' attitudes, awareness or behaviour that need changing, nor just specific details of the existing educational system that need piecemeal tinkering with: the whole system needs to be overthrown.

However, thinkers in the second set have been criticized, especially by right-wing writers (see, for example, Palmer 1986). Such critics have, perhaps paradoxically (see Oldman 1987), seen Marxist antiracists as dominated by ideology and as degrading education to indoctrination. But it is surely not indoctrination to teach basic values like liberty or antiracism in an open, documented and reasoned way.

The point is sometimes made that *anti*racism suggests a negative and narrow approach. However, racism is a negation (of rights and respect, for instance), and a negation of a negation is positive. Antiracism means not just attacking racism, but replacing it with equality, freedom, informedness, respect, etc. The question for me is to what extent and in what ways education can genuinely contribute to a thorough-going transformation of society, so that society might be more equitable, more humane, and more positively self-transforming – but without sacrificing a rich diversity to a bland conformism.

Antiracist approaches generally have also been criticized for being inappropriate, exaggerated or counterproductive. For instance, Lynch (1986: ix) has termed many such approaches 'strident and confront-ational'. However, perhaps one needs often to distinguish style, vocabulary and strategy from content, rationale and intention. Or perhaps, not a rejection, but a different analysis, of antiracism – and so, in the first place, of racism – is needed. Our discussion in the previous chapter indicates that it would certainly be an error to minimize the existence or extent of racism, or to see it purely in individual or personal terms. The analysis of racism put forward there has implications for multicultural and antiracist education.

THE SITUATION *VIS-À-VIS* 'ETHNIC' MINORITIES IN BRITAIN

We have seen that existing concepts of 'multicultural', 'pluralist' 'multiracial' and 'antiracist' education are open to criticism. Much basic conceptual clarification, including clarification of goals and tasks, is needed. I shall therefore seek to develop and ground what I mean by 'multicultural and antiracist education' – with particular reference to Britain. This requires the clarification of 'multicultural', 'antiracist' and 'education'. This in turn requires the clarification of some basic social values, in particular equality and openness, and of certain underlying and related concepts, such as the human person, society, pluralism, culture, 'race', racism, ethnicity and ethnicism. Furthermore an understanding of the specific society (Britain in particular) and its relation to the wider 'global village' is necessary. 'Multicultural and antiracist education' is just a (somewhat cumbersome) term for the education which is appropriate, given certain basic human, social and educational values, to present-day British society, and to other societies, in view of their 'multicultural' nature and of the corresponding or underlying social realities, which include racism and ethnicism.

An important starting point then is the understanding of the specific society: in particular, Britain. So, the first proposition of my argument points to several characteristics of British society (and indeed of many other European and non-European societies across the world). These are: cultural and ethnic diversity; racism and ethnicism, or racist and ethnicist closedness; and, closely related to this, inequality along racist, and ethnicist lines.

This is not the place for a comprehensive analysis of British society. For example, Britain is a class-structured society and this is very much relevant to the operation of racism and ethnicism in Britain – and indeed to the forms that the incorporation of cultural pluralism takes. No doubt racism and ethnicism, and even cultural pluralism, would take different forms in other types of society. However, I do not accept that racism or ethnicism can be reduced to social class or adequately accounted for simply by a class analysis, even though there are parallels, commonalities and interaction between these phenomena. A class-structured society is not necessarily racist or ethnicist (while a classless society may be), and racism and ethnicism operate across social classes. In addition as Hall *et al.* (1978) have maintained, post-Empire Britain has suffered a crisis of identity, and this is an important factor in understanding 'race' relations in post-war Britain. This thesis fits in well with the notion that racist and ethnicist frames of reference are central in the definition of identity. However, my present purpose is a limited one; not a detailed social analysis but a brief indication, with particular reference to Britain, of the broad characteristics that specifically define it as a society in which 'multicultural and antiracist education' is needed. It is even beyond the scope of the present work to document in detail the cultural and ethnic diversity, the racist and ethnicist 'ideologies', and the inequality.

On the first point, the Swann Report (DES 1985a), for example, has argued strongly that Britain is a 'plural' society. A society can be culturally plural in many different and complex ways. Ethnic pluralism includes the notion of 'groups' seeing themselves, or being seen as, 'ethnic' groups (see below). Not only are there middle class and working class, and various local and regional cultures or sub-cultures in Britain, there are also many different cultural strands going back to population movements and culture contact over the ages, as well as to more recent immigrations of White and of Black people. The more recent Black ethnic minority groups in the widest sense only constitute 4.5 per cent of the population, but it is their presence which has been socially defined as problematic. It is the widescale reaction to their presence which has resulted in the debates about multicultural and antiracist education. These 'Black' minority ethnic populations, as already briefly indicated in Chapter 1, are themselves very diverse, consisting of many cultural, religious and linguistic groups originating from rural and urban areas in many countries around the world. They also cover a wide social class spectrum (see for example, Rose *et al.* 1969; Figueroa 1971; Figueroa 1982; Lashley 1981; Cole 1983; Linguistic Minorities Project 1985; DES 1985a; Parekh 1988). In the ILEA alone, for example, the number of languages spoken by pupils, as a first language, has been found to be over 180 (ILEA Research and Statistics 1989).

As far as racism, ethnicism and inequality along racist and ethnicist lines are concerned, the previous chapter has set out some relevant historical evidence. Chapters 6–9 will also provide relevant data with specific reference to the education system in Britain. Beyond this, some of the many studies which document the inequality of 'Black' minority ethnic groups (in terms of such indices as unemployment, socio-economic status, housing and education) are: Hill (1967); Daniel (1968); Rex and Moore (1967); Castles and Kosack (1973); Figueroa (1974, 1984a and 1984b); Smith (1977); Verma and Bagley (1975); McIntosh and Smith (1974); Husband (1982); Sivanandan (1982); Milner (1983); Brown (1984); and DES (1985a). Such studies also document or infer the existence of discrimination, 'prejudice', stereotypes and racism – though authors vary in their conceptualization. Some other works which provide evidence specifically of 'prejudice', stereotypes or racism are Bagley (1970), Bagley and Verma (1975), Brittan (1976), DES (1981), Davey (1983) and Brown and Gay (1985). It is certainly common in everyday life, in administrative practice and even in academic discourse, for 'race', 'ethnic group' and related concepts to be used as organizing or accounting concepts, with little or no question as to their exact meaning or validity.

ETHNICITY, ETHNICISM, 'RACE' AND RACISM

In view of the varying conceptualizations that different authors use, and so as to clarify my interpretation of the data and hence my understanding of the 'multicultural', 'ethnicist' and 'racist' characteristics of Britain, it is necessary for me to develop further my understanding of several related concepts, in particular those of 'ethnicity', 'ethnic group', 'ethnicism', and 'ethnicist frame of reference'. These are especially important since in many contexts the relevance of racism is often rejected or minimized. For example, even though there has recently been a resurgence of fascism in Europe, the focus on 'intercultural', 'multicultural', or 'migrant' education on the continent is often in terms of 'ethnicity' and perceived cultural differences rather than of 'race', 'racial' differences or racism.

The closely interrelated concepts of 'ethnicity', 'ethnic group', 'ethnicism' and 'ethnicist frame of reference' parallel those of 'race', 'racial group', 'racism' and 'racist frame of reference'. 'Ethnicity', like 'race', refers not just to objective 'characteristics' of 'groups', but especially to constructed 'identities' resulting from collective processes of categorization, definition and identification – whether other-identification or self-identification. Similar collective interpretive processes operate in the case of both 'race' and 'ethnicity'. In the case of 'race', these interpretive processes involve a deterministic ideology (see, for example, Rex 1982). In the case of ethnicity, the extent to which this is so may vary. In the first case, actors believe or implicitly accept that there is an 'essential' link between real or fictional *'natural'* features and certain social, historical, cultural or personality 'facts', real or imagined. In the second case, there tends to be an assumed 'essential' link between real or fictional *cultural* or *historical* features and other social, historical, cultural or personality 'facts', real or imagined. Hence, like a 'racial group', an 'ethnic group' is a social construct in the sense that certain cultural or historical characteristics – real or supposed – are, in effect *given* a social significance (meaning and importance) that they do not necessarily have. Indeed, the focus is often on differences which, as such, are (socially and culturally speaking) of a relatively superficial or trivial nature – such as food, dress or folklore.

However, the parallel of ethnicity and ethnicism with 'race' and racism is not perfect. 'Natural', physical or 'biological' characteristics (or ancestry) do not of themselves necessarily have any social significance, whereas culture and history by their very nature do. 'Race' is inherently a distortion, being a (false) construct of racist thinking, racist relations and racist systems. But 'ethnicity' may represent a group self-definition in 'good faith'. Not all 'ethnic' constructs are, in any strong sense, 'ethnicist'.

Gordon (1964: 24) defines ethnicity in terms of a 'sense of peoplehood'. An 'ethnic group' is thus for Gordon 'a group with a shared feeling of peoplehood' (Gordon 1964: 24). Clearly, however, such a sense of peoplehood is socially constructed by those sharing in it. It involves a collectively constructed identity and shared myths. Such a sense of peoplehood is true of ethnicity as self-definition, and tends to be true of ethnicity as genuine cultural or historical commonality. Nevertheless, it is not just the facts of history or culture, for example, that are important but how these are selected, highlighted, distorted, interpreted – and even invented. A sense of peoplehood, however, does not necessarily obtain in the case of an 'ethnic group' which has been defined as such by others.

Any self-identification necessarily involves a differentiation of the self from the other. Thus any 'in-group' identification at least implicity involves the identifying, categorizing and defining of an 'out-group' even if only an undifferentiated one. But this other-identification does not necessarily tally with the way those others identify themselves. When we look at others and refer to them as this or that 'ethnic group', we are involved in an interpretive process which does not necessarily respond to the 'objective facts' nor to the interpretive process of those others. What is referred to as an 'ethnic group' may sometimes be nothing more than a category. Thus, people sharing essentially the same culture (or history) might be socially defined and related to as constituting more than one ethnic group. On the other hand, people who differ from each other in certain important cultural, or historical, respects – like the various groups in Britain with roots in the Indian sub-continent – might be socially defined and related to as constituting one 'ethnic' group: the 'Asians'.

A 'race' as such has not got the same cultural or historical basis for a sense of peoplehood as an ethnic group (except a purely other-defined 'ethnic group') has. Even more so than 'ethnic groups', 'racial groups' are frequently only categories. But they, too, may be genuine social groups. This may occur, for example, where those comprised under the so-called 'racial' category actually define themselves in 'racial' terms – that is, at least implicitly, by reference to 'natural' characteristics like physical appearance, genetical inheritance or ancestry. They would then, like an 'ethnic' group, have a sense of peoplehood, but one appealing to 'race', phenotype, etc. Similarly, even without any 'racial' self-definition, the so-called 'racial groups' may actually come to form collectivities or groups as a result of the way they are treated, and the positions and roles they are ascribed in the society. Besides, pre-existing 'minority' (or relatively powerless) communities or groups might subsequently adopt, or be attributed a 'racial' identity. And, of course, the powerful 'group' may, at least implicitly, define itself in 'racial' terms. A 'group' or collectivity may be both 'racial' and 'ethnic' in so far as both 'natural' and 'cultural' or 'historical' features may be central at least implicitly, in the collective self- and other-defining, interacting or interrelating.

'Ethnicity', then, as used here refers not just to the sense of peoplehood a collectivity or group has and to the corresponding interpretive and usually distorting processes of self-definition; but also to the related identities ascribed, rightly or wrongly, to others (or to oneself by others) on the basis especially of historical or cultural features, real or imagined.

Ethnicism, like racism, involves assumptions, often only implicit and unstated, which are false, distorted, misapplied or overgeneralized. Besides, like racism, it applies at the closely interrelated individual, interpersonal, cultural, institutional and structural levels. It is not just a matter of an individual's perceptions, beliefs, ignorance, stereotypes, attitudes or prejudice but is closely tied to a group's self- and other-definition and to intra- and inter-group interactions and interrelations. The social constructing is not just an ideological operation but takes place through material social relations, through processes of social interaction and allocation. It interlocks with, flows from, sustains and produces social structures, social articulation.

The 'ethnicist' frame of reference fulfils similar functions to the racist frame of reference. These include the production and reproduction of hard boundaries, closedness, inequality, and enhanced freedom for some but reduced freedom for others. In addition, the use of 'ethnicist' language – which is not usually considered objectionable – can also serve to camouflage racism at all levels (see Reeves 1983 on the related concept of discursive deracialization).

In brief, what I am suggesting is that in so-called 'multicultural' societies (such as Britain) the situation is complex. It is characterized by cultural pluralism – differences in lifestyles, languages, religions, social values, behavioural norms, kinship and family patterns, etc. It is also characterized by plural ethnicity – that is, by a plurality of ethnic group identities. More critically, however, it may be characterized by ethnicism, racism, closedness, inequality, exploitation, conflict, etc. – *and* by forces for equality, respect, solidarity, freedom, etc.

THE HUMAN PERSON, SOCIETY AND THE BASIC VALUES OF EQUALITY, FREEDOM, OPENNESS AND SOLIDARITY

The second main proposition in my argument assumes that inequality, restricted freedom, closedness, ethnicism, racism and the like are socially undesirable. Antiracism, antiethnicism, pluralism, openness, constructive interaction, collaboration, solidarity, equality and freedom are basic human and social values.

This is not the place to attempt the large task of a thorough-going justification of such values. Nor is it my task here to discuss the question of whether such justification is even possible. In my view, however, the situation is somewhat similar to that with language. One can only speak about language by using language. Similarly, one can question the validity of one's knowledge only through one's knowledge. Likewise, one can only justify these basic values in already assuming them or at least the domain of values. The starting-point must inevitably be 'arbitrary', and there will be a certain unavoidable circularity. But not all circles are vicious: some are virtuous. It is at least useful to indicate something of the philosophical and sociological 'bases' of these values, and thereby something more of the content that I wish to suggest for multicultural and antiracist education.

Our grounding of these values, and our understanding of education, must rest on our understanding of the human person and of society. Although I cannot hope to discuss such basic notions in detail here, I have already in the previous chapter outlined my view of the human person as a situated, free, intentional being who is inherently social. Similarly, I have delineated society as a mutual and articulated holding-together and differentiating, a mutual interacting and interrelating, of such individuals. As any individual is always in relation to some other individuals, they network and constitute groups. These groups themselves articulate and interrelate. However, the individual does not precede the social; neither can the social or the individual be accorded priority one over the other. The pursuit of other-advantage or of group-advantage is as basic as, and is inseparable from, the pursuit of individual advantage. Besides, the only motivation is not the pursuit of advantage. One is also guided by moral, ethical and social imperatives.

Culture is the (open) set of lived 'principles' which, looked at abstractly and retrospectively, can be seen to animate and regulate social interaction, this intentional 'holding together at a distance'. Culture – and likewise my social situation – both makes possible *and* limits my every action. These views imply that values such as equality, freedom, pluralism, openness and solidarity are basic dimensions of the human person and of society, and are basic values. They are something like 'preconditions' – or indispensable dimensions – of the social, and deserve to be cherished, defended and actively promoted. Without these, the human person would be diminished and the social would be less constructive, less fulfilling.

As far as the value of equality is concerned, this refers not to sameness, but to equity – that is, to the recognition of relevant differences and the disregarding of irrelevant ones in social interaction and in the allocation of social 'rewards' and social position. If this principle of equality – that is, of equal rights – is not accepted, everyone (indeed society itself) is potentially under threat. If 'might is right', even the present 'strong man' is open to threat from the next 'strong man'.

It is a common error to identify equality with sameness, or even with the notion of the lowest common denominator. For instance, Warzee (1980: 2) writes that educationally 'the Belgian state does not discriminate between Belgians and foreigners . . . criteria of competence alone (fluency in the language, cultural level, knowledge) differentiate among pupils'. This is not, as Warzee calls it, an 'egalitarian principle', but the opposite, because it means that 'Belgians and foreigners' are being assessed, and probably taught, with no or inadequate regard for relevant differences, such as language spoken.

Rex (1987b), in his attempt to clarify the concept of a multicultural society, also fails to develop the concept of equality and so slips into the error of equating it with sameness. He does not seem to distinguish between different and differential. It is crucial, however, that the notion of equality should include equal respect and equitable treatment for *difference*. The right to be different should not be denied because of abuses of it. In fact, apartheid violates the fundamental values of both equality and freedom.

Rather than sameness, equality means fairness – that is, giving full recognition to everyone's rights and legitimate needs, and inseparably taking into account relevant similarities and relevant differences, relevant resources and relevant disadvantages. Ultimately this means a system in which everyone has a fair say, for there needs to be some fair way of deciding what is a 'legitimate need' and what is 'relevant', and even of weighing one right or one relevant consideration against another. If any one person or party had control over this they could manipulate everything to their own advantage and to the disadvantage of others. Furthermore, another basic right is freedom, and this includes the right of everyone to have a fair say in determining one's own destiny, and that of one's society. In other words, equality includes equality of rights and equality of powers; but in both cases equality means the principle that relevant similarities and relevant differences should be given due recognition, always within the framework of being fair to all parties.

Banton (1983: 390–7) discusses equality in terms of a dichotomy: 'fair shares for groups' as against 'fair shares for individuals'. He considers the former 'undemocratic' because, he says, individual freedom would be curtailed. It would, he claims, be necessary 'to prevent anyone changing groups or forming new ones' (Banton, 1983: 390) once equality among groups had been achieved. Similarly, he says, it would also be necessary 'to keep each group the same relative size' and 'to operate quotas' for various occupations (Banton, 1983: 390). This *reductio ad absurdum* is not very convincing. First of all, to reiterate, equality does not mean sameness. Second, when groups change, equality would only require that certain other things might also need to change, such as the share of resources or of votes. To treat groups equally means, ultimately, that each group should have a fair say in the affairs that affect it. This does not preclude change.

Banton (1983: 396) seems to grant that public policy on the basis of 'fair shares for individuals' should seek 'to eliminate any unfavourable treatment of individuals based on their assignment to particular categories when membership is not a justifiable ground for differential treatment'. Thus, to place a child into a lower stream simply because he or she is Afro-Caribbean, or to place a child in a corrective unit simply because his or her behaviour patterns are culturally different, is to take irrelevant differences into account.

But this is only half of the story. The other half is that individuals should also be given equally favourable treatment when membership of some category *is* a justifiable ground for different treatment. For instance, if people belong to different linguistic groups, then they have to be addressed, and taught, in different languages if they are to understand and learn. Hence, to teach everyone through the medium, say, of French or Flemish when half the class only speaks Arabic or Italian, is not equality but just the opposite, because relevant differences have not been taken into account.

The principle involved here is a modified form of Aristotle's principle of proportionate equality. Thus, Aristotle (*Politics*, Bk III, Ch IX, 3 – my italics) says: 'Justice is relative to persons; and a just distribution is one in which the *relative* values of the things given correspond to those [the *relative* values] of the persons receiving'. In other words a person who deserves more should be given more, and one who deserves less, less.

One problem here is with 'deserves' or 'relative values'. The examples Aristotle gives suggests that he has in mind the type of situation where rewards are being distributed for performance. But often it is not easy to compare two different performances. Besides, a performance will not only be a function of innate ability and effort – but also of other factors which may lie outside the control of the performer, such as education and socio-economic conditions (see the discussion of the 'under-achievement' of 'Black' people in Chapter 9 below). Furthermore, situations in which the issue of equality arise do not always correspond to those of a performance. For instance, what might be at stake is whether needs are the same, and if not, how one is to decide whether quite different needs have been equally met.

Whatever the difficulties in practice, the principle is too narrow if it means: more to those deserving more and less to those deserving less. First, there is not always a question of more or less, as what is at issue might be of a qualitative, rather than a quantitative, order. Second, there is not always a question of 'desert' – at least in the sense which implies the rewarding of effort or performance.

Durkheim has pointed out two different conceptions of equality. The first he sums up as 'to each according to his merit'; and the second as 'to a certain extent men should be equally treated despite their unequal value' (Durkheim 1910 in Pickering 1979: 68, 72). The first conception means treating people the same if they are equally meritorious, but differently if they are different in (relevant) merit. The second conception seems to assume that there is some basic underlying similarity between people who otherwise differ, and also that these differences are not here considered relevant. The principle, as I formulate it, encapsulates both of these conceptions – but also goes beyond the notion of 'merit' and incorporates equal respect, not only for basic similarity, but for relevant difference.

Equality, then, implies: the same treatment, position, award, or whatever, to parties which are exactly similar (in the relevant respect – whether this is a performance, innate ability, social circumstance, or a quality, etc.); but different, though fair or somehow 'comparable', treatment, etc. to parties that are non-trivially different in the relevant respect (of whatever type that might be). The difficulty in practice still remains here with what is meant by 'relevant', 'fair', 'comparable' and indeed 'non-trivial'. In any case, the basic point is that equality does not mean sameness or uniformity, but 'fairness' or 'equity'. That is why procedures are needed which permit everyone to contribute to determining such issues, but in impartial ways. Again this points to the close relation between equality and freedom.

Those who are less equal are also less free: they have fewer options and fewer resources. Freedom is the power to determine one's actions and situation – and in a measure to make oneself – but always with and through others. Freedom is a basic human and social dimension and value. Only a free agent could pursue goals deliberately. Only for a free agent could it make sense to enter into means–ends calculations. Only a free agent could be responsible. Only the free can have rights. Only for a free agent does it make sense to speak of a mutual 'taking account of', and this, as we have seen is characteristic of the social. However, this mutual 'taking account of' also means that this freedom is limited. The other, the concrete situation, one's own previous choices and actions, the existing patterns and structures, the existing culture – all simultaneously define possibilities *and* limitations.

Openness to difference enhances freedom. To 'take advantage' of opportunities, one must rely on others, act with others. But to interact one must be open. Only maximum openness makes possible maximum interaction and maximum 'achievement'. *Even* the maximization of self-interest requires the maximization of other-orientation. Solidarity is openness in its fullest sense – that is, positive acting together, supporting each other. In this sense solidarity is not identical to, but overlaps with, Durkheim's understanding – especially with organic solidarity (see Durkheim 1888: 9–11). Through openness and solidarity across differences and boundaries, much can be learned, gained, achieved, realized. Indeed, through such openness and solidarity, racist and ethnicist frames of reference and racist structures might begin to be undermined.

It is a common error to think that openness to other cultures means uncompromising relativism. That all cultures are equally valid is true at one level, but can also be misleading. It may be more accurate to say that in some ways cultures are incomparable, or at least not directly and immediately comparable, whilst at the same time being equivalent to each other. Hence, at a deep-structure level, I would suggest that one can find many commonalities across the most diverse cultures, as Lévi-Strauss's work suggests (see, for example Lévi-Strauss 1966, Merleau-Ponty 1960, Badcock 1975 and Sperber 1979; see also Lloyd and Gay 1981). All cultures face the same basic 'problems' – such as the relation to time and nature and the relation between the individual and the community (see Kluckhohn and Strodtbeck 1961). However, there are also great differences between cultures. These relate to specific geographic, historical and social situations, and to specific 'solutions' to the basic 'problems'. Each culture approaches and solves problems in ways that tend to be appropriate for its specific circumstances. To be open is to appreciate this, and to accept the culture for what it is and as far as possible on its own terms. Above all, to be open is not just to seek out commonalities and to build bridges, but also to accept other cultures in their differences.

However, this does not imply a naïve relativism according to which 'anything goes'. All cultures have a validity. But this does not mean that every detail of every culture is to be accepted. For example, if our culture is racist or ethnicist, then we should seek to change those aspects of our culture. All cultures are complex, living systems. All cultures have a history, and undergo change. All have strong points and weak points, and all probably incorporate some conflicting principles and contradictions. Being open means being questioning, critical of one's own and of other cultures, but in a positive and constructive way.

It would seem to me then that groups can be open in at least three different ways. One is freely to admit new members from outside the group. Another is to be willing to admit new ideas, new values, etc. (this includes the notion of being constructively critical). The third is 'to agree to disagree' – that is, to recognize and accept difference as legitimate, and to collaborate with those who are different without necessarily seeking to change them. As already stated, this does not necessarily imply an absolute relativism. Every culture is committed to what is 'true' and 'correct'.

None of these three ways of being open necessarily leads to a diminution or loss of group identity. New members will tend to adapt to the group. Converts to a religion, for instance, adopt the creed and practice of the religion. Also, intermarriage does not necessarily lead to a breakdown of group identities. Many groups practise exogamy without the group losing its identity. On the other hand, new ideas, or values etc., accepted into a culture will change that culture – at least to some extent – but will not necessarily lead towards its loss of identity. In any case, new ideas, values, etc. drawn from outside a culture will themselves be changed when assimilated into it. Furthermore, changes generated from within may lead to a transformation, but that is not the same as a loss of identity. Finally, simply accepting other cultures as legitimately different in no way necessarily leads to change resulting in loss of identity in the in-group.

PLURALISM

These ideas are important for the issue of pluralism, and the notion of a plural society deserves some further comment here. A plural society is an articulated society, and pluralism in a wide sense can take many different forms. All societies are plural in varying degrees and varying ways. A plural society in Furnival's (1948) – and Smith's (1965) – narrow sense is only one type of plural society. It consists of several quite separate, more or less self-contained communities, each with its own institutions. The individual members of these communities only meet in the market place, and the society is held together – in the original form of this theory – by a colonial power.

Although it is often asserted that pluralism inherently poses a problem for social cohesion, it has not, and perhaps cannot, be demonstrated that the greater the pluralism the greater necessarily the threat to cohesion. Complexity – for example, that of a living organism – does not automatically imply problems of cohesion. Pluralism is not necessarily socially centrifugal. A strong government, in particular by a colonial power (see Furnival 1948), or overarching values – and thereby perhaps at least an attenuation of pluralism – (see, for example: Banks 1981; Banks and Lynch 1986; Bullivant 1981; and DES 1985a) do not provide the only ways of maintaining the cohesion of a plural society. The greater the interdependence of the component 'groups', sectors or classes of the plural society, the more robust will be the cohesion of the society even despite basic conflicts – conflicts of 'objective' interests, for example – between these 'groups', sectors or classes. Above all, the greater the openness of the component 'groups' or sectors, the greater the diversity that can hold together in one society.

Gordon (1964) has distinguished between cultural pluralism and structural pluralism. Cultural pluralism means the existence of several different cultures within the same society. Culture, however, according to Gordon:

> refers to ... the ways of acting and the ways of doing things ... passed down from one generation to the next ... Culture, in other words, is the ... norms of conduct, beliefs, values, and skills, along with the behavioural patterns and uniformities based on these categories ... plus ... the artefacts created by these skills and values.
>
> (Gordon 1964: 32-3)

Structural pluralism, on the other hand, means the existence in one society of several separate, total sets of crystallised or patterned social relationships. Social relationships include primary and secondary group relationships. Primary group relationships are 'personal, informal, intimate, and usually face-to-face', and involve 'the entire personality, not just a segmentalized part of it' (Gordon 1964: 31). Secondary group relationships tend to be 'impersonal, formal or casual, non-intimate, and segmentalized' (Gordon 1964: 32). Gordon equates structural pluralism with the existence of several separate groups or communities each with its own network of institutions or organizations, permitting 'primary group relations to be confined within its border throughout the life cycle' (Gordon 1964: 39 – see also p. 34).

He considers that in a society of immigration like the United States there is a strong tendency to cultural homogeneity despite a marked tendency to structural pluralism. In other words, although separate groups or communities having separate identities and serving as separate primary group systems persist, the vast majority of these tend in fact to adopt a common 'American' culture.

Furthermore, Gordon (1964: 235-238) argues that the tendency to 'structural pluralism' or 'structural separation' (that is the existence of several groups across which there is a lack of intimate primary group relations) 'tends to promote ethnically hostile attitudes' (Gordon 1964: 236). Thus prejudice is perhaps 'endemic' where there is such 'structural separation' (Gordon 1964: 238). Indeed, Gordon (1964: 236) holds that:

> structural separation of ethnic groups, brought about in part by the prejudices of the majority and in part by the desire of most such groups to maintain their own communal identity and subculture, can proceed to a point which is dysfunctional both for the creation of desirable attitudes and relations between the two groups and for the workable operation of the society itself.

Now, one may readily agree with Gordon that cultural pluralism cannot exist without structural pluralism. Martin (1978: 55 and 215) also makes this point. However, it is difficult to see how structural pluralism could persist – as he claims (Gordon 1964: 77 and 81) – without at least some measure of cultural pluralism. Specifically with regard to the USA Gordon's assertion of the strong tendency to cultural homogeneity can be questioned. As Glazer and Moynihan (1963) have pointed out, the 'melting pot' did not happen. Also Harris (1979) has shown that ethnicity has been 'rediscovered' in the USA.

It is, furthermore, not at all clear that structural pluralism would be inherently dysfunctional or conflictual. The existence of several primary group systems (whether they all differ from each other culturally or not) does not necessarily lead to conflict. No doubt there will be conflict in a plural society in which the articulation is along ethnicist or racist lines. But this is not simply a function of difference or articulation. What matters rather is the extent to which the policies, practices and frames of reference of the 'majority' are closed, distorting or subordinating; the extent of social inequality and restricted freedom; and the political awareness of 'minorities'. Critically, frustration and alienation, and thereby conflict, are likely to arise from the experience and awareness of social inequality (for example, in employment, unemployment, housing and education). Also, as Smolicz (1984: 135) points out, conflict arises from the frustration of having a separate ethnic identity, but being denied the means, for instance appropriate curricula, of feeling 'whole persons in a cultural sense'.

A final point here is that conflict itself is not necessarily 'dysfunctional'. It can be destructive; but it may also be positively productive. Moreover, conflict may be a necessary pre-condition, means, or at least correlate, of structural change – and such change may be advantageous.

These views challenge Banton's position that competition as between groups necessarily tends to produce conflict, and that harmonious relations between groups can only be achieved to the extent that competition takes place as between individuals (see Chapter 1 above). This seems to imply that only by the loss of their separate identities can groups live harmoniously together. The implication seems to be that group difference necessarily tends to produce conflict, that this is necessarily dysfunctional, and that a plural society is necessarily and inherently one of conflict and instability.

On the contrary, I am suggesting that differences do not of themselves lead to conflict, that what conflict arises is not necessarily dysfunctional, and that a plural society is not necessarily unstable. The situation is complex. As Price (1969: 215) has observed 'there may be complete assimilation in some things . . . accommodation in other things . . . and conflict in others' – and I would highlight that in some things there may be acceptance of difference as such.

Banton states, indeed, as already indicated, that what counts is not just the fact of difference, but the ascribing of 'cultural' importance to it. However, he seems to consider that when 'groups' encounter, cultural importance will be assigned to differences and there will be competition and conflict. On the contrary, differences can also be complementary or can lead to fruitful collaboration and creative interaction, especially in a context of equality. Even inequality of itself does not automatically and necessarily lead to conflict. What leads to conflict is not just the inequality or the difference, or even just that differences (supposed or real) are assigned social significance. Rather, conflict arises from the extent to which the differences are negatively evaluated (or are irrelevantly or inequitably used as a basis for social allocation) and such evaluation (or allocation or the inequality) are apprehended as unjust. Hence inter-group harmony does not require the breakdown of boundaries in the sense of the diminution of distinctive identities, or even in the sense of the permeability of the boundaries by non-members. Rather, for fruitful and 'harmonious' intergroup relations, it is necessary that groups accept differences as such without negatively evaluating them or assigning them irrelevant or distorted social significance, and it is necessary that there should not be suspicion between the groups. It is in this sense of acceptance of differences, and of mutual trust, that groups need to be open. Of course, it is also necessary to rectify inequalities.

It is also inadequate to think in terms of the sharp dichotomy Banton (1983a: 393–4) has drawn between 'preserving' distinct cultures and developing a cultural 'commonality'. According to this conception, each group would, in the former case, be pressed into intensifying its distinctive ethnicity, and people would be encouraged to think that their cultural characteristics are genetically based. Also, 'high' culture would suffer – apparently because only 'ethnic' culture would be encouraged. Banton has depicted this 'preserving' of distinct cultures as a situation of inherent conflict, of very sharp boundaries and with little potential for new developments. He seems to imply that the only alternative to this would be one of cultural 'commonality' and of a tendency for cultural distinctiveness to disappear. Banton (1983a: 395 and 397) does mention the notion of 'group-based policies . . . constructed on a voluntary foundation' and of 'voluntary groups resulting from inclusive processes', where 'every adult could seek membership of any group'. It is not clear, however, whether Banton thinks that such groups would all end up having very much the same culture. That would seem implicit in his general argument. My contention is that cultural distinctiveness can be maintained without ossification, without necessarily in-built conflict, especially of a dysfunctional type, and without racist or ethnicist assumptions. Cultures can be distinctive, but open and dynamic. The aim would not be to preserve each of the cultures as it happens to be; but to permit each to develop in its own way, on an equal footing with others. This might include developing through interaction with other cultures – which would not necessarily lead to the interacting cultures ending up as one.

Of course, cultures are not in fact always open, and different ethnic and so-called 'racial' groups are often not equal. It seems to me, however, that such things as openness, solidarity and equality, along with freedom (and the correlate to these, pluralism) rather than the maximization of self-interest (or 'commonality' or merely 'racial harmony') must be the aims of policy. Only in this way can the rights and humanity of all individuals, as members of different groups, and the rich potentialities of human and social diversity be realized.

Rex (1987b), in his discussion of the concept of a multicultural society, draws a distinction between the 'public domain' and the 'private domain'. The 'public domain' must be 'unitary', must have 'a single culture based upon the notion of equality between individuals', while 'the private domain . . . permits diversity' (Rex 1987b: 228). This, however, is another one of those abstract, distorting dichotomies like subject–object (see Merleau-Ponty 1945, 1964); individual–social; mechanical solidarity–organic solidarity (see Bernstein 1971: 66); and process–product. Analytically, these all seem at first sight attractive, but as soon as one examines them carefully one finds that things are much more complex, interactive and less clear-cut than they suggest.

Rex tends to equate the 'private domain' with communal matters, where he allows cultural diversity. But if the public–private distinction means anything, it could also be drawn at the communal level. 'Law, politics and economy' – which he sees as the main institutions of the 'public domain' (Rex 1987b: 222) also apply in the communal sphere. Rex, in fact, having set up the private–public dichotomy is then forced into conceding that the real world 'breaches' it (Rex 1987b: 223). He also acknowledges that education pertains both to the 'public' and the 'private' domains (Rex 1987b: 225), and indeed gets into difficulties by assuming that there is some inherent conflict between 'large scale society' and 'the culture of minorities' (Rex 1987b: 226).

Rex (1987b: 220) in effect assumes that diversity in the public domain must automatically mean differential rights. But in my view there is no inherent conflict between the 'culture of equality' and 'cultural diversity'. The culture of equality is not the preserve of 'the majority culture' – nor of the ruling classes, which Rex (1987b: 227–8) comes close to implying. Multiculturalism as a social value means that each individual should be treated equally – that is, equitably – irrespective of irrelevant cultural difference or similarity, but taking appropriate account of each person's (and of his or her group's) specificity because: (1) each culture is worthy of respect; and (2) each individual is equal as a person. It is possible – indeed it is the ideal of multiculturalism – to have diversity *and* equality. I agree with Rex's final point that 'the new social order of the multi-cultural society is an emergent one which will result from the dialogue and the conflict between cultures' (Rex 1987b: 228). This must mean, however, that this dialogue and conflict must touch the 'public domain' and not just the 'private domain'. In the ideal of the multicultural society what matters is that all sectors, groups, classes, and cultures should be equal parties in determining the 'public' order. Rex's distinction of 'public' and 'private' domains falls apart. At the very least one would need to be able to account for how these 'worlds' of the 'public' and 'private' domains relate to each other: the same people inhabit both.

EDUCATION AS AN INSTRUMENT TO PROMOTE EQUALITY, OPENNESS AND FREEDOM

It is an important job of the school to help pupils grow in an open and egalitarian culture and to help them achieve an equal place in and make a full contribution to society. The school likewise needs to enhance the pupils' freedom by empowering them in various ways. It therefore also needs itself to operate in accord with these basic values of openness, egalitarianism and respect for freedom. Thus, the next main proposition in my argument states that education is an important instrument that can help combat inequality, ethnicism and racism, and promote such values as equality, freedom, openness and constructive interaction and collaboration.

A brief word is needed at this point on 'education'. Rex's (1987b: 223) view of education as having the three functions of selecting individuals for occupational roles, transmitting skills 'for survival and for work in industry', and transmitting 'moral values' is too narrow. We need to distinguish between the goals of education and the institutionalized processes. The goals of education need to be seen within the context of the earlier statements about society and the human person. Thus, education is for me concerned with the development of the whole person as an individual human person *and*, inseparably, as an active social being in a specific, concrete cultural and socio-historical situation, which that person can influence, change and transcend even though he or she is constrained and shaped by – and in a sense for – it.

Education is concerned with what one might call the growth of consciousness. This means a growth of self and of self-consciousness, which is also inseparably a growth of social consciousness, since self-consciousness occurs through social interaction. Education is growth in critical awareness (see Freire 1969) – that is, awareness of oneself, of others, of one's own and others' assumptions, situation, social and political reality, limitations and potentialities. Education is not just about 'handing on' specific knowledge and values, a specific culture, but also about developing basic cognitive, evaluative, cultural and social skills and orientations, such as, in particular, openness, egalitarianism and responsibility. It is about developing the faculties of questioning and the ability to see the strengths and weaknesses of one's culture (and of other cultures) and to reject the anti-social and the distorted – such as racist and ethnicist assumptions.

However, it is important not just to remain at the level of basic skills, knowledge and values. Education needs to help each person develop the specific knowledge and skills that he or she needs in the specific society, in order to play a particular active and rewarding part and to 'make a living'.

Schooling, the institutional processes of formal education – with (among other things) their selective and allocative functions – do not automatically achieve these goals. The school may, indeed, work in the opposite direction, and may function to maintain, produce or reproduce social inequality, closedness, and ethnicist or racist frames of reference. The case study reported below in Chapter 7, for example, suggests that ethnocentrism, ethnicism or racism and inequality were probably reproduced in the school studied. Indeed, Althusser (1971) has argued that the school is an ideological state apparatus. Thus, if racism is in the interest of the dominant class – which controls the state – the school would operate to reproduce this racism.

However, Althusser has overstated the case. If the school can be used as an instrument for maintaining the social order, it has within it the potential for affecting, and so also for changing, that social order. The school is not a monolith. There are conflicting forces within it – teachers with different political views, for instance. Similarly, in the education system more widely there are important conflicting forces. The impact of the school will largely depend on the balance between such forces. Moreover, the school 'transmits' knowledge and skills, and also 'transmits' or at least reinforces, values. More basically the school is an important, formal, context for the growth of consciousness. If ways can be found of 'transmitting' knowledge and skills equitably, of 'transmitting' certain values rather than others, and of encouraging a growth of positive, questioning, open and humane consciousness, then the school could, at least indirectly, be an important instrument of change.

EQUALITY, OPENNESS AND MULTICULTURAL AND ANTIRACIST EDUCATION

However – and this is my next proposition – specific educational policies, programmes, organizational arrangements, strategies and practices are needed in present-day Britain (and in other countries), in order to promote the social and human values I have indicated and to achieve the educational goals I have outlined, and will consider further below. When I speak of 'multicultural and antiracist education' it is this complex of educational goals and tasks – and the related educational policies, programmes, organizational arrangements, strategies and practices – that I have in mind.

I cannot pursue here the many issues and details of policy and its implementation, although some relevant points will be raised briefly in these respects. I will, however, now elaborate somewhat the educational goals and tasks of 'multicultural and antiracist education' as understood here.

I have suggested that Britain is a culturally and 'ethnically' plural society characterized by racism and ethnicism (as well as a liberal tradition). The education provided must be appropriate to this situation, assuming that the human individual is inherently social and that education has individual and social aims, and assuming also the basic values (among others) of equality, freedom, openness and solidarity – and, inseparably, of pluralism, antiracism and antiethnicism. My position rejects the dichotomous notion that multiculturalism and antiracism are at opposite ends of some imagined continuum. The social reality is much more complex than that. The education that is required must be multicultural *and* antiracist. To this extent I am in agreement with Parekh (1986). Moreover, it is important to go beyond apparently negative formulations, such as antiracism or countering 'Black underachievement'. Broadly speaking, the goals and tasks of multicultural and antiracist education may be summarized under the complex and closely interrelated principles of pluralism, equality, freedom, openness and solidarity. This includes countering or working against imposed uniformity, oppositional separatism, inequality, exploitation, manipulation, coercion, closedness and intergroup animosity.

With regard to equality, the aim is not just equality of opportunity. More basically, the aim is that, as a human person, one's diverse rights and needs should be met equitably. The aim is genuine equality across difference. Equality of opportunity is a means towards the more basic forms of equality. It is not sufficient just to focus on the 'inputs' and to hope about the outcome. Specific measures need to be taken to try and ensure specific outcomes and to meet the diverse rights and needs of all parties – especially of the minority ethnic population of Caribbean and Indian subcontinent background, since the society has constructed them as the 'problem'.

The interrelated goals of pluralism, openness and solidarity are not only desirable in their own right, but should help contribute (at least indirectly) to educational and social equality. Freedom means here not just freedom *from* racial harassment, ethnic abuse, inequitable assessment procedures etc., but freedom to *be* different, to *be* oneself. More basically, it means being empowered for autonomy.

Now these basic aims need to be seen first and foremost in relation to the pupils. But the implications of these aims also need to be worked out in relation to all the other parties involved in the process of education and in the complex set of institutions which is the school system. They need to be applied to all aspects of the school: assessment procedures, the curriculum, teaching methods, materials, classroom organization, the organization and staffing of the school, etc. All of this implies a rather complex matrix which cannot be worked out in detail here.

However, on the basis of the argument that has been sketched out in this chapter the main tasks of multicultural and antiracist education may, in outline, be seen as including the following, as far especially as the pupils are concerned:

1 providing a good general education for all, including the promotion of the necessary cognitive, value, social and personal development, and skills;
2 making a fair provision of 'marketable' skills for all, taking care not in effect to prepare some 'groups' simply for low-status jobs or second-class citizenship;
3 seeking specifically to rectify any existing educational inequalities or disadvantages affecting any group disproportionately, but especially 'Black' groups – such as, poor attendance, drop out, poor achievement in reading, writing, computation or otherwise, or over-representation in 'sin bins', among lower streams or in non-examination school-leaving classes;

4 promoting sufficient competence in the dominant culture to avoid disadvantage – but without accepting the dominant culture uncritically and without attacking or neglecting the pupil's own culture where different from the dominant one;

5 teaching an official language (English in England) to a high standard;

6 making 'community languages' available to all;

7 teaching mother tongue;

8 promoting insight into, appreciation of, constructive questioning of, and growth in the pupil's own culture;

9 promoting knowledge, appreciation, acceptance and constructive questioning of other cultures, both in their similarities to and differences from one's own culture;

10 overcoming ignorance, stereotyped thinking and narrow (or negative) attitudes;

11 raising awareness of and seeking to transform racist, ethnicist and ethnocentric behaviour and relations;

12 raising awareness of and seeking to replace racist and ethnicist frames of reference with more critical, discerning and open-minded ones;

13 promoting greater insight into and understanding of the nature of racism, ethnicism and ethnocentrism, and of 'race' and ethnicity as social constructions;

14 promoting a better understanding within a broad historical context of the society one lives in, especially of its plural, democratic, racist, ethnicist and class aspects, and of developments (especially in the post-war era) relating to immigration and 'race' relations;

15 in general, developing openness, knowledge, understanding, critical thinking, respect, positive interaction, constructive collaboration and friendliness across cultural, 'ethnic' and other differences, without necessarily seeking value consensus or change in one or other party.

QUESTIONS OF STRATEGY

This is a large and difficult programme, one that cannot best be undertaken merely by isolated individual teachers or educators, nor merely on a voluntary or piecemeal basis. One must seek to involve the normal channels of the education system. The programme indicated is not, however, an impossible utopia. It is essentially a definition of 'good education' expressly taking various relevant specifics into account – as good education needs to.

It is not sufficient, though, to define basic goals and aims and to identify the educational tasks. One needs – and this brings me to my final set of propositions – to devise the necessary strategies for moving forward. This means technical strategies – for example, ways and means within the classroom of raising awareness of and transforming racist frames of reference. But it also means management and change strategies. Many questions of pedagogy and of educational management, organization and innovation – and more widely of social change – thus arise here. For present purposes I can do little more than list some of the important strategies, although it should be stressed that some of these can be seen not only as strategies (pedagogical or not), but also as substantive aims within the broad goals of pluralism, equality, freedom, openness and solidarity, etc., and in particular of developing a fair and equitable education system.

Pedagogically, it would be essential to develop and use curricula, materials, teaching approaches and assessment procedures which are unbiased and free of racism and ethnicism, and which positively challenge racism and ethnicism, and promote the desired values. They would need to be sensitive to, and build on, the pupils' cultures, in general taking positively into account the heritage and experience of the whole range of majority and minority ethnic groups – including the communal experience and history of all these 'groups'. As far as the minority ethnic pupils are concerned, it would be important to use their mother tongue, or any suitable language of which they have adequate grasp as a medium of instruction, especially in the early stages of education, if these pupils are not to be handicapped. Furthermore, it is not sufficient to restrict one's vision to the classroom. Even, for example, the physical environment of the school should reflect the multicultural and antiracist principles.

Each school should develop, adopt and publicize an explicit multicultural and antiracist policy, and should establish a structure, such as a working party with some status and power, to ensure the implementation of the policy and the monitoring and further development of the programmes devised. A systematic approach will need to be taken to examining especially the curriculum, teaching resources, assessment and other procedures, rules, arrangements, organization and structures within the school so as to identify and eliminate any source of discrimination, whether direct or indirect, intentional or unintentional, and so as to identify and promote any strong or potentially strong features from the point of view of the values and criteria built into our argument and especially in the list of tasks above.

Central to the educational endeavour, after the pupils (and the parents), are the teachers, the education administrators and all the other education personnel in the system. It is these, and in particular the classroom teacher, who in practice control and shape the pupils' education. The teacher in particular is an important 'significant other', an important definer for the pupil – as well as an important source, enabler and gate-keeper. Thus, the expertise, knowledge, skills, values and frames of reference, etc. of the classroom teacher – and of all these other education personnel – are of central importance. It is therefore essential to institute staff recruitment and development programmes so as to try and ensure among all staff the same values and qualities aimed at for the pupils, and the relevant knowledge and skills. Moreover, schools should endeavour as far as possible to ensure a fair representation of minority ethnic members, especially of Caribbean and Indian sub-continent background, on their staffs and on their boards of governors, since these bring a particular perspective and experience, and since questions may remain about how equitable the school itself is unless these are adequately represented. Similarly, it is important that minority ethnic members, in particular those of Caribbean and Indian sub-continent background, should be adequately represented as far as possible at all levels of the education system.

Teacher education and the education of administrators and other personnel in the education system have an important role to play in furthering multicultural and antiracist education. This teacher education itself – and the education of the other personnel in the education system – would need to be informed by the values, and to measure up to the criteria, indicated in this chapter. This raises the wider issue of multicultural and antiracist higher education in general, for in the consecutive model of initial teacher education, regular undergraduate programmes are *de facto* an integral part of the education of teachers for those undergraduates who subsequently opt for teaching through the PGCE (Post Graduate Certificate of Education) route, and of course other personnel in the education system are also graduates. In any case it is high time that institutions of higher education gave serious attention across the board to issues of multicultural and antiracist education. *Mutatis mutandis* a similar case can be made out for multicultural and antiracist higher education as has been made out in this chapter for compulsory school education. However, this is not the place to develop that argument.

Chapters 5 and 6, in particular, and Chapter 7, more indirectly, explore some of the relevant points relating to teacher education. Chapter 9 also has implications for teacher education. Apart from teachers and other education personnel, the examination system also has a great impact on the curriculum. If it is biased, it can unfairly restrict the chances of minority ethnic members, in particular those of

Caribbean and South Asian background. Chapter 8 therefore reports on a study relevant to the impact the examination system can have, unfairly, on the life chances of certain minority ethnic groups.

However, first of all, Chapter 4 reviews critically the Swann Report (DES 1985a) since it has made a significant contribution to the debate on multicultural and antiracist education for all, on the situation of minority ethnic pupils and indeed on teacher education – all issues that are central to the concerns of this book.

4 A critique of the Swann Report

INTRODUCTION

The Swann Report (DES 1985a) marks what may well prove to be a watershed in multicultural and antiracist education in Britain. A massive document (well over 800 pages all told) produced by the Committee of Inquiry into the Education of Children from Ethnic Minority Groups, it is supported by several important reviews of research, commissioned from the National Foundation for Education Research (NFER) by the Committee (Taylor 1981, 1987, 1988; and Taylor and Hegarty 1985 – see Chapter 9 below). It has also aroused extensive debate (see, for example: Chivers 1987; Commission for Racial Equality 1985; National Antiracist Movement in Education 1985; Haydon 1987; Mebrahtu 1987; Troyna 1988; and Verma 1989). Furthermore, it has directly or indirectly stimulated or supported various forms of action, including: DES national priority INSET courses; ESG (Education Support Grant) projects; the inclusion of relevant items in the GCSE national criteria; the adoption by many local education authorities (LEAs) of multicultural policies; and the paying of some attention by the National Curriculum Council to multicultural issues.

The Committee of Inquiry was established by a Labour government in 1979. It had its roots in concerns expressed by the 'West Indian Community' (DES 1985a: vii) in the 1960s and 1970s about the way their children were treated in the education system. As a result, the Select Committee on Race Relations and Immigration (House of Commons 1977: para. 57) strongly recommended the setting up of a high level inquiry into the educational 'underachievement of children of West Indian origin'.

In fact, however, the government established the Committee with rather wider terms of reference, namely to 'review . . . the educational needs and attainments of children from ethnic minority groups' taking account of relevant factors outside the education system (DES 1985a: vii). The Committee was also to consider issues of monitoring 'the educational performance of . . . ethnic minority groups', and were to give 'early and particular' attention to 'pupils of West Indian origin' (DES 1985a: vii).

Although the Committee interpreted these terms of reference widely – and thus focused on 'education for all' – this background history and the emphasis on ethnic minorities, and especially on 'under-achievement' (rather than, say, on antiracism, or structural accounts, or the education of the 'majority') had a strong and limiting influence on the final Report.

An interim report (the Rampton Report, DES 1981) focused specifically on 'West Indian children in our schools'. (Black British educationalists have often raised a question about this 'our': are not the Black British, and in particular British born youngsters of Caribbean background, part of 'us'?) This interim report highlighted so-called 'West Indian underachievement' (that particular issue will be taken up in the last chapter of this book) and emphasized the factor of racism. However, it also identified and explored several other factors, and strongly indicated that there was 'no single cause . . . but rather a network of widely differing attitudes and expectations on the part of teachers and the education system as a whole, and on the part of West Indian parents' (DES 1981: 72).

The work of the Committee was arduous and sensitive. There were many resignations in its long life. After the interim report was published, a new chairman, Lord Swann, emerged.

SUMMARY OF THE SWANN REPORT

The Swann Report contains sixteen chapters plus the conclusions and recommendations, a preface, a summary of the interim report, a range of very useful annexes to various chapters and several appendices. The main message of the Report is expounded primarily in Chapter 6. Chapters 1 to 5 lay the basis by considering: the nature of British society today; racism; educational achievement and underachievement of 'West Indians' and 'Asians'; and the history of the response in policy and practice to immigration and 'ethnic minorities', including recent developments – or non-developments – in 'multicultural education'. Chapters 7 to 9 pick out certain 'major areas of concern' for particular attention. These are: language (especially English as a second language, and mother tongue); religious education and related issues; the issue of separate schools; teacher education and staff development; and the employment of ethnic minority teachers. Chapters 10 to 16 consider children from Chinese, Cypriot, Italian, Ukrainian, Vietnamese, 'Liverpool Black', and 'Traveller' (i.e. Gypsy) backgrounds.

The argument of the Report may be summarized somewhat as follows. Since the Second World War, the response of the education system to immigration and 'ethnic minorities' has moved broadly from 'assimilationism', through 'integrationism', to 'multiculturalism' (DES 1985a: 191–9). It became clear in the 1960s and 1970s that neither an 'assimilationist', nor an 'integrationist' approach had successfully met the needs of the 'ethnic minorities', nor had these minorities been 'absorbed' into the society. However, the 'multicultural' approach which thus developed was confused and open *de facto* to criticism on various counts. In practice it focused on 'ethnic minorities', and impinged only on schools in multiethnic areas.

This is far from satisfactory, for Britain today is a plural society – one particularly important aspect of this being the society's multiethnic nature (DES 1985a: 3–8). All the ethnic minority groups reviewed demonstrate a strong sense of identity (see DES 1985a: 760). What is required is an approach which:

> enables all ethnic groups, both minority and majority, to participate fully in shaping the society . . . within a framework of commonly accepted values, practices and procedures, whilst also allowing and, where necessary, assisting the ethnic minority communities in maintaining their distinct ethnic identities within this common framework.
>
> (DES 1985a: 5)

This is a pluralist approach, and its watchword is 'diversity within unity' (DES 1985a: 7–8). 'A multi-racial society such as ours would . . . function most effectively and harmoniously' on the basis of such pluralism (DES 1985a: 5). However, 'the major obstacle' (DES 1985a: 8) to the realization of such a pluralist society is racism – as seen in 'individual attitudes and behaviour' as well as in the 'more pervasive "climate" of racism' (DES 1985a: 36), including 'institutional policies and practices' (DES 1985a: 8). All the ethnic minority groups reviewed reported the experience of racism (see DES 1985a: 761). Moreover, there is evidence of 'underachievement' among most of the ethnic minority groups, not least among the 'West Indians' (see, however, Chapter 9 below). Furthermore, the evidence to hand indicates that this cannot be accounted for by IQ, therefore the explanation must be sought in a complex of factors, encompassing socio-economic 'deprivation' (DES 1985a: 71–6) and 'racial prejudice and discrimination' (DES 1985a: 89–90).

In view of these various considerations, the Swann Report argues strongly for an educational approach, and hence for a teacher-education and staff-development system (DES 1985a: 541–99), which stress 'the relevance of multicultural education to all children' (DES 1985a: 226). The Report usually refers to this simply as 'education for all' (DES 1985a: 315–326). This means 'educating *all* children, from whatever ethnic group' (DES 1985a: 316) with the interrelated aims of:

1 helping them understand 'the shared values of our society as a whole' (DES 1985a: 316);
2 helping them appreciate and respect the diversity of cultural identities and 'of lifestyles and cultural, religious and linguistic backgrounds' in Britain and the world (DES 1985a: 323 and 316);
3 encouraging them to develop 'positive attitudes towards the multiracial nature of society, free from . . . inaccurate myths and stereotypes about other ethnic groups' (DES 1985a: 321);
4 helping them 'to develop . . . a flexibility of mind and an ability to analyse critically and rationally the nature of British society today [pluralist and interdependent] within a global context' (DES 1985a: 324);
5 promoting in them 'an appreciation [sic] and commitment to the principles of equality and justice' (DES 1985a: 320);
6 enabling them 'to contribute positively to shaping the future nature of British society' (DES 1985a: 316–17) – working within the 'commonly accepted' framework (see DES 1985a: 5);
7 helping them 'to gain confidence in their own cultural identities' (DES 1985a: 323), enabling them 'to determine their own individual identities, free from preconceived or imposed stereotypes of their "place" in . . . society' (DES 1985a: 317);
8 helping them develop 'both a national identity and indeed an international global perspective' (DES 1985a: 322).

Furthermore, 'a good education must reflect the diversity of British society and indeed of the contemporary world' (DES 1985a: 318). It must combat racism, and, within this, identify and remove 'those practices and procedures which, work, directly or indirectly, and intentionally or unintentionally, against pupils from any ethnic group' (DES 1985a: 319, 320). It must provide 'true equality of opportunity' for all (DES 1985a: 325). Hence it must cater for all individual educational needs, including 'any particular educational needs' of ethnic minority pupils (DES 1985a: 317). This would include, where appropriate, English as a second language. Pastoral needs must also be attended to – so as to avoid, for example, conflict between the requirements of pupils' 'fundamental religious beliefs and the provisions of the school' (DES 1985a: 326). These goals can be achieved only if the curriculum and indeed the whole work of the school are *permeated* by the 'multicultural perspective' (DES 1985a: 323). Moreover, both initial (DES 1985a: 557) and in-service (DES 1985a: 583) teacher education must likewise be permeated.

These principles – the Swann Report continues – have implications for evaluating and developing the curriculum, for formulating school and educational policies, devising strategies and making organizational changes, and, in general, for managing change at all levels of the education system and the LEAs, from the DES down to individual schools. Among other things, these principles imply the need for political education in so far as the basic principle is that of preparing all pupils for adult roles in a pluralist democracy. Moreover, of prime importance are the implications relating to the 'hidden curriculum'. These involve, in particular, 'the ethos' which the schools present and 'their attitudes and policies towards . . . the "pastoral" needs of their pupils at the interface of the home and the school' (DES 1985a: 340).

With respect to language issues, the Swann Report (DES 1985a: 413) argues for 'a greater awareness of the language needs of all children and for recognition . . . [of] the positive aspects of the multilingual nature of society today'. Pupils' concept of language should be broadened: they should not 'see it solely in terms of "English"', and should be educated into 'a real understanding of the role and function of language in all its forms' (DES 1985a: 419). However, the Report also argues that 'the key . . . to academic success and . . . to participation on equal terms as a full member of society, is a good command of *English* and the emphasis must therefore . . . be on the learning of English' (DES 1985a: 407). The Report (DES 1985a: 416) fully supports the notion of 'language across the curriculum as important to the education of all pupils' – and, in particular, of minority ethnic pupils. Good teaching adapts itself 'to the particular linguistic needs of the class or indeed the individual pupil' (DES 1985a: 414).

Within this context, the Report also argues against any form of 'separate provision' in the teaching of English as a second language (DES 1985a: 389–92). This should be seen as an integral part of language education, 'as an extension of the range of language needs for which *all* teachers . . . should . . . given adequate training and . . . support, be able to cater' (DES 1985a: 392). Among other things separate provision: tends to mean the injustice of a restricted curriculum; may not in any case meet 'language needs perceived by class teachers' (DES 1985a: 391); and may have negative effects both on

English language competence and on socialization – because of the minority ethnic child being separated from normal school life and from the majority of their peers.

On the question of mother-tongue (or community-language) provision, the Report (DES 1985a: 397–413) distinguishes between bilingual education, mother-tongue maintenance and mother-tongue teaching. By 'bilingual education' is meant 'the use of a pupil's mother tongue [or "community language"] as a medium of instruction alongside English' (DES 1985a: 399). By 'mother-tongue maintenance' is meant doing work with minority ethnic pupils on their mother tongue or community language in the primary school. 'Mother-tongue teaching' refers to teaching 'community languages' as an integral part of the secondary curriculum to any pupil who might be interested.

The Report takes the view that linguistic diversity is a 'positive asset': all schools have 'a role in imparting a broader understanding of our multilingual society to all pupils' (DES 1985a: 406). Moreover, 'the linguistic, religious and cultural identities of ethnic minority communities' should indeed be fostered (DES 1985a: 406). Nevertheless, the Committee rejects any idea of 'bilingual education in maintained schools', and regards 'mother tongue maintenance . . . as best achieved within the ethnic minority communities themselves rather than within mainstream schools' (DES 1985a: 406). However, it 'wholeheartedly' favours 'the teaching of ethnic minority community languages, within the languages curriculum of maintained secondary schools, open to all pupils'.

With respect to religion, the Report (DES 1985a: 465–98) supports a wide-ranging, non-denominational religious education, but opposes any denominational religious instruction in the school. Religious instruction should be left to the community. Religious education, however, can play an important part in preparing all pupils for multiethnic Britain, and in countering racism. The Report (DES 1985a: 498–517) also rejects the notion of separate 'ethnic minority' schools – in particular Islamic and 'Black' schools – while noting the right enshrined in the law for such schools. It considers that such schools would be divisive and might undermine the case for multicultural education for all. However, it calls for the retention of some single-sex schools – as that would partly cater for some of the religious and cultural sensibilities of, in particular, Muslim parents. In general, schools should be more sensitive to and respectful of the religious and cultural requirements of the different communities. Also, the education and teacher education systems should do much more to rectify the underrepresentation and unequal position of ethnic minorities in the teaching profession.

CRITICAL COMMENTS

Diversity within unity

In my opinion, the Swann Report is much to be welcomed, and provides a good and particularly significant staging post from which to move forward. It handles a very complex and sensitive topic in a broad and constructive way. Most of the themes I have developed in the previous chapter are addressed. Nevertheless, some major criticisms may be made of the Report – due in particular to some of its emphases, to some of its conceptualizations, and to certain central ambiguities (and even contradictions) built into it.

The Report (DES 1985a: 4) distinguishes between two theoretically 'extreme forms' of relationship between the 'majority' and 'minority' groups. These are 'assimilation' and 'separatism', both of which the Report rejects. 'Full assimilation' means the minority group losing 'all the distinctive characteristics of its identity', and being 'absorbed within the majority group'. 'Separatism' means the separate groups existing and operating each within its 'own separate "compartment"'.

But this is too stark and simplified a division to be of much use. Constructive interaction depends on strong separate identities. A strong cultural identity assumes some measure of separate social organization. Moreover, this issue is not just that of the relation between 'the majority' and 'the minorities'. There is also a question of the interrelation between minority groups, and, above all, of cross-cutting interrelationships. Relationships that cut across ethnic groups (or segments of ethnic groups) do not necessarily tend to destroy ethnic group identity or organization, but help to establish a wider 'organic' organization. The social reality is complex, dynamic and open.

The way in which the Swann Report attempts to deal with some of the complexity, and to find a 'balance' between assimilationism and separatism, is to focus the argument on the desirability of pupils understanding 'the shared values of our society' (DES 1985a: 316) while at the same time appreciating cultural diversity. The emphasis thus seems to be on pupils learning about cultural diversity (in a framework of unity), and, beyond that, developing (laudably) 'a flexibility of mind and an ability to analyse critically and rationally the nature of British society today within a global context' (DES 1985a: 324). However, the 'nature' of British society seems to be taken as given. Furthermore, it seems to be seen essentially in terms of a diversity of 'lifestyles and value systems' (DES 1985a: 324). Thus the focus is not on such matters as the right to and the value of separate identities, which schools should therefore support; nor on societal structures such as inequality to be overcome or structural racism to be dismantled. Many of these (or related) aspects are admittedly mentioned, but without being taken as major organizing concepts. The main concerns seem to be with *cultural* diversity, within social *unity*.

There is, indeed, a central ambiguity in the key notion of 'unity within diversity'. Some passages seem to go quite far in extolling diversity, whereas others seem to be preoccupied with unity. The diversity intended seems to be merely that of lifestyles, whereas the unity seems to assume the continued hegemony of traditional British institutions, practices, procedures and law. What, then, is the essential difference from the assimilationist and integrationist positions rejected by the Swann Report itself?

The Report argues for a democratic pluralist society as 'socially cohesive and culturally diverse' and 'as seeking to achieve a balance':

> between ... the maintenance ... of the essential elements of the cultures and lifestyles of all the ethnic groups within it, and ... the acceptance by all groups of a set of shared values distinctive of the society as a whole.

(DES 1985a: 6)

However, as I have argued in Chapter 3, one cannot really separate the social and the cultural that sharply. Indeed, social coherence as argued by Swann means the sharing of common values and of common ways of proceeding. But this means sharing of cultures since values and norms are central aspects of culture. If culture means anything more than quaint and visible manifestations (like calypso and curry), and if it means religion and language (and therefore values, world-views, conceptual systems, etc.), then it cannot be separated from social organization and social practice. At the least, the cultural and the social are symbiotically interrelated. The cultural is not just an epiphenomenon, but is built into the simplest and most fundamental of social practices, relations and structures. It seems to me there can be and is unity in diversity, but this is so both in the social and in the cultural.

Swann states more than once the need for 'a framework of commonly accepted values, practices and procedures' (DES 1985a: 5–6). This implies both cultural and social sharing. The questions, however, that Swann does not clearly resolve are: *which* framework of values, practices and procedures, *whence* such a framework, and *how* is its development and functioning envisaged. Although Swann (DES 1985a: 7–8) speaks of 'an amalgam of all the various forces' and rejects the notion of the minority communities being assimilated 'within an unchanged dominant way of life', it remains at best unclear whether or not 'the shared values distinctive of the society as a whole' refer to the traditional, dominant ones already in place. If so, then the 'balance' achieved will be one of assimilation to the 'majority' group. If not, what precisely is the conception being put forward? Is it the notion of a 'melting pot' – i.e. a completely new (but unitary) culture and set of mechanisms – developing? Or is it the notion of the sum of all the values and procedures that might happen to be similar across the different groups? Or is it a very general framework of basic values such as: pluralism, democracy, egalitarianism, antiracism and humanitarianism? Or is it merely a procedural framework – namely, that all groups and interests constantly contribute to a dynamic process?

Power

A crucial question in this matter, which the Swann Report tends to neglect, is that of power. The issues are complex. What 'balance' can one expect to be achieved between the cultures of different groups if one of those groups is much more powerful than the others? It seems to me that several conditions would probably need to be met for cultural pluralism to prosper.

Among other things, each group would need to have some power base, and to mobilize that power. Power, indeed, rests on many different bases. Group power is not just a matter of size. It depends also, among other things, on the strength of group identity, on group cohesion, organization and action, on the establishment of and access to networks, on the level of education and the access to knowledge and information, on access to and control of the media (i.e. to the flow of information and the shaping of ideology and images), on the accumulation of capital, on the holding of or control over exchangeable resources, on the control (which may take different forms) of the means of production and distribution (of *desiderabilia*, values, ideology, conceptualizations, beliefs).

Alternatively, or additionally, the weaker groups would need to 'join forces' in their common interest. The dominant group would need to see power-sharing as in its interest, and/or would need to subscribe to basic democratic, egalitarian or humanitarian values. Furthermore, there would need to be adequate procedures for accomplishing and safeguarding such values. The situation would naturally be dynamic. If such procedures were enshrined in law, however, that would give them greater force and stability.

Racism, 'underachievement' and inequality

Related to the Swann Report's neglect of power is its highlighting of the individual, attitudinal and cognitive dimensions of racism. Thus the main concern seems to be with the prejudice, stereotypes and ignorance of individuals. Although institutional racism, inequality, name-calling and racist attacks are referred to, they are not central to the discussion or the recommendations. Yet racism is a particular system of inequality and exploitation, with an 'underpinning' that reaches deep into the culture. In school, therefore, it is not sufficient – though it is desirable – to raise awareness, overcome ignorance and change attitudes. The very images and assumptions of the culture (its frames of reference) and, in particular, the very structures, procedures, mechanisms and processes of the school and of the education system generally, also need addressing. Research (for example, Pettigrew 1969) has long since shown that information campaigns by themselves are ineffective. Hence it is misconceived to think of countering racism merely in terms of teachers seeking to 'dispel present ignorance' (DES 1985a: 88).

Another related point is the salience given to ethnic minority (especially 'West Indian') 'underachievement' – rather than to their *inequality* within the education system. As will be suggested in Chapter 9, this preoccupation with 'underachievement' is a symptom of the racist situation, reinforces negative stereotypes, misdirects the debate excessively towards questions of individual characteristics (especially 'IQ') and cultural 'deficiencies', and away from the crucial issues of processes and structures. What are the grounds for asserting (DES 1985a: 87) that 'the very different school performances of Asians and West Indians seem likely to lie deep within their respective cultures'? Is this kind of statement not itself a part of the problem? Moreover, the 'underachievement' data offered by the Swann Report, (as we shall see in Chapter 9) are themselves open to important criticisms, not least to the lack of sophistication in the way they were collected and are analysed.

Cultural preservation

There are now some other specific points that I would like briefly to take up. The first is the insistence that it is not the job of the school 'to reinforce the values, beliefs and cultural identity which each child brings to school' (DES 1985a: 321), nor to preserve cultures (DES 1985a: 322–3). The Swann Report suggests two main arguments here for this view. The first is that 'cultural preservation' would entail a narrow education, one that was monocultural rather than multicultural. The second is that cultures are dynamic, and so seeking to preserve them would be self-defeating.

However, I would maintain first of all that to be able really to understand, respect, appreciate and relate to other cultures and identities one must be secure in one's own culture and identity. One must stand somewhere in terms of values, assumptions, conceptions, etc. Hence, strengthening children in their cultures is far from antithetic to opening them to other cultures: their own culture is the only means they have of approaching other cultures – as well as of reflecting on this, their own culture. Like a bridge, a culture – i.e. an identity, a language – is both a means of contact and that which separates. What is necessary, as I have argued in Chapter 4, is that one should approach both one's own culture and other cultures in a questioning and positive way.

I agree with the Swann Report (DES 1985a: 322) that 'an education which seeks only to emphasise and enhance the ethnic group identity of a child, at the expense of developing both a national identity and indeed an international, global perspective, cannot be regarded as . . . multicultural'. However, the dichotomy established here provides a snare. It is possible to enhance the ethnic group identity of children *and* to develop their national and international identities, including openness to and appreciation of other cultures. Indeed, as already suggested, the former is necessary for the latter: it is the only ground one has to stand on.

I agree therefore that schools should be 'encouraging the cultural *development* of all their pupils, both in terms of helping them to gain confidence in their own cultural identities while learning to respect the identities of other groups' (DES 1985a: 323). But this can be done only if schools are open to different cultures. *De facto*, schools are enacting, reproducing, legitimating, and teaching the 'dominant culture' all the time. If they do not make special efforts to include minority cultures as well, they will simply continue to be monocultural and to teach monoculturalism. Especially in schools where minority ethnic children are present, failing to make such special efforts would in fact amount to a strong message of rejecting, non-valuing or even despising their cultures.

The argument that cultures are dynamic and should not therefore be 'preserved' is unfortunately an example of sophistry. Of course, if by 'preserve' one means 'encapsulate' or mummify, then the argument applies both to the 'dominant culture' and to the others. But that is not an argument for excluding any express use of, approach to, or any operational assuming of, minority cultures any more than it would be for excluding the 'dominant culture'. Rather, it is an argument for approaching and including the various cultures as all being living, dynamic systems.

Language

Similar observations can be made about the Report's views relating to 'community languages'. Completely to reject any consideration of any form of bilingual education, particularly in the early years of schooling, and furthermore completely to reject the 'maintenance' of mother tongue in the primary school is in effect to send out the message that the 'community languages' are of no great importance. The position of the Swann Report in these regards undermines its protestations about the positive values of multilingualism and the equal validity of all cultures in their own right (see, for example, DES 1985a: 323 and 406). Indeed, this stance must necessarily put at least some linguistic minority children at a definite educational disadvantage, thus also undermining the Report's advocacy of equality of opportunities for all (see, for example, DES 1985a: 5). Perhaps the Report assumes that bilingualism would necessarily retard proficiency in the main language (English) of the society. But such an assumption is not substantiated, and probably only seems to have force because Britain has traditionally been a monolingual society. In the world at large, however, bilingualism is the norm (Spolsky 1978: 17). The case for bilingualism is reviewed, for example, by Saunders (undated).

Cummins (1981) has shown the crucial importance of bilingual education for minority language children. Beltz (1985) has also found that the use of first language enhanced self-esteem and cultural maintenance (not to be equated with 'encapsulation'). Furthermore, initial language and reading instruction in the mother tongue actually assisted with the learning of the 'dominant language', English. Finally, using mother tongue as a medium of instruction in various subjects while the child was still learning English would help to ensure concept development.

Separate schools

Again, similar points may be made with reference to the debate about separate schools. If Church of England, Roman Catholic and Hebrew schools correspond to certain basic rights and are allowed, why should other minority ethnic groups be treated differently? Will this not send out negative messages about them and their cultures, including their religions? Moreover, there already exist *de facto* unplanned separate 'Black' schools, or schools that are overwhelmingly 'Black' but not necessarily so through the choice of the Black community. It would be better if Black schools could develop where there was a positive wish for, and commitment to, them on the part of the Black community, and in particular of Black parents. Furthermore, the majority of schools in Britain are monoethnic 'all-White' schools. If they can be permeated by a multicultural and antiracist approach, why should it not be possible for the same to be true of, for instance, 'Black', or Muslim or Sikh monoethnic schools? Why if Church of England schools, Roman Catholic schools, Hebrew schools, and 'all-White' schools are not divisive, should 'Black' or minority ethnic or minority religious schools necessarily be?

SUMMARY

In summary, the Swann Report has made a valuable and substantial contribution to the debate about education for a 'multicultural society'. It has stimulated much thought and action. To my mind it points basically in the right direction by stressing the positive advantage of a multicultural society and the need for all pupils to be aware of cultural diversity and to have respect for other cultures. Likewise, it is right in calling for equal educational opportunities for all, and in saying that both individual and institutional racism must be countered. However, in some respects, its emphases need redressing – in particular to give greater weight to equality and antiracism. Furthermore, some of its central concepts (pluralism, equality, racism) require sharper analysis. Finally, some of its stances, especially in relation to cultural 'maintenance', language issues and the 'separate schools' debate, seem to be in conflict with the Report's basic pluralist philosophy.

5 Can teachers be taught?
Can attitudes be changed?

One set of issues which the Swann Report focused on, as we have seen, was to do with teachers and teacher education. Clearly, the education which children actually get depends most immediately on the teachers in the classroom. Questions therefore of the attitudes of teachers, of whether there is ·a link between their attitudes and the academic performance or the attitudes of pupils, and of whether and how these matters should be researched are of some significance. Underlying these questions are also those of attitude change which relate not only to teachers, but also to pupils and to the population at large: such questions as whether attitudes can be changed and whether and how one may go about trying to change them in the process of education. In this chapter I will consider some of the broader issues, but discussing them specifically in relation to teachers.

I take as a convenient focus one of the main conclusions which Tomlinson (1981: 68) put forward in a review of the research context to teacher education for a multicultural Britain, namely that 'there would seem to be *no* need for further research on teacher attitude and opinions'. Tomlinson has since written fuller literature reviews in the field of multicultural education (for example 1983) and has not repeated this opinion. The present chapter is therefore intended less as a critique of Tomlinson's considered views than as a discussion of some of the important issues involved in such an opinion. Although Tomlinson is not entirely explicit about her reasons for putting forward this view, she seems to imply, perhaps, four main ones, as follows: enough research has already been carried out in Britain on teacher attitudes, opinions and expectations in this connection; further research of this type is likely to antagonize teachers; it is difficult to establish a link between academic performance and teacher attitudes, opinions and expectations; we cannot, anyway, hope to change such attitudes, opinions and expectations.

First of all she expresses the opinion (1981: 56) that teachers 'perhaps too often, have been the objects of research and exhortation concerning their job in a multi-cultural society'. But in fact relatively little has been done in Britain to study the extent and nature of teachers' attitudes, opinions and expectations relating to multiculturalism and racism. Such attitudes, opinions and expectations which might be held by others involved in education have also hardly been the focus of research. It is, after all, a sensitive and difficult area to study. Tomlinson (1981) herself identifies only some eight British studies concerned specifically with these issues. Taylor (1981: 195) has also remarked on the paucity of research in Britain into teachers' attitudes towards ethnic minorities. Many aspects of this important matter seem not as yet to have been researched. It is a useful first step (see Tomlinson 1981: 59) to have established, as Brittan (1976) has done, that teachers tend to stereotype children of West Indian background and to perceive them 'as of low ability and as creating discipline problems'. Edwards' study (1979) – referred to by Tomlinson (1981: 61) – linking such attitudes to speech types as an identifier is also important.

Much more research remains to be done, however, as will I hope become more apparent in what follows. In general terms we need not only to know more about teachers' attitudes, but especially to seek greater conceptual clarification, and a greater understanding of: the social roots of teachers' attitudes; the educational consequences, if any, of these attitudes; the mechanisms which might be involved; and the ways in which, directly or indirectly, negative 'forces' can be countered or removed and positive ones introduced or supported (see Newcomb and Charters 1952: 244–6, though I am critical of the mechanistic and algebraic character of their conception).

But would research into such issues simply antagonize teachers, who 'might justifiably begin . . . to reject their scapegoat label' (Tomlinson, 1981: 68)? Not necessarily. This depends on how it is done, with what sensitivity, and within what conceptual framework. To study the attitudes of teachers is not necessarily to attach to teachers a 'scapegoat label'. Their attitudes might be conceptualized, not on an individual pathological model, but as arising within certain social systems and contexts, and as being but one element performing certain functions within the existing structure and within the existing network of interrelations.

More research certainly needs to be done, as Tomlinson (1981: 68) recommends *with* the active co-operation of teachers – and by teachers themselves. For example, collaborative action research, perhaps combined with some form of consciousness raising, might be appropriate. Similar issues may be raised about how others in the education system – especially pupils and parents – are perceived, treated or involved in the research process. In social research one must always be on guard against depersonalizing the respondents and the social reality under investigation – both for ethical reasons and because otherwise the social reality will be falsified. Hence, not only should researchers enter into a partnership with teachers and not only should teachers 'do research', but also researchers and teachers should enter into a research as well as an educational partnership with pupils and parents. Researchers and teachers should not treat minority ethnic children and communities merely as problems or as objects of study. This raises questions, for instance, about participative research.

The third reason that Tomlinson (see 1981: 57) seems to have in mind for saying that there is no need for further research into teachers' attitudes is the difficulty of establishing a link between pupils' academic performance and teachers' expectations, attitudes and opinions. Tomlinson (1983: 74) repeats that 'the links are difficult to frame empirically'. However, this is a general point, since attempting to establish 'causal' links presents a basic difficulty for social science research. It is not a reason for discontinuing research, but for developing more appropriate conceptualizations of social research and of the research problems, and more appropriate research approaches, designs and methods. Actually, Tomlinson herself readily accepts that 'Rist's (1970) work in the U.S.A. *demonstrated* a link between teacher expectations of some black children and their subsequent poorer performance even where the teacher was herself black' (Tomlinson 1981: 5, my italics). She also points out that, after careful documentation, 'Rogers (1981) . . . concludes that there is sufficient evidence to demonstrate that teacher-expectancy effects will *sometimes* take place' (Tomlinson 1983: 74). In Britain, however, we have so far hardly attempted to investigate what link there might be between teachers' expectations and the academic performance of Black pupils, or under what circumstances and through what mechanisms such a link might operate.

The fourth point Tomlinson (1981: 60) makes is that 'attitudes and expectations are nebulous characteristics which are not amenable to change'. She subsequently (1983: 78) only modulates this, saying that they are 'nebulous characteristics . . . not easily amenable to change'. It is a discussion of this point of the impossibility (or at least difficulty) of attitude change, in particular on the part of teachers, that mainly concerns the rest of this chapter.

It is, of course, no easy, simple or straightforward matter deliberately to bring about changes in attitudes (see, for instance, Lewin 1948, Newcomb and Charters 1952, Deutsch 1968, Raven 1968, and Pettigrew 1969); but to acknowledge this is quite different from asserting that attitudes and expectations cannot change, or that there is no point in carrying out research in this field. There is, indeed, a debate about attitude change. Nuttin (1975), for instance, lends support to Tomlinson's view. However, all of Nuttin's evidence comes from contrived experimental situations. Also, there is a large corpus of literature (see, for example, Zimbardo and Ebbesen 1969) to support the alternative view.

A classic example of a study documenting and exploring attitude change is the Bennington College study by Newcomb (1943) (see also Newcomb and Charters 1952). In Britain there is a growing body of work by Bagley, Verma and others on influencing 'racial' attitudes in the classroom (see, for instance, Bagley and Verma 1972, and Verma and Bagley 1979). Verma and Bagley (1979: 140–1), in a study measuring changes in 'racial' attitudes among groups of pupils who had been taught 'race relations' according to three different strategies, found that under the first strategy (the neutral chairman) 'the experimental group changed significantly in the direction of tolerance', that similar changes occurred under the other two strategies, and that only in the third strategy (drama) were none of the changes statistically significant. Tomlinson (1981) mentions none of this, and the very brief references she makes (1981: 62) to this type of research in Britain are only to dismiss it as documenting the *difficulties* of eliminating 'racial' tension and ill-feeling via teaching. Tomlinson does subsequently (1983: 96–7) mention such research briefly – but again within the context of the difficulty of realizing positive attitude changes.

Schon (1973) has convincingly argued that every innovation enters a 'plenum', not a vacuum – a plenum of attitudes, value assumptions, beliefs, norms, etc. If curriculum development for education for a multicultural society is to take place successfully in Britain, one must understand and somehow take account of the existing plenum. Curriculum development is not a simple straightforward technical affair concerned merely with objective, non-contentious, 'factual' matters (see, for instance, MacDonald and Walker 1976, and Whitehead 1980). Attitudes – and other 'nebulous characteristics' of the social process, which is curriculum development – must not be ignored. Tomlinson herself (1981: 67) criticizes Stone (1981) for attacking the stress sometimes given by White teachers of Black children to the affective at the expense of the academic. This suggests that for Tomlinson the affective relationship between the White teacher and the Black child is important. Surely then, the teacher's attitudes are important. Hence, it would seem desirable to understand them, how they work, in what contexts they arise, what consequences they may have, and how they may change.

It seems to me that one ought to investigate the whole issue of how teachers may influence their pupils' attitudes, both negatively and positively – and, linked to this, how teachers' attitudes may be influenced. One needs to know how teachers may be able to help pupils to be more open-minded, more fair-minded, more respectful of difference, etc. Crucially, too, one needs to inquire into how teachers themselves and student-teachers may be helped to become aware of and change any narrow-minded, racist, ethnocentric, or stereotyped attitudes or beliefs that they may have. Furthermore, while I agree with Stone (1981) that it is wrong to assume that teachers' (or 'society's') negative, ambiguous or narrow attitudes and expectations concerning Black people will more or less automatically result in similar negative, ambiguous or narrow Black self-concepts, nevertheless, teachers' attitudes and expectations may have important negative consequences – in complicated ways – for Black pupils' identity development and academic performance within the British education system. It is essential to know more about such matters.

In the research that is necessary, the conceptualization of attitudes (especially racist attitudes) requires careful attention. As I have argued earlier in this book (see in particular Chapter 2), the concept of a shared frame of reference – and more particularly of a racist or ethnicist frame of reference – as an integral feature of social interaction and of social structures is more helpful than a concept merely of individual attitudes and especially of 'prejudice' understood as a rigid, hostile rejection on the part of an unhealthy personality. Newcomb and Charters (1952: 210ff) also see attitudes as largely determined by frames of reference, and consider that changing attitudes is primarily a matter of changing frames of reference.

As we have seen (especially in Chapter 2), frames of reference form a lived, integral part of the social reality. Thus they have a social history, and change over time. It should therefore be possible to influence the rate and direction of their change by, for instance, influencing the group, its institutions, the roles within the group, a member's prestige or standing within the group, events affecting the group, information available to it, awareness within the group, or even group membership, or what groups are taken as reference groups. Besides, these shared frames of reference, being largely tacit, may contain many hidden ambiguities and inconsistencies, and this can assist the process of change.

For instance, 'raising consciousness' so that people become aware of inconsistencies can lead to changes in attitudes or frames of reference.

Another important point is that since frames of reference consist of basic assumptions and standards, and fulfil primary personality and social functions, it would be counter-productive simply to attack them or to try and destroy them. Instead, one must seek to build new frames of reference which can *replace* existing ones, or else one must aim to *modify* existing ones.

If these ideas are largely correct, much would seem to follow with reference to any process of trying to help teachers or pupils change their frames of reference. For instance, it is not sufficient to work only at the level of the cognitive: one must also involve lived experiences, values, feelings, actions. Also, as indicated in the previous chapter, a mere information campaign is not enough (Pettigrew 1969: 281) – although information has got a part to play. Again, rather than techniques aimed purely at the individual (see, for example, Deutsch 1968, and Raven 1968), some sort of group involvement is necessary. For both of these reasons T-group and other small group techniques might be useful (see, for example, Hunter 1971, and Katz 1978). However, if one can go beyond such 'artificial' or short-lived groupings, one could expect the gain to be greater. For example, can different members of the community actually be helped to realize the interests they have in common and to work together towards common goals? Deutsch and Collins (1951), for instance, found that interracial attitudes and relations were better in interracial housing where the different occupants had to work together towards certain common goals. It may also be that the various community groups, such as WELD (Westminster Endeavour for Liaison and Development), which have sprung up at various times around Britain, have often served to change the attitudes of, and to inform, those who took part in them – although they have not been studied from that point of view. WELD grew out of the initiative of a group of teachers at a school with a high proportion of Black pupils – the Westminster Junior School in Handsworth, Birmingham. WELD functioned within a small neighbourhood area round the schools, and held regular meetings in a local pub (see Adeney 1971, and Rex and Tomlinson 1979: 256).

It has also been maintained (for example, Pettigrew 1969: 280–1) that antiracist legislation, in constraining people to behave in certain ways, actually leads to a change in attitudes. Similarly, policy statements by the appropriate authority figure might provide the right context for a change in frames of reference. Following Blumer (1961), I have already argued that the big event or the well-known public figure might play a particular role in the forming of frames of reference (see Chapter 2). One could therefore also expect similar factors to serve in the changing of frames of reference. Specifically in schools it seems to me that staff development and curriculum change have been facilitated by the Swann Report (DES 1985a), the policy statements of teachers' unions and the policy statements of LEAs. More work needs to be done in developing models to realize such changes. In my experience INSET can be a good tool for raising awareness, possibly helping to transform frames of reference, and initiating and informing curriculum development.

Apart from being concerned with how schools – as well as teacher training institutions and other educational institutions – could help *change* attitudes and frames of reference, we must also look very closely at whether schools, teacher training institutions and other educational institutions might in fact be *teaching* or at least *reinforcing* negative, narrow or ambiguous attitudes – or negative, closed or subordinating frames of reference regarding minorities (see, for example, Milner 1975: 212ff, and Chapters 6–9 below), and we must try to develop ways of overcoming this. More research is needed into the factors which may be reinforcing racist or ethnicist frames of reference in the ordinary English school – or, indeed, in teacher training and other educational institutions. Apart from the frames of reference of the teachers, what part is played by, for instance: the curriculum; text-books; assessment and selection procedures; streaming and setting; school hierarchies; and such practices as withdrawal arrangements or the creation of various groupings? (See, for example, Lacey 1970 on the 'production' of sub-cultures within the streamed school, and Siegel and Siegel 1966 on group membership, reference group and attitude change.)

In brief, far from concluding that no more research is needed into teachers' attitudes, or that attitudes are not amenable to change, we need to do much more research and development work relating to these issues. Moreover, this work needs to be linked with other necessary research and development, such as work on the attitudes of *teacher-educators*. However, as I have already argued, the issues in the fields of 'race and ethnic relations' and of multicultural and antiracist education are not just to do with attitudes but also inextricably with frames of reference, interpersonal relations, institutions, procedures, social and educational inequality, etc. Research into, and development work on, attitudes and attitude change must incorporate and be incorporated into research and development work on such essential aspects as these. Since Tomlinson wrote in 1981 there have been some relevant research developments in the field of education in Britain, and some of these will be discussed in the remaining chapters of this book.

6 Student-teachers' images of Black people and of education for a multicultural society

A case study

INTRODUCTION

It is my view that where racist or ethnicist frames of reference operate in the classroom or school they can have an important impact on pupil development and performance. They tend to inform school processes and organization and to impinge on the socialization process, influencing the developing beliefs and frames of reference of the pupils generally. In addition, they may substantially, if subtly, affect the treatment accorded to, and the assessment of, ethnic minority pupils – as well as their achievement. If we accept the importance of the hidden curriculum, and of teacher expectations (Rosenthal and Jacobson 1968; Pidgeon 1970; Rubovits and Maehr 1973; Tomlinson 1983:73–7), one of the first steps for us should be to find out what images teachers and those entering the teaching profession have of Black people and of multicultural or antiracist education.

Yet, as we saw in the last chapter, there has been little research, in Taylor's words (1981:195), into the 'delicate issues' of teachers' attitudes generally to ethnic minorities. Much more specific information is also needed, as she indicates, about teachers' attitudes towards particular groups – such as those of West Indian background. The lack of research data is even greater as far as the attitudes and frames of reference of the up-coming generation of teachers is concerned. One interesting study was carried out by Edwards (1978) with twenty student-teachers. When presented with tape recordings they judged what was in fact the same speaker, a Barbadian, as less intelligent when she spoke in Creole than when she spoke with an English working-class accent.

The present project was thus set up partly to try and explore the frames of reference of student-teachers concerning especially people of West Indian and Asian background in Britain. It was carried out with post-graduate certificate of education (PGCE) students at one British university between 1982 and 1984.

Until 1982 there had, for several years, been an option in 'education for a multicultural society' available each year to these students. This typically lasted 8 weeks in the summer term, and was usually taken by only a dozen or so students. Apart from this, the only specifically 'multicultural' content to the PGCE course was provided by one of a series of introductory plenary lectures in the first term. Perhaps, in addition, some of the subject tutors will have touched on relevant issues from time to time. In 1981–2 it was decided to organize the option unit on 'education for a multicultural society' in such a way that all of the PGCE students could participate in it even if it was not one of their chosen options. Hence two one-day conferences on convenient days replaced the eight weekly classes. It was also thought that this more intensive format would be more effective.

Partly as an evaluation of this programme, and partly as an attempt to explore the issue of student-teachers' frames of reference, students were asked to complete a questionnaire before and after this programme. In the following year, 1982–3, a similar but somewhat reduced exercise was carried out. In 1983–4 the one-day conferences were organized *in addition* to the more usual (but somewhat abbreviated) option unit programme. The research and evaluation aspects were also expanded.

Only data from 1983–4 are discussed here. In that academic year an introductory plenary lecture on education for a multicultural society was given as usual in the autumn term. There was also an introductory session later on that term for those students electing for the option unit on education for a multicultural society. The two one-day conferences were run during the summer term, one at the beginning of May and the other in the middle of June, about two weeks before the end of term. Several guest speakers participated in these. The option unit sessions took place during the weeks between these two conferences. The spring term was dedicated, as usual, to teaching-practice.

Three questionnaires were administered, the first at the beginning of the introductory plenary session in the autumn term, the second at the beginning of the first one-day conference, and the third towards the end of the second one-day conference. They were all to be completed on the spot, but absentees were followed up through the student pigeon-holes or even through the post.

The questionnaires sought to explore perceptions of and attitudes towards 'Black' ethnic minority people and towards education, and teacher-education, for 'multicultural' Britain. They likewise probed knowledge about immigration, about British 'race relations', and about 'multicultural' Britain. They also helped to evaluate the programme on education for a multicultural society.

The focus in what follows is mainly on. the student-teachers' perceptions of and attitudes towards 'West Indians' and 'Asians'. Selected findings and quotations are reported mainly from the second questionnaire. The selections have been carefully made so as to provide a fair spread of views expressed and a fair picture of the overall findings. The quotations are verbatim, including any vagaries of spelling or grammar.

There were 102 PGCE students in 1983–4, all training to be secondary school teachers. Eighty-six, eighty-nine and sixty-five of these (representing response rates of 84, 87 and 64 per cent) completed the first, second and third questionnaires respectively. The reduced response rate for the last questionnaire was largely due to the late date during the academic year at which it was administered.

There were far more females than males taking the PGCE course (63 per cent female as against 37 per cent male) and the sex distribution among the respondents to the second questionnaire was very similar to this (66 per cent female, 37 per cent male). The distribution among the respondents by main teaching subject also closely matched the corresponding distribution among the total population. Only about one-third of both the population and the respondents were taking arts subjects.

The self-attributed social-class background of the respondents to the second questionnaire was, as one might expect, predominantly middle class (69 per cent). Nevertheless, 28 per cent did describe themselves as being of working-class background. The remaining 3 per cent represented no response. In the year concerned, the PGCE course included no Asians or West Indians. All of the students were White, and the vast majority were English. Indeed, more than one respondent remarked on the absence of students other than Whites. One female respondent admitted that she was 'very surprised and disturbed by the fact that the PGCE course consists of white students only'.

FINDINGS

Contact with ethnic minorities

The second questionnaire started with four open-ended (sentence-completion) questions, headed by the general rubric: 'Please write as much or as little as you wish in response to the following items'. The first question then read: 'My experience of Blacks in Britain is . . . '. The

Table 6.1 Percentage of respondents having Asian or West Indian schoolmates
or friends (n = 86)

	None/ Very few	Some	Fair Number/ A lot
Schoolmates	81	12	7
Friends	70	22	8

commonest response to this was: 'limited'; and respondents quite often
made it clear that they were ignorant about Black ethnic minority
people. About two-thirds of the respondents had clearly had little
contact with 'Blacks', and only about one-tenth had had quite a lot of
contact with them. It also transpired from other information obtained
from the first questionnaire that most of the student-teachers had gone
to schools with very few if any Asians or West Indians (see Table 6.1).
Similarly, they had very few if any such friends. Two respondents with
very little contact replied as follows to the open-ended question:

> very limited, having been to almost an all white school and living in
> an all white community.
>
> *(Female)*

> quite limited, despite living in Birmingham for 3 years.
>
> *(Female)*

One respondent with quite a lot of contact wrote:

> Since I live near Southall I come into contact with them regularly. I
> must admit maybe as a result of my parents prejudice I don't like the
> fact that now more than half our road has coloured people living in
> it – There seems to be little if any communication on the other hand.
> On the personal level I have quite a few very close good friends who
> are coloured but I don't see them that way.
>
> *(Female)*

Sometimes the respondents considered that what little contact they had
experienced had been with 'atypical' Black people: that is, with students,
professionals, the trading class, with rich or educated Black people. An
example of such a reply was:

> limited to a few friends at University – tend to be well educated and
> rich.
>
> *(Male)*

Images of 'Asians'

The second open-ended question at the beginning of the second questionnaire read simply: 'When I think of Asians I think. . . . '. This produced many stereotypes (or clichés) about 'Asians' but not too many negative ones. One respondent acknowledged that he thought 'of clichés', and also replied as follows:

> Curry, complex but intriguing religions, colourful clothes, arranged marriages, very strict and polite formal manners (particularly East Asians). In general, rather quiet and reserved.
>
> *(Male)*

Words relating to business and trade (e.g. shops, restaurants, hard-working) came up most frequently, being mentioned by 45 per cent of the respondents. Some examples of replies which included such references were as follows:

> of hardworking people (shops open until late, open all hours – in Brum).
>
> *(Female)*

> of mostly tradespeople and have the impression that they are more serious about making a living and supporting each other than some white families . . . that I don't know enough about them to say anything very relevant . . . of how it strikes me when I go back to Leicester from Southampton and how my parents say they want to move before they retire as they feel they don't belong so much any more.
>
> *(Female)*

> of excellent cheap shops that are open after hours, curries and demure looking women.
>
> *(Female)*

Culture and related items such as religion, dress and food were also mentioned by almost a third (30 per cent) of the respondents. For instance, two of the student-teachers wrote:

> of shopkeepers and a culture I don't understand.
>
> *(Male)*

> of a group of Asian people in Britain. Generally, an area of a city with Asian shops and temples, terraced houses . . . bright colours, interesting smells, music.
>
> *(Female)*

Reference was occasionally made to the restriction of womenfolk, arranged marriages, etc. (12 per cent of respondents); to the family (over

10 per cent); to close-knit communities (10 per cent); and to difference or alienness (6 per cent). Some further examples of responses were as follows:

> of a closely knit family with the father at the head of the household and the mother as dominated by her husband. Quiet rather insular people.
>
> *(Female)*

> of areas of the country which have a predominance of Asians within the community (e.g. Leicester, Bradford) who maintain a closed Asian society.
>
> *(Female)*

> of housing areas which are almost entirely Asian; areas which I would feel out of place in.
>
> *(Female)*

Some answers simply identified particular countries, nationalities or ethnic groups – most often, but not exclusively, referring to people from the Indian sub-continent. For instance, one respondent wrote:

> of areas such as Pakistan, India and Bangladesh, though several other third world countries also come to mind.
>
> *(Male)*

Images of 'West Indians'

The third open-ended question read: 'When I think of West Indians I think. . . .'. The images held of 'West Indians' contrasted substantially with those regarding 'Asians'. Some respondents specifically contrasted the two. For instance, one reply to the question about Asians was as follows:

> of fairly middle class families, certainly more so than West Indies, and with a fairly strong sense of family, but fairly well-integrated into English life (viz. don't live in ghettos, speak good English).
>
> *(Female)*

Another respondent similarly had this to say in answer to the question concerning West Indians:

> of open, gregarious people, more vocal about their culture. They also seem to integrate less well in the classroom and society than Asians for example.
>
> *(Female)*

On the other hand, yet another respondent wrote the following about West Indians:

of them as being more closely integrated with 'white' society and a more established part of Britain's cultural community.

(Female)

As with the question about Asians, some respondents also acknowledged here that their replies ' were clichés or over-generalizations. One person wrote of:

happy go lucky people, with a sense of humour. West Indian cricket team: Viv Richards, etc. (I know these views are totally generalised).

(Female)

This same person commented later:

I realise I view Asians and West Indians very differently for no really logical reason (I don't really know very many).

(Female)

The commonest image of the West Indians included such categories as sport, music, carnival and easy-going – 46 per cent of the respondents mentioned at least one such item. References were also quite common to Rastafarians, their dreadlocks, woolly hats, music (reggae) and ganja (marijuana) – 32 per cent of respondents referred to such items. Two typical replies were as follows:

very lithe, fast bowlers. Rastafarians in Lewisham high street.

(Male)

of reggae music and clubs where you can listen to this; lots of young West Indians hanging around the Bullring shopping centre in Birmingham with their symbol of identity – large cassette recorders + loud reggae music – of the Rastafarian culture – of bright colours.

(Female)

Besides, 12 per cent mentioned unemployment or menial jobs, while 10 per cent found West Indians threatening, aggressive, rebellious and the like. For instance three other respondents wrote:

of rhythm, care-free nature, cricket, inner-city depression, caused by large numbers of unemployed.

(Male)

again in clichées [*sic*]; music comes to mind first, tea-cosy like head-wear, groups of young men hanging round street corners, talking in loud voices, making me feel slightly uneasy.

(Female)

of them doing very menial jobs . . . transport.

(Female)

The following two replies highlight contrasts and apparent inconsistencies or contradictions built into some of the images held of West Indians. This phenomenon was not so noticeable in replies about Asians.

of pimps, and prostitutes freezing on the street corners in the snow while the men drive round to 'make sure they are OK'. But also of my friend who is appalled by the way he sees others behaving, I also think of strict, puritanical, pentecostal churches.

(Female)

of a somewhat brash, aggressive form of self-justification tinged with the unknown aspects and the impression that many of the younger blacks have such an enormous chip on their shoulder at an earlyish age that even if you try to be friendly or open they treat you with some distrust, OR open, warm and friendly yet still somehow different.

(Female)

Contrasting images of West Indians and Asians

Questions with fixed-alternative answers, including the semantic differential technique, were also used in addition to the open-ended questions. In the semantic differential question, placed towards the end of the second questionnaire, respondents were asked to rate Asians and West Indians on twelve adjective-pairs: Not musical/Musical; Unfriendly/ Friendly; Rate education lowly/ Rate education highly; Slow learners/ Quick learners; Strong/Weak; Speak English well/Speak English badly; Academically gifted/Not academically gifted; Bad at sports/Good at sports; Good at mathematics/Bad at mathematics; Well behaved/Badly behaved; Quiet/Noisy; Linguistically deprived/Linguistically gifted. Of course, the respondents had the option of replying at the 'neutral' mid-point of the scale – or of simply leaving the question blank.

In fact the incidence of mid-point replies and of no response was high. This suggests an unwillingness to generalize. Indeed, several respondents made comments about this question indicating that they did not want to use stereotypes. Three examples of such comments follow:

This encourages generalisations which I don't want to make.

(Female)

I don't believe its possible to generalise to the extent that section 5 [the Semantic Differential section] demands.

(Male)

I didn't like page 7 [the page with the Semantic Differential] so I just aimed for the middle.

(Male)

Nevertheless, it is interesting to consider the results for any given adjective-pair or dimension relating to the Asians and West Indians, where for either of these 'concepts' (Asians, West Indians) the non-response together with the mid-point replies represented less than 50 per cent of the respondents. The images indicated by the responses along such dimensions fit in with the data already seen from the open-ended questions.

Thus the respondents tended to see the West Indians as musical, noisy, good at sports and friendly (Table 6.2). By contrast there was a tendency to see the Asians as rating education highly and as quiet and well behaved. It may also be noteworthy that on balance there tended to be what might be taken as a negative perception of West Indians on three items. It may be significant that these were: noisy, rate education lowly, and badly behaved. There was only a small tendency to rate Asians badly on one item – and that was: bad at sports.

Contrasting images of Asians and West Indians also appeared in the replies to a series of other attitudinal type questions, only a fraction of which can be mentioned here. Thus the Asians were often seen as keeping themselves to themselves, but hardly so the West Indians. Also, although West Indians and Asians were often seen as disadvantaged, this was even more likely to be the case regarding West Indians. Furthermore, the West Indians were frequently thought of as Black, whereas the

Table 6.2 Percentage of respondents seeing West Indians and Asians in specified ways (n=89)

| | West Indians | | | Asians | | |
	Yes	NR	No	Yes	NR	No
Musical	83	16	1	24	62	15
Noisy	69	29	2	1	42	57
Good at sports	67	29	3	9	71	20
Friendly	60	35	6	34	53	13
Rate ed. lowly	34	58	8	6	30	64
Badly behaved	27	64	9	2	42	56
Speak English well	26	58	16	36	44	20

Note: NR = No response and replies indicating the mid-point of the scale

Asians were not. 'Blacks' (i.e. West Indians?) in turn were seen as having a chip on the shoulder and a higher than average crime rate by almost a third of the respondents, with over a third not committing themselves.

Images of the 'majority' population

Partly so as to have a point of reference, and also to explore the respondents' perception of the incidence of racism, questions were asked about the 'majority' population. There was, for instance, an open-ended question (the fourth question in questionnaire number two) similar to the two open-ended questions concerning West Indians and Asians. It read: 'When I think of the majority population in Britain I think . . . '. Perhaps at least partly because of the context of this question, many of the respondents (53 per cent) referred to 'the majority' as being 'white'. Some wrote simply 'of whites'. Two other examples of replies were:

> of white non religious Anglicans, fish and chips and factories.
>
> *(Female)*

> of it as quite free thinking, liberal etc. But I generally think of it as white. Although I think of Americans as both black and white!
>
> *(Male)*

Some respondents actually commented on the context of the question – as, for instance, in the following two replies:

> mainly of white people as the word majority lends itself to being contrasted with minorities.
>
> *(Male)*

> I'm not sure what you mean by majority since this questionnaire is investigating multicultural aspects, do you mean the white pop. [i.e. population]? . . . I wouldn't like to make generalisations on the basis of colour. I think most people in Britain want to be happy, secure and peaceful. Black or white.
>
> *(Female)*

Occasionally, the very notion of 'the majority' was expressly rejected. One person wrote:

> that most of the population is a mixture of all sorts. Throughout history different races have invaded the country like the Romans and Danes, so there is not such thing as a majority population.
>
> *(Female)*

Table 6.3 Percentage of respondents agreeing or disagreeing with the specified items (n=89)

	SA	A	U/NR	D	SD
British are fair-minded	1	40	24	28	7
Prospects of 'racial' peace are good	0	30	48	20	1
Notion of 'race' is suspect	9	36	38	13	3
Normal to be suspicious of the stranger	12	60	11	16	1

Note: SA = strongly agreed; A = Agreed; U/NR = uncertain/No response; D = Disagreed; SD = Strongly disagreed.

Some 18 per cent of the respondents alluded to social class. For instance, two wrote:

> of the white, middle classes.
>
> *(Female)*

> of middle class white families who live in box like houses on estates with 2.2 children a car a fridge, T.V., and dissatisfied with what they have, wanting to get 'more and more' money. Tolerant of coloured people but not wanting to live in their area.
>
> *(Female)*

There was also a range of questions with fixed-alternative answers concerning the 'majority population', the British, Britain and various related issues. For instance, more than a third of the respondents disagreed with the express statement that 'on the whole the British are a fair-minded people' (Table 6.3). One-fifth thought that the prospects of 'racial' peace in Britain were not good. Almost three-quarters (72 per cent) thought it was 'a normal human tendency to be suspicious of the stranger'. Yet 45 per cent agreed that although people differ physically and culturally, the notion of 'race' is suspect.

Racism

Other respondents (some 12 per cent) expressly saw the 'majority' as ignorant, biased, discriminating, ethnocentric or racist. Some of the relevant replies were as follows:

> they're white and racist.
>
> *(Female)*

Table 6.4 Perception of extent of racism (1) in Britain, (2) among teachers
(percentage of respondents, n = 86)

	Great deal/ Very great deal	Fair amount	None/ Little	No response
In Britain	36	56	8	0
Among teachers	5	51	42	2

of mainly white English people who think that their culture is the only
one with any validity. Their sense of superiority and crusade has been
justifying the imposition of their culture upon others for centuries.

(Male, Irish)

Massive Ignorance (inc. [including] me, of course).

(Female)

what a prejudiced lot we are, and such prejudice seems to be that
nurtured by others rather than based on personal experience.

(Male)

Some questions were also asked specifically about the incidence of
racism. For instance, in the first questionnaire in 1983–84 there were
two separate questions about the occurrence of racism: (1) among
people in Britain today; and (2) among teachers in schools today. The
vast majority of respondents thought there was some racism among
people generally in Britain today (Table 6.4). Although half of the
respondents also thought that there was a similar incidence of racism
among teachers, many of the student-teachers were clearly less willing
to attribute racism to teachers than to the public at large.

The future

An open-ended question towards the end of the third and last
questionnaire asked: 'What do you think is the main issue during the
next decade or so concerning Britain as a multi-ethnic society?' One-
fifth of the respondents gave answers which assumed the existence of
racism, prejudice or Black–White antagonism. More than one in ten
assumed cultural conflict. Many giving such answers were concerned
that the racism or conflict should be overcome. One person rejected the
notion that Britain is a multicultural society. She wrote:

I don't see Britain as a multicultural society. I see it as a society with
a dominant Christian/Anglo-Saxon culture (despite the claims of
secularism) with an increasing duty towards the minority cultures in

its midst. I think the main issue in the next decade will be to provide for the needs of young people whose origins may well be otherwise, but whose birth-place and upbringing take place in this country and to help them to relate the two principles.

(Female)

In other words, the assumption here seems to be that the 'problem' is one faced by *ethnic minority* people caught 'between two cultures'. Some other views about the 'main issue' in the future were as follows:

Sexism of other cultures.

(Female)

We need to oppose 'fundamendalist' movements in Asian and West Indian communities.

(Male)

The problems of unemployment which will possibly be more severe amongst the ethnic minority groups, and the continuing tension between groups as problems of unemployment and poorer living conditions continues.

(Female)

Jobs; 'Ghetto' regions in the inner cities; Police and generally 'Authority'. Equal opportunities.

(Female)

Equal opportunities for all, without positive discrimination for ethnic minorities.

(Female)

Accepting that we do live in a multi-ethnic society and not just ignoring it, or thinking that it is only limited to certain areas such as London or Liverpool.

(Female)

Reluctance of 'English' people to accept others of different races.

(Female)

Lack of knowledge and understanding of other cultures.

(Male, Irish)

Many (almost a quarter) referred specifically to some aspect of education, although often they referred to other issues as well. For instance, two respondents wrote:

Combatting racism, i.e. educating people so that they lose their prejudices.

(Male)

The main issue is concerned with the education system – As soon as multicultural education is a common factor in *all* schools, integration, I think, will be much less of a problem.

(Female)

Attitudes towards multicultural education

What then did the student-teachers understand by 'multicultural education' and what were their attitudes to it and to related issues? We have seen that on the whole the student-teachers had little contact with, were ignorant of, and tended to hold biased and stereotypic images about Black people. Nevertheless, they often manifested a positive orientation towards 'multicultural education'. This was no doubt in part stimulated by the 'education for a multicultural society' programme and especially by the questionnaires. Quite possibly most of the respondents had hardly thought of the issues previously. It seemed clear that just having to complete the questionnaires often raised awareness and interest, and helped to bring assumptions and images into question. For instance, one person wrote at the time of the second questionnaire:

Having virtually no contact/experience with people of any of the ethnic minorities in question (why?) I don't feel I can completely answer this questionnaire, but I realise that I haven't even thought about many of the questions, and feel I should take a stronger interest in the matter.

(Female)

In replying to this questionnaire most of the respondents agreed that all subject teachers should ask themselves what the implications of multicultural education might be for their teaching (Table 6.5). Most also

Table 6.5 Whether respondents agreed with specified items (in percentages, n = 89)

	SA	A	U/NR	D
All teachers should consider implications of multicultural education for them	36	49	15	0
Teacher education should include multicultural education	30	62	7	1
Teacher education should include how to combat racism	25	57	11	7

Note: SA = Strongly agreed; A = Agreed; U/NR = Uncertain/No response; D = Disagreed.

thought that teacher education should include aspects of multicultural education, and should deal with how to combat racism.

However, in answer to the third questionnaire in 1983 – 4, some of the respondents also made some less than positive comments about 'multicultural' education. For instance, one thought that:

> too much fuss is made about 'ethnic minorities' (labelling various 'types', identifying their problems etc.)
>
> *(Female)*

Another said that:

> All this interest in multicultural education is very good – but surely – if not to be too cruel – 'Charity begins at home'. Sort out our own problems in Education as a whole before concentrating on a minority group who have chosen to join our society.
>
> *(Female, of French background)*

Apart from such negative comments, it became clear that most of the respondents, even though they might have had a generally positive orientation, tended to think of 'education for a multicultural society' in relatively narrow cultural terms. For instance, in reply to an open-ended question about this in the first questionnaire, only a small minority referred to equality (5 per cent) and even fewer to antiracism or the combating of prejudice (3 per cent). By contrast, some 65 per cent referred in some way to culture; while 21 per cent spoke non-specifically in terms of promoting integration, understanding, respect or tolerance. Almost a quarter thought of multicultural education as being concerned with the needs of ethnic minorities, as teaching about ethnic minority cultures, or as coping in classrooms or areas which contained ethnic minorities. Only 12 per cent indicated that they thought multicultural education was for all.

The same question was asked again in the third questionnaire at the end of the PGCE course. The overall tendency to think mainly in terms of culture or of ethnic minorities – rather than in terms of equality, antiracism or the education of all pupils – was still apparent, although it had been somewhat attenuated. It may be, however, that even greater changes had taken place among the respondents than the shifts in their answers seemed to suggest. For instance, one student-teacher replied to the question about 'education for a multicultural society' in the third questionnaire, as follows:

> My own feelings have not changed a lot but their practical application and specificity has – greatly. It helped me broaden my view.
>
> *(Male)*

A selection of other replies to the question about education for a

Table 6.6 Selected replies to questions about the meaning of 'Education for a Multicultural Society'

First Questionnaire	Third Questionnaire
(Female)	
Educating people to understand the different cultures amongst which they live.	Preparing children of all cultures to go into a multicultural society being aware of the differences, but not prejudiced because of the differences.
(Female)	
An education which recognizes the different cultures and therefore the different needs of children. An education which teaches an understanding of different cultural groups, in order to move towards an undivided society.	1. Equal opportunities for all races. 2. A knowledge of other races, cultures etc; and an ability to empathize with these.
(Female)	
Education about the Asian, West Indian ... subcultures and what influences them. Removing fear of different communities and acceptance of each other as human beings.	An education for everyone that draws from and acknowledges the richness and diversity of our multicultural society and which builds respect.
(Female)	
Coping with the problems of many races in the classroom, and the difficulties of children not necessarily having the same first language, and the same background.	Teaching children to respect others who are not of the same culture, to reduce prejudices and anti-racial feelings and to help produce a more socially stable society.
(Female)	
An education for everyone regardless of race, colour or creed.	Awareness of other people's cultures, but not necessarily integration.
(Male)	
Educating within a tolerant and enlightening environment, conducive to racial harmony.	An education for whites and non-whites which develops an understanding and tolerant relation between the two.

multicultural society are set out in Table 6.6. For each respondent quoted, the reply to the first questionnaire (early on in the course) is given on the left, and that to the last questionnaire (at the end of the course) on the right.

CONCLUSION

The 'multicultural' teacher-education programme – to which the research reported here was linked – was of limited duration, did not permeate the teaching-subject work of the PGCE students, and was otherwise methodologically limited. Thus a critical comment on this programme, one of the few made by any of the respondents, was as follows:

> Most of the sessions were reasonably interesting, but more positive ideas for the new teacher would have been useful. It may have been useful to split into small discussion groups at some stage.
>
> *(Male)*

Yet the programme did, in fact, generally seem to have positive educational outcomes for the student-teachers. As already indicated, the very use of the questionnaires seemed to play not only a research but also an educational role. Some of the typical comments on the programme made by the student-teachers were as follows:

> I particularly enjoyed finding out about Creole, and the background to West Indians coming to this country (and how West Indies developed). I was stimulated about covert racism – something I'd never thought about much. Looking at ways this could be conveyed, and discerned was interesting.
>
> *(Female)*

> I hadn't really given the subject much thought, if any at all before these sessions. They opened my eyes to some problems which could arise and hopefully I will be better prepared.
>
> *(Female)*

> [I gained:] An understanding of the purpose of education for a multi-cultural society. An appreciation of the various cultures within our society.
>
> *(Female)*

> I think just getting someone to examine his or her own attitudes/responses is a rewarding exercise – so I think particularly the questionnaires a good idea.
>
> *(Female)*

> The sessions dispelled a lot of myths and reveal cultural elements about which I was ignorant.
>
> *(Female)*

Very valuable in making you realise, that no matter how smug you are about your own racial tolerance, there is a long way to go.

(Male)

Three important questions now arise. In view of the limited contact with Black people, what is the source of the stereotypic images about them, and of the biased attitudes towards them? What are the likely educational consequences of the holding of such images and attitudes by future teachers? What are the implications of the findings reported, and of the answers to these two questions, for teacher-education?

First of all, one possible source of the images and attitudes regarding West Indians and Asians may be over-generalization from the respondent's own limited experience. For instance, one person replied to the open-ended question about Asians in the following way:

of tight immigrant communities and tradespeople. I have taught English to an Asian woman, and am, I think, prejudiced against Asian men, from hearing of her experiences, but that, I realise is a dangerous generalisation. I have other good Asian friends and think of them as industrious – tending to loyal almost 'servility'.

(Female)

Another, similar source of images and attitudes may be over-generalization from the more public activities of some members of the particular 'group' – like reggae bands among West Indians, and corner shops among Asians. An important source, however, is undoubtedly interaction with one's own in-group members. For instance one respondent has already been quoted above in the section on 'contact with ethnic minorities' as saying that maybe it was as a result of her parents' prejudice that she didn't like seeing 'coloured people' now living in more than half 'our' road in Southall. Another respondent – quoted in the section on 'racism' – referred to prejudice being 'nurtured by others rather than based on personal experience'. Related to this, several respondents referred to the influence of the media on their views. One wrote:

I have had very little experience with people of other cultures. I believe myself to be non-racist. But I also believe the media and other things make people, who have not had experience of cultures, biased against coloured people in Britain.

(Male)

The second question which arises concerns the likely educational consequences of the ignorance of the student-teachers and of the stereotypic images and biased attitudes they often hold. My postulate is that such images and attitudes form part of the frames of reference which define, structure, and orientate social interaction. Moreover, the assumptions, images and attitudes of significant others are likely to influence the course of events. Also, since social interaction is likely to flow more smoothly when the frames of reference of the powerful are accepted, these may be at least partly 'internalized' by the less powerful, and by the newer or more junior social actors. Besides, those members who fit the positive assumptions and expectations of these frames of reference are likely to be the most 'rewarded' within the system.

Now, teachers are in a position of power and are 'significant others' *vis-à-vis* the pupils, who are the newer or more junior actors. Hence teachers' frames of reference, including their assumptions, images and attitudes – are likely to have particular impact on the learning process of the pupils, on their development and on their achievement. Just as some of the student-teachers probably learned stereotypic or biased attitudes about ethnic minorities from their parents, so they may pass these on, not only to their own children, but also to their pupils.

Where these pupils are members of minority ethnic groups, these images and attitudes – at least where they are clearly negative or subordinating – might be resisted, especially as they may not tally with the home experiences of these youngsters. Nevertheless, the development – or growth of consciousness – and the educational performance of these pupils might suffer. Not only the stereotypes and biased attitudes but also the ignorance of the future teachers could negatively affect the development and performance of such pupils.

Conversely, in addition to the teachers' stereotypes or biased attitudes – and, more generally their frames of reference – being passed on to or reinforced among the 'majority' pupils, the operation of such frames of reference could also tend relatively to enhance the performance of these 'majority' pupils, at least in mixed classrooms or mixed schools. This would tend to occur if and to the extent that the 'majority' pupils were more likely to share the teachers' assumptions or fit the teachers' images of the 'ideal pupil'.

Of course, given the class nature of British society (reflected in some of the student-teachers' responses) social class would also be a significant variable here. In other words, just as the operation of ethnicist or racist frames of reference – often deeply embedded within the institutions – may work to the detriment of some groups and to the advantage of others, so will the operation of classist frames of reference, of classist institutions, disadvantage some and advantage others. Similarly, sexist frames of reference work in the society and in schools against women and in men's favour. Such ethnicist, racist, classist and sexist frames of reference, institutions and structural relations can be expected to interact in complex ways.

A further, related point is that different minority ethnic groups might be differently affected. The effect on the different groups would be in part a function of the nature or contents of the images and stereotypes held by teachers and other powerful actors within the education system (as well as of class and gender differentials). As we have seen, however, different images are held of different groups. Thus the images of West Indians as noisy, easy-going and threatening or rebellious could be expected to work to their disadvantage in school settings. On the other hand, the images of Asians as rating education highly, as quiet, well-behaved and hard-working would be to their positive advantage in classroom and school interaction. Perhaps these contrasting images would operate more strongly in schools, and especially in classrooms with appreciable numbers of both 'West Indian' and 'Asian' pupils.

There is in fact some evidence, whatever its limitations, to suggest that many Asians do well in the British education system whereas the performance of many West Indians is below average (for example, DES 1985a – see Chapter 9 below). There is also some research evidence that corroborates the relationship I am hypothesizing of stereotypes, or racist and ethnicist frames of reference (as well as of class or gender), with treatment and performance within the education system (for example, Carrington 1983; Tomlinson 1982; Bagley 1971; Driver 1980), as we shall see in Chapter 9 below.

The final question that needs to be briefly raised here concerns teacher-education. Since the results reported have identified both ignorance and stereotypic thinking, two major tasks for teacher-education (whether pre-service or in-service) for a 'multicultural' society would seem to be: (1) overcoming the student-teachers' ignorance about ethnic minority people, plural Britain and indeed the plural world; and (2) bringing to awareness, challenging and transforming the student-teachers' stereotypes, biased attitudes and assumptions – in brief, their frames of reference. To these two tasks there needs to be added a third major one: (3) seeking to provide the student-teachers with the ideas, resources and skills to overcome ignorance, to combat racism and ethnicism among their future pupils and within the education system, and to promote a good education and genuine equality for all. In the approach to the first two tasks the student-teachers could learn much that would be useful to the third. In all three tasks the postulated in-group source of the frames of reference, and their shared and largely tacit and taken-for-granted nature, would call for a sensitive, probing, interactive and group-work approach. In particular, in view of the need to work at the level of the group, and in view of the centrality of the subject-based groups on the PGCE course, it would seem important that at least some of the multicultural and antiracist work on the PGCE course should be done within the subject groups. The teacher-education institution also needs to reflect on and examine itself (and its workings) so as to ensure that it is not itself characterized, however covertly, by institutional ethnicism or racism. It will become apparent from the next chapter that there is, as one student-teacher remarked, 'a long way to go' not only for student-teachers and institutions of teacher-education, but also for practising teachers, for schools and for their pupils.

7 Racism in school

A case study[*]

INTRODUCTION

This chapter reports on a case study of a 'multiethnic' school, focusing especially on teachers' and pupils' frames of reference. It also raises questions about 'achievement' among 'Black' pupils, and indicates that frames of reference which might well have an adverse effect on the progress of minority pupils do seem to be common among teachers and White pupils in the school studied. Some of these issues will be further pursued in the final chapter of this book.

The case study was carried out in a small 12–16 co-educational comprehensive school, code-named Townview, mainly during the summer term of 1982. Located in a provincial town in an LEA with a percentage of Black people lower than the national average, Townview was an inner-city school in a Victorian building with good recently added craft and gym facilities and ample space (due to falling rolls). The headmaster estimated at about the time of the study that about half of the near 400 pupils were of Asian background (that is, with roots in the Indian sub-continent, including East African Asians). Something under one-tenth of the pupils were of Caribbean background. Most of the others were White and mainly British, though many different nationalities were represented in the school, including a small number of Vietnamese and Chinese. Two of the cleaning staff in the school were 'Asian'. So was the home-school liaison officer. Otherwise all of the staff, academic and other, were White. One 'Asian' and one 'West Indian' had been appointed to the board of governors for the first time at the beginning of 1982.

Up to about the time of the field-work there had for years been little turnover in the academic staff. The main exception was that a new headmaster had assumed duties at the beginning of the 1981–2 school year. He had previously worked in an area with a large Black population and seemed committed to 'multicultural' education. The school was run on formal lines, and offered a largely traditional fare academically with little account taken of the changes that had occurred over the years in its make-up. However, although the school uniform was enforced, concessions had been made: turbans for boys and trousers for girls, both in the approved colour. Pastoral care in the school was based on mixed-ability tutor groups, with one tutor in each year acting as year head. The small size of the school naturally set limits on the curriculum.

There were three streams throughout the school, with the A stream as the top academic stream and the C stream as a 'remedial' stream. The C stream also provided English as a second language, though it is not clear how good this provision was. Where numbers warranted it, as for instance in the second and fourth forms at the time of the study, there were also A1 and A2 streams. These designations did have the implied hierarchical significance. There was, however, some setting across A and B streams in the fourth and fifth forms. On the whole, only the A streams were considered to be examination classes, although quite a lot of the B stream pupils and even some of the C stream pupils took CSE examinations. GCE 'O' level examinations were taken mainly by pupils in the A1 stream, although a small number of A2 pupils also took them. The examination boards used were London for the GCE 'O' level and Southern Regional for the CSE. The C stream classes followed a less subject-based curriculum than the A and B streams, and often the C stream teachers would be expected to teach more widely across the curriculum than is usual in a secondary school. All classes, including 'remedial' classes, sat formal, written, internal examinations at the end of each academic year.

The school was located in an old run-down, decreasingly residential area. The pupils' parents belonged mainly to the Registrar General's occupational classes IV and V. In September 1982 over 15 per cent of the school roll were receiving free meals. According to the previous headmaster, in an interview in November 1980, the Black children came mainly from good, stable homes, while the White children were often problem children from poor, broken homes.

We decided to focus on the first and penultimate years in the school, the second and fourth forms. Since we were interested in high and low 'achievement' (as seen, in particular, in the terms of the school) we wished to include upper and lower stream classes in both of these years. Furthermore, we decided that we had to limit our observations mainly to English and Mathematics classes. These two subjects may be considered as basic. Moreover, all pupils in the school took them.

In the event, since one of the teachers did not want an observer in his class, 2A1 could not be studied. Initially, therefore, 2A2, 2C, 4A1 and 4C were chosen. However it soon became clear that it was desirable to observe 4A2 as well. Later, 4B was added, as it transpired that it was seen as the 'problem' class in the school. Hence the entire fourth year was covered. Altogether 119 second- and fourth-form pupils were studied: 34 second-formers and 85 fourth-formers. There were 57 South Asians, 44 Whites, 8 Vietnamese and Chinese, 7 West Indians and 3 others. There were no West Indians in 2C or 4C, which were small classes (7 and 12 pupils respectively) consisting mainly of Asians.

In all, 33 lessons of 45 minutes each – mainly in English and Mathematics – were observed. Swart taught some English lessons, and set some written work in this connection. For example, he taught a lesson on Wole Soyinka's poem, 'Telephone Conversation'. Pupils provided some biographical information, and did sentence-completion and word-association tests. Their records and previous reports, as well as their final internal marks and reports for 1982, were studied. Thirty-six pupils were interviewed. Also the school's GCE and CSE results were obtained for the years 1980–3.

The headmaster, one of the two deputy head teachers, one other teacher and the home-school liaison officer were interviewed. Many informal conversations were also held with teachers, especially in the staff-room. Questionnaires were given to the 25 academic staff, but only 17 responded. Finally, teachers' personal constructs (Kelly 1955) regarding their pupils were obtained from ten volunteers.

TEACHERS

What frames of reference, then, did teachers at Townview School seem to have which may come into play in their interaction with and assessment of pupils, and in general in their curricular decisions in the broadest sense, and which may thereby help to shape and mould the course of events and especially the school careers of the pupils?

In order to explore these frames of reference – the 'backdrop' against which teachers might perceive pupils and interact with them – one of the approaches we tried was an adaptation of Kelly's role-construct, repertory-grid method. Although unfortunately only ten teachers were willing to respond, an interesting picture emerged. These teachers seemed to perceive their pupils primarily in terms of their work habits and classroom behaviour rather than in academic – or expressly ethnic – terms. The teachers' chief concern seemed to be with maintaining the normative order of the school, and the dominant values of middle-class society.

Only two teachers seemed to see their pupils expressly in ethnic or 'racial' terms: one teacher labelling them either 'West Indian' or 'Not West Indians' and the other teacher referring to pupils' colour ('White boys', 'Coloured') and to minority cultural forms of dress ('turban', 'plaits', 'juggas', 'pyjamas'). Thus it might seem that 'race' and ethnicity were not salient in most of these teachers' minds when considering their pupils.

This is not, however, necessarily to gainsay that Townview teachers have frames of reference pertaining to 'race', ethnicity or culture. First of all, one needs to bear in mind the sophistication of these respondents: they might want to shy away from matters of 'race' or ethnicity. Again, as already noted, these respondents were self-selected. It may well be that 'race', ethnicity and culture were more salient in the thinking, perceiving and acting of those teachers (over half in the school) who declined to take part in this aspect of the research. Furthermore, ethnicity, culture or 'race' might constitute an unthematized but organizing construct – that is, in Polanyi's (1958) terminology they might be part of the subsidiary awareness, or in Merleau-Ponty's (1945) terminology, part of the *cogito tacite* – and may thus not necessarily be identified even by the role-construct method. In fact, at least five teachers in conversations at various times during the observations, and in their responses to the teacher questionnaire, did seem to demonstrate such frames of reference. Teachers often spoke about the 'problem' of the attendance of Sikh girls and about the Sikh system of marriage which created 'problems' for girls at the age of sixteen.

One quite senior teacher spoke of the overt expressions of racism in the staff-room from 'a *very* small number of staff – small but influential, though', with whom this teacher had had to argue. Also, after the draft report of the present study was given to the headmaster for staff comment, this teacher and one other member of staff asserted in interview with Figueroa that racist views were common among the teachers. One of these two staff members stressed in particular the low turnover of the staff, and said that it was especially senior and key members of staff who were racist. Professionally, he said, they cover up their views on 'race'; but these had long-term effects on the curriculum and the hidden curriculum.

The other staff member effectively pointed to the monocultural and ethnocentric, if not racist, frames of reference that seem *de facto* to inform the life of the school by observing that the school 'pays lip-service to minorities by having entertainment evenings; generally though, British/Western culture is regarded as the major and superior culture'. A good deal of other information collected also pointed to culture-bound, ethnocentric or racist frames of reference on the part of the teachers. Few of them seemed to be really sensitive to the implications of the cross-cultural situation, to see the related issues as being of central importance, or to be making any sustained effort to adapt their teaching accordingly.

One teacher felt that the pupils themselves wanted to learn English ways of looking at the world – as though that was excluded by a multicultural approach or automatically implied their being divested of their own cultures. Perhaps, too, the implication was that 'English' ways of looking at the world were homogeneous and unchanging. This teacher also felt that while it was 'expected by the [recently appointed] headteacher and some other teachers to make this a multicultural school' there was not enough money for adequate resources, and furthermore many of the pupils 'themselves don't want it'. Another teacher seemed to feel threatened, and responded to the teacher questionnaire somewhat defensively, saying that there was, 'a lack of tolerance of OUR culture and morals by many children'. Both of these teachers seem, at best, to be unenthusiastic about 'multiculturalism' – although for almost opposing reasons: one saying the children want to learn 'English' ways, the other that they are not tolerant of 'our' culture. In any case, would not teachers who seem to feel threatened – like the second of these two teachers – perhaps be hampered from working to best advantage with Black pupils?

The Asian home-school liaison officer pointed to cultural differences as a source of miscommunication and conflict between teachers and Asian pupils. She referred to an incident where a teacher became furious with an Asian girl for replying 'yeah' instead of 'yes, miss', even though the girl did not mean to be impolite. The Asian pupils, though accustomed to strictness, are not accustomed, she said, to 'that kind of formality'.

Some of the remarks made by pupils also seemed to point to a lack of sensitivity by teachers towards cultural differences. For instance a Sikh girl said in interview: 'They call me "skiver" – pupils and teachers. It won't help to talk to the teachers – they won't know anything about it'. In this case the sense of a gulf between the mainstream culture of the school and the pupil's culture was great. The pupil felt that teachers operate according to their own norms and hence are not able to enter into her conception of reality. More importantly, the pupil felt the injustice of being labelled deviant for what is only different behaviour, but is in effect 'wrong' in the teachers' eyes (and in the eyes of many fellow pupils culturally different from herself). A Caribbean pupil, talking about the gulf between a teacher's language and his own, said:

He puts words harder than what they seem . . . he says the single word, then he says the higher word that all goes with it, then I don't understand it . . . If you try and get him to explain it, he just says you must shut up and get on with your work.

Apart from such remarks by staff and pupils, observations in the classroom provided a rich source of information. In a Form 2 Home Economics class one Asian girl responded to the request for decoration for a trifle by bringing in ready-mixed cake icing: she had never seen a trifle, and the teacher had clearly not been sensitive to the cultural gap here. Moreover, the exercise books of these girls contained only English recipes, such as cottage pie, which many pupils would never eat at home. The girls had even more insensitively been required to draw cuts of pork and beef irrespective of religious belief. In general, the text books in use were distinctly Anglocentric, making little reference to Black people. Somewhat curiously the book entitled, *Living with Others: Rules and Responsibility* (Jordanhill College of Education 1980), which was in use in the school, made no reference at all to ethnic minorities.

It also seemed clear from classroom observations that there were many attempts to get pupils to conform to what the teacher saw as the acceptable norms of behaviour. For instance, the teacher often projected herself or himself as trying to teach 'manners'. Exclusion and the threat of exclusion from the class seemed a common method of dealing with disruptive or non-conforming pupils. Four such exclusions were observed, involving three different classes and three different teachers. In each case the speed with which the pupils – one White girl, two Asian boys and a Caribbean boy – were told to leave was striking. The exclusion, it seemed, was being used as an instant method of control that was remarkable in its finality.

In a Form 2A2 class, pupils were doing exercises from textbooks. A White girl said in a loud voice to a Caribbean boy: 'Up yours . . . '. Without comment the teacher sent her out. In a 4B class discussion an Asian boy called out across the class and was sent out without comment or discussion. This was the first time he had committed an offence or had had to be reprimanded. In a Form 4A1 class the only Caribbean pupil, a bright boy, was sent out at great speed without any reason being given. When the teacher was questioned about this afterwards, she said that 'he was turning around' and 'was warned'. When the boy was approached about the incident he considered it unusual:

some guy made a remark to another boy. I turned round . . . and she said 'Get out of the class' just because I looked at him.

Sometimes, as in this case, exclusion seemed to be used more to make an example of someone than in strict justice, for sometimes other pupils seemed to need reprimanding more than the one excluded.

The final example of an exclusion was also observed during a fourth-form class. The following sets out all the utterances the teacher used to control pupils and the times at which they were made.

2.12 p.m.   *(to White boy)*: Sit here!

2.13 p.m.   *(to first Asian boy)*: Sit here, A— *(quietly)*

2.31 p.m.   *(to first Asian boy)*: What about you, *(to control him)*

2.33 p.m.   *(to West Indian girl)*: B—, why were you laughing during the first part?

2.34 p.m.   *(to first Asian boy)*: A—, be silent!

2.34 p.m.   *(to second Asian boy chanting 'Ba-ba')*: Get out. *(calmly)* You've made no contribution to this lesson, other than that – if you don't want to contribute, get out.

Here the first Asian boy is called to order three times, but the first time the second Asian boy opens his mouth he is sent out. When approached about this incident after the lesson, the teacher said that the second Asian boy had made a racial slur. (Clearly 'ba-ba' would mean 'ba-ba black sheep' with a range of racist connotations.) The teacher was undoubtedly acting with the best of intentions.

One could, however, question using exclusion to deal with 'name-calling'. Certainly, if racist frames of reference tend to be shared by a community and tend to operate at the level of a group taken-for-granted, simply coming down heavily (and inexplicitly) on an individual may have little lasting and positive impact. Perhaps some form of more explicit awareness-raising with the class would be helpful. Maybe, too, various forms of collaborative cross-group interaction would be fruitful. Moreover, racist name-calling and racist harassment in general, need to be dealt with within the context of a school policy and of established school procedures. The school needs to make its complete disapproval of such behaviour clear, but there need also to be guidelines about positive and constructive ways of dealing with such behaviour. Such disapproval and such guidelines need to be placed within the general context of the school's stated approach to pastoral and disciplinary matters, and to multiculturalism and antiracism. And all of this needs to be set within the general educational policy and philosophy of the school.

Another facet of some of the incidents observed is that they seemed to point to certain pupils having perhaps become targets for being more easily or more regularly excluded from lessons than others. It also seemed that perhaps this was associated with a teacher image of the 'ideal pupil' (see Becker 1952) and with teacher stereotypes of certain pupils in relation to this 'ideal'. Thus a 4A1 Asian boy complained that teachers had an unfair image of him as one who 'chatters'. He said that if you have a bad name it goes round the staffroom and the teachers look out for you. They always 'picked on' him and the Caribbean boy in his class, he said, while a lot of other pupils got away with chattering.

This Caribbean boy said how he always got into trouble with a certain teacher:

> even for nothing; and the whole class used to say 'Why does she pick on you for nothing?' . . . When I first came into the classroom, all I did was say *one* word, . . . she said . . . 'you sit where your sister used to sit, and you chatter like your sister.' She never used to like my sister . . . and my sister was clever.

The importance of conformity to the teachers' view of how a pupil should behave also seemed apparent, as might be expected, from the comments teachers made on the reports of 'promoted' or 'demoted' pupils in the classes studied. Thus, without exception, all of the 'promoted' pupils (one White girl, one Asian girl, and five Asian boys) were described as co-operative and in terms highlighting good behaviour. On the other hand, the four White and three Asian boys 'demoted' were consistently described as displaying non-conforming patterns of behaviour. It may be significant that no girls were 'demoted' and no Caribbean pupils 'promoted'. Perhaps also significantly, the one Caribbean (a boy) who was 'demoted' had a mixed report. Some teachers mentioned 'chatty behaviour' and an 'attitude of indifference', while others made comments such as: 'likeable boy, meticulous, carrying out senior responsibilities well, marked improvement from chattering'. In general, teachers' comments in end-of-year reports seemed to indicate that the teachers tended to define the 'ideal pupil' more in behavioural than in intellectual or academic terms.

We would suggest that if pupils do not accord with or conform to the apparent assumptions about the 'ideal pupil', or are not seen as so doing, they are more likely to be negatively labelled and stereotyped. Also, less is likely to be expected of them academically, and their academic performance is less likely to be recognized and rewarded. Thus an Asian boy seemed to link conforming behaviour with teacher approval, and to consider that non-conforming behaviour somewhat lowers the pupil's worth in the teacher's eyes, despite academic worth. He said:

> If you're good [at school work] and chatter a lot, [the teacher] don't

help you, but [another pupil] don't mess about, and so the teacher allows him to borrow stuff and all that.

Besides, since the teachers' notion of the 'ideal pupil' is inevitably culture-bound, it may be that some groups are more likely than others to be disadvantaged (or advantaged) by its operations.

We have seen that many of the Townview teachers seemed to lack awareness of, sensitivity to and informedness on cross-cultural and related issues. Perhaps they were not even convinced about their importance. One notable exception was an experienced mathematics teacher. Both researchers observed his teaching at different times. He clearly had a good relationship with his class, and was quietly in full control. He used Hindu and Arabic number systems in teaching place value. This was no mere gimmickry. He considered that place value is better learned when pupils have to cope with unfamiliar numbering systems. He arranged things so as to ensure that all of his pupils were working in at least one unfamiliar (and one familiar) script. He also took care to place mathematics in its world-wide historical context. He made the point, for instance, that the crucial introduction of zero and of our familiar decimal system was made, not by Europeans, but by the Hindus and came to Europe via the Arabs. He also taught transformation geometry using traditional Arabic (Islamic) and Hindu patterns.

Apart from him, however, the main teachers who seemed convinced of the importance of 'multicultural education', or who seemed to be doing anything at all to adapt their teaching, were the senior religious-education teacher, the senior remedial teacher and the new headmaster. A multi-faith syllabus was being used in religious education. However, the senior remedial teacher was about to retire, partly for health reasons, but partly also it seemed from a sense of tiredness, and of having tried to raise the issues in the school and the community with little success.

The reality of the situation was that this school, which for many years had had a large proportion of pupils with roots in the Indian sub-continent (and other Black or ethnic minority pupils), had never as a body discussed the basic issues nor sought to formulate an appropriate policy. The school had never embarked upon a systematic examination of its curriculum, methods, materials, books or assessment procedures within the changed context so as to attempt at least to guard against racist and cultural bias and to ensure genuine educational equality for all of its pupils. Instead, it seemed to pursue a policy of 'inexplicitness' (see Kirp 1979) – hoping cultural differences and racist problems would disappear or not surface noticeably if ignored or played down.

We had hoped that submitting our draft report to the school for comments by the staff would have provided the opportunity for the school as a body to discuss these issues. However, pursuing his cautious approach, and despite his own awareness, commitment and deep understanding of the issues, the headmaster only gave the report limited circulation within the school. No general staff discussion was encouraged, and none took place. It might be that the headmaster felt constrained by his new LEA and area, which had not up to that time been in the forefront of 'multicultural education'. It may also be that he considered that his staff were not yet ready, and perhaps he hoped to institute staff awareness and discussion of the issues in the near future. In the meantime, however, many of the pupils may already have gone through the system without their needs and rights having been met, without having realized their full potential or without having been adequately prepared – as far as lies within the limited power of a school – for contemporary, multicultural society with its institutional racism, racist tensions and democratic ideals.

Besides, while proceeding on the tacit policy of inexplicitness – that is, of ignoring cultural differences, different cultural requirements and racist tensions – one is, in effect, proceeding in a monocultural, ethnocentric and racist manner. In effect, the different cultures are not approached as of equal worth. And racist beliefs and tensions are, in effect, at least winked at. On the whole, it would seem, then, that perhaps many of the Townview teachers were operating within largely unquestioned frames of reference (i.e. White, British, middle-class, monocultural, ethnocentric) which were, at best, not entirely appropriate within the context of their school. Apart from this, it would seem that at least some of them were operating within ethnicist or racist frames of reference.

PUPILS

Although it proved not surprisingly difficult to get at whatever racist frame of reference there might be among staff, there was a good deal of evidence for such a frame of reference operating among pupils. Their responses to a word-association test for nationalities and religions displayed a good deal of in-group and out-group stereotyping. The Whites, the Asians and the Caribbean pupils mainly tended to see each other in a negative or narrow way, and themselves in a positive light. However, Asians and Caribbeans seemed to have somewhat less negative images of each other than of the English. They also agreed in referring to 'Englishmen' as 'prejudiced', 'fascists' or 'racial'.

White pupils sometimes focused on colour of skin with reference to 'Indians', 'Pakistanis' and 'West Indians'. They also demonstrated a negative attitude towards these 'nationalities', but perhaps especially towards Indians and Pakistanis. They associated words like, 'smelly', 'dirty' and 'noisy' with all three. They also referred to the Pakistanis and Indians in terms such as: got fleas, wank-heads, breed like rabbits, annoying and donkeys. But they tended to cast the West Indians in a more 'positive', though narrow, happy-go-lucky mould with constructs such as: good laugh, good dancers, fun-loving and sense of humour.

Similarly, the Asian pupils tended to associate music, sport, 'coolness' and style with West Indians. They also referred to such ethnic and phenotypical features as: Rastamen, black curly hair and dreadlocks. Negative constructs included: dirty men, bossy, pick on you, swear, and talk behind your backs. But the Asians also specifically described West Indians as 'good', 'helpful' and 'not prejudiced'. By contrast, Asian pupils saw 'Englishmen' as: prejudiced, fascists, boring, greedy, prostitutes, drunkards, trouble-makers and cruel. (Many of these pupils, perhaps especially the Asians, lived in the nearby 'red light' district.) But they apparently considered 'Englishmen' as sharing with West Indians such characteristics as being: dirty, bossy and two-faced. And, of course, they referred to the English as White.

Like the Asians, Caribbean pupils associated with 'Englishmen' such terms as: prejudice, racial, National Front and British Movement. Some other negative constructs they associated with 'Englishmen' were: snobs, vandals, dirty-minded and sex-minded. But they also saw them as 'strong', 'nice' and 'friendly'. The Caribbean pupils did not mention prejudice or racism with reference to 'Indians' and 'Pakistanis'. However, they highlighted phenotypical and ethnic characteristics such as: coloured, speak different language, turbans, mosque and samosa. Less frequently they also produced modified negative constructs like: some dirty, sometimes unkind and not very good.

As far as group self-images are concerned, the White pupils tended to see 'Englishmen' in such positive terms as: good-looking, kind, thoughtful and clean. They also used constructs with social class or ethnic connotations, such as: snobs, posh, pubs, business people and bowler hats. Some of the positive terms used by Asians about 'Indians' and 'Pakistanis' were: good, clean, kind, rich, fair, good cooks, fearless, clever, don't pick on others, got style, well-reared, honour and helpful. They also referred to themselves to some extent in ethnic terms: 'Muslims', 'Allah'. Caribbean pupils also saw themselves in a positive light, and perhaps in 'ethnic' terms, but in a way that seemed to parallel somewhat the narrow image that both Whites and Asians often seemed to have of them. Thus Caribbean pupils tended to associate with 'West Indians' terms such as: cool, dread, magic reggae music, good sense of humour, Iry na Rasta and Bombo Klaat. 'Iry na Rasta' means roughly, 'They're great – they're Rastas' (i.e. Rastafarians). 'Bombo Klaat' is a strong Jamaican swearword, and is perhaps reproduced here for its Creole and 'in' connotations. It is interesting that some of the other children, especially Asians, also used variants of this expression to refer (no doubt in a friendly way?) to 'West Indians'.

These data suggest that racist and ethnicist frames of reference were common among the pupils. Information from observations and interviews supports this conclusion. Racist comment was often heard flying across the classroom, sometimes out of earshot of the teacher. But often the teacher seemed to hear and yet ignore it. Sometimes teachers seemed to consider it of little importance. Or else they were at a loss to know how to deal with it. A fourth-form Asian said that the deputy headteacher had caned pupils for it, and that teachers often speak to their pupils about it. The West Indian boy in 4A1 said that the deputy headteacher had given them a talking-to about it. As we have seen above, teachers also resorted to exclusion for name-calling. Yet, from our observations and from what pupils said, name-calling continued to be rife, and was sometimes clearly very hurtful.

One exchange which the teacher did not seem aware of took place in a fourth-form class between a White boy and an Asian boy:

White: Shut up you top-knot black dick! This is not Brixton.
Asian: We rule this area!
White: You've got fleas in your top-knot!
Asian: We've got history in our knots!

When asked later about this 'name-calling', this Asian boy said that it had been happening in his class since second form (the first year in the school), and that Asian pupils were especially hurt when their parents and families were referred to. Another fourth-form Asian boy also said that it hurt when someone said something 'really bad about you like about your mum and dad'. But he claimed that the name-calling had begun in the third form when the pupils realized that the teachers were not really strict. Nevertheless, some second formers also reported on name-calling. One Vietnamese boy felt sorry for himself when called 'Chinkie'. An Asian boy was called 'top-knot', 'geordie', 'turbine' or 'turban dioxide'. He reacted, and the term 'fatty' drew anger.

The Caribbean boy in 4A1 asserted that *'everybody'* name-called. Certain Asian pupils – and it would seem implicitly White pupils as well – called him 'racialist names . . . like "rubber-lips" and "gorilla" . . .

things that they call coloured people'. But he didn't care – 'only if they calls me "nigger": that's the one name I can't stand, and I goes mad (and) beats 'em up'. One incident that the teacher ignored occurred when she enquired of an African boy with a bandaged arm what had happened, and several pupils shouted out, 'He was swinging in the trees, Miss! In the jungle!'. We observed in 4B one attempt by the teacher to pick up on name-calling; but it was not very inspired or skilled.

Teacher (to White boy): A –, you call names. Why?

White boy: To hurt them.

Teacher: Why?

White boy: Because I hate 'em.

Teacher (to Caribbean girl): It's become a habit. Do you do it because you hate people?

Caribbean girl: Only in school.

Teacher: Why do you sit in your groups?

(referring to the seating arrangement with boys on one side, and girls on the other) Why not next to B –? *(Vietnamese boy)*

White girl (mocking): Because he doesn't understand us.

(general giggling)

Caribbean girl (disparagingly): He can't understand us – he can't talk English.

Vietnamese boy: I can! *(this silences girls)*

Asian boy: He won't argue! We'll beat him up!

Teacher (to Sikh girl): C –, you'll be embarrassed – Yes? Because of your religion? Yes?

(referring to this girl's not sitting next to boys). You think your religion won't allow it?

Asian boy (makes a disparaging remark about Sikhism, ending with): It's all superstitious!

Second Asian boy: What's he saying about me?

Teacher (to second Asian boy): D –, why do you always think people are talking about you?

While this teacher was prepared to raise the question of name-calling, pupils had received very little by the end of the lesson except a platform to fling insults to and fro.

Some of the pupils, especially some White pupils and some 4A pupils, played down name-calling and racism in the school. According to a White fourth-form boy, name-calling was 'just to wind people up and annoy them – something to do for a laugh'. Several Whites and Asians thought the school was good as it tried to bring the various 'races' into harmony. A 4A White girl said everyone in the school lived 'in harmony without colour prejudices', and a 4A Asian girl asserted that 'there's not many racialists around here'.

Many of the staff also seemed either to play down racist tensions in the school or not to be aware of them. Nine out of sixteen staff respondents had not noticed any 'racial/cultural' tensions in the school during the year. Of the seven who had, most only mentioned teasing, ragging, name-calling or childish squabbles. The home-school liaison officer said that in 9 or 10 years she had only heard of four major instances – racial incidents as such – and none had been on school premises. Yet some pupils, Asians and Whites, boys and girls, perhaps especially from 4B, seemed to harbour some very hostile feelings: 'We hate English people' (4B Asian girl); 'School is crap because there are honkies about' (4C Asian boy); 'Perhaps Townview should not have so many Paki' (4B White girl). 'Paki' is a common disparaging name applied generally to Asians (and sometimes even more widely).

These pupils live in a racist world in which feelings often run high. Many pupils gave vivid accounts in written work set by Swart of racist strife in their neighbourhood. Swart in fact uncovered some disturbing conflicts. For instance, although the soccer matches during the break-times of Whites and West Indians vs. Asians were usually in good spirit, he witnessed a chase of two White fourth-form boys by 'The Tribe' (a group of 4A1 Asian boys). The intention was obviously to harm these two, but they managed to escape. When Swart tried to unearth the meaning of the chase, he met with extreme evasiveness. However, one of the White boys chased said how he hated the 'Pakis' who came to 'take away the Whites' jobs in this country'.

CONCLUSION

This case study has shown that racist and ethnicist name-calling was common in Townview School. It also provides evidence of other forms of racist harassment and of racist and ethnicist frames of reference, especially among pupils. Other studies show that such findings are by no means unique (for example, DES 1985a: 234–6; Wright 1986; Gaine 1987: 2–8; CRE 1988: 10–14; Kelly and Cohn 1988; and Tattum and Lane 1989).

The case study has also shown that Townview School had hardly begun to face up to the basic issues involved in antiracist and multicultural education. Classroom work had hardly been adapted as necessary. The teachers themselves, although certainly concerned with their pupils as individuals, seemed little aware of some of the basic issues and realities – or at least seemed to give them little importance. They also seemed to be ill-equipped for many of the difficult tasks they faced. But then what specific preparation, training or support had they received?

The ethnocentric, ethnicist and racist frames of reference which teachers, and especially pupils, seemed to manifest might well have negative effects, directly or indirectly, on pupil performance, as suggested in the previous chapter. Wright's study (1986) supports such a likelihood as far as teachers are concerned and will be discussed in Chapter 9, where data on achievement from the Townview case study will also be presented. Any negative effect on pupil performance might also be a function of the extent to which the school's notion of the 'ideal pupil' does not correspond to the pupils' cultures – or to the stereotypes held about those cultures. Again, like the contents of the frames of reference this might vary across the different groups, and so help to account for differential performance.

Quite apart from any question of the effects on educational achievement, however, it is critical – on wider educational, social and value grounds – for incidents and realities (such as this chapter has reported) to be dealt with urgently, fundamentally and sensitively. Racist, ethnicist or ethnocentric behaviour and arrangements in the day-to-day life of the school could help to reinforce, or even to socialize into, racist, ethnicist or ethnocentric frames of reference and forms of behaviour – and could also lead to the alienation of Black pupils.

NOTE

* This chapter has been written jointly by Peter Figueroa and L. Thomas Swart, and is based on a study initiated by Figueroa and carried out mainly by Swart under Figueroa's direction. In preparing this chapter Figueroa has drawn on Figueroa and Swart 1986 and 1983, and Swart 1983, and has also gone back to the raw data.

8   Bias in examinations[*]

EXAMINATIONS AND INEQUALITY

School-leaving examinations can be considered as the culmination of the assessment and allocation process within the school. My postulate is that frames of reference such as those for which we have found evidence among pupils, teachers and trainee teachers will also be incorporated in the very examination system. As a result, despite all efforts at objectivity and fairness, this examination system may itself tend in effect to be biased. It may thus tend to work more to the advantage of some and to the disadvantage of others, and, more specifically in a multicultural but unequal and racist society, to the disadvantage of the minority ethnic pupils and especially of those seen as most problematic.

In England the examinations boards not only devise the school-leaving examinations and assess the scripts, they have also had a great influence on the curriculum through the syllabuses which they determine. Even with the National Curriculum they may still have a substantial influence on actual practice. Yet these boards – even in their more recently reorganized groupings and even in reference to the General Certificate for Secondary Education (GCSE) – have been slow to devise policies and practices which address the specific educational needs and rights of ethnic minorities, or which deliberately seek to avoid ethnocentrism, to combat racism and to further positive and creative interaction between the different cultures and 'groups' (see, for example: Little and Willey 1981; Schools Council 1981; File 1983; and DES 1985a: 350–1).

It is thus important to review relevant syllabuses and examination papers, assessing their appropriateness to present-day 'multicultural' Britain. Hence, in the first part of this chapter we will consider some evidence from a study of some examination syllabuses and papers for the Certificate of Secondary Education (CSE). This will then be briefly supplemented and updated by some reference in particular to the more recent General Certificate of Secondary Education.

SREB HISTORY, CSE MODE 1

The focus in the first part of the chapter will be the CSE History syllabuses and examination papers of the Southern Regional Examinations Board (SREB). The data here are drawn from a project which also investigated the parallel SREB syllabuses and examination papers in English and Mathematics. The SREB was one of thirteen boards awarding the Certificate of Secondary Education. The examinations leading to this Certificate were the most frequently attempted school-leaving examinations in England. The CSE existed in three 'modes', of which Mode 1 – devised, set and assessed by the boards themselves – was the commonest. The overall aim of the project was to consider whether the Mode 1 CSE examinations were adapted to contemporary 'multicultural' Britain. The syllabuses, examination papers, marking schemes and regulations for the period 1978–82 were investigated, with the emphasis on 1982 (see SREB 1976–80; 1978–82; 1981 and 1982).

Questions we were interested in included such as the following. How culturally suitable and sensitive are the examination papers? Is there explicit or subtle support for racist stereotypes, beliefs or values in the papers or syllabuses? Do the examination questions adequately respond to and reflect the backgrounds and cultures of the ethnic minority communities? Does the structure of the examinations have a preponderant 'White' British bias? Are ethnic minorities conspicuous by their absence, or do they feature only in certain roles and situations? In what light are minority cultures in Britain or the cultures of other countries seen? What cultural values are implicit? Is there any reference to multiethnic Britain? If so, is it satisfactory? Is there any bridging between the pupils' cultures or experiences and the syllabus? How are the marks, content and structure distributed from year to year, and is this likely to affect ethnic minority candidates more disadvantageously than ethnic majority candidates?

History is a subject which can easily be given a narrow, ethnocentric or nationalist orientation (see DES 1985a: 235). This is because history is closely linked to a collectivity's identity and myths. At the same time it offers insights and opportunities, and can highlight difference, similarity, universal rights, bias – and in general the complexity of truth and evidence – in a particularly striking way, especially in a multicultural context. It is 'polymorphous': that is, it permits varying selection, definition and interpretation from a variety of points of view. Does school history reflect this? In the interests of 'objectivity', honesty, openness, positive interaction and equality, it ought to – not least in a multicultural situation. Children should have some critical idea of the history from which they, and others, come. School history should be appropriately wide, polyvalent *and* critical in orientation.

The syllabus options or sections

Until 1980, SREB Mode 1 History consisted of six syllabus options or sections with a preponderance given to British history. In 1981 limited changes were introduced towards a more manageable syllabus and one somewhat less narrowly focused on Britain. Two sections were dropped – 'Prehistoric Britain to *c.* 1500 AD' and 'Britain and the World 1789–1914' – while one new section on 'Contemporary Affairs: the World since 1945' was added. The total number of sections was thus reduced to five:

A *c.* 1450 to the End of the Seventeenth Century;
B British History *c.* 1760 to the Present Day;
C The World 1900–1964;
D Contemporary Affairs: the World since 1945;
E British Social and Economic History from *c.* 1750–1964.

The arrangements in 1982 were identical to those in 1981. However, some of the changes were merely window-dressing. For instance, section C was identical with a section previously entitled 'Britain and the World since 1900'. Furthermore, the contents of the syllabuses and the incidence and weighting of the questions still showed a strong bias towards Britain, Europe and the western powers. For instance, in the 1982 syllabus three out of the five options, Sections A, B and E, had a largely British focus. A fourth option, Section C, also tended to take a European, or at least a superpower, perspective. Only Section D, 'Contemporary Affairs: the World since 1945', dealt with a wide variety of nations – but here too there was quite a strong European or superpower bias. Although four of the five sections included the post-Second World War period, it was only in Section D that 'immigration' to Britain was mentioned – and that very briefly. Section A, '*c.* 1450 to the End of the Seventeenth Century', was characterized by a history of 'discoveries', and made no reference to the lucrative slave trade.

In none of the sections was 'race relations' or 'civil rights' in Britain or the 'Black British' expressly mentioned. Yet there has been a Black population in Britain continuously since at least the beginning of the sixteenth century. Indeed, in 1596 Queen Elizabeth I noted 'that there are of late divers blackamores brought into this realm, of which kind of people there are already here too manie', and directed that 'those kinde of people should be sente forth of the land' (see for example Walvin 1973: 8). Despite this and other efforts at 'repatriation', there was by the nineteenth century a substantial Black population in Britain which by then had 'permeated most ranks of society, through the length and breadth of the country' (Walvin 1973: 72). Over the centuries there were many prominent Black people in Britain – such as Olaudah Equiano (born 1743 in Biafra and enslaved at the age of 10), who was active in the anti-slavery movement, and William Cuffay (1788–1870), who was a leading Chartist (see, for example, Ethnic Minorities Unit, Greater London Council 1986, especially 20–5, 32–5, 40–3 and 48–50).

The first half of the eighteenth century was not covered in any of the options. The importance of slavery, of the plantation system, of the colonies (especially of the Caribbean and India), and of past or indeed recent immigration for British economic, social and military history was not acknowledged. Yet the industrial revolution and the prosperity of Britain at that time were founded to a large extent on the wealth transferred from the colonies (see, for example, Williams 1944, Rodney 1972 and Fryer 1984: 15–17, 33–8).

Altogether, no great salience was given to India and perhaps less to Black Africa – while, apart from Cuba, the Caribbean was ignored. Moreover, the references to such countries tended to be from a British or western point of view, and to be stereotyped. In the whole syllabus the word 'Caribbean' occurred only in Section D – and there it was bracketed with South America and linked to the concerns of the 'great powers' and to 'poverty and population'.

Examination papers and questions

On the positive side, the examination papers made use of pictures and illustrations. Also, there was some variety in the types and formats of questions. Different points of view were sometimes solicited, and some choice was permitted. Moreover, project work was a possibility. (This provided a great opportunity, although we were not able to investigate its actual use.) All of this could help cope with the range of experience and perceptions of the candidates, and so could contribute to the fairness of the examination.

Nevertheless, there were many problems. For example, in the twenty-two history examination papers for the years 1980 and 1982, there were thirty-one pages of illustrations portraying people; but only five of these pages showed non-white people. They were all from the 1982 Paper 2 of Section D, 'Contemporary Affairs', and none of them showed non-whites in Britain or in any other western country. They depicted: Chinese people (two pages); a Vietnamese family; Mrs Indira Gandhi (see question below); and Black workers with a White trainer. In this last case the question was on the 'Third World', and the photograph was labelled, 'Agricultural training in Africa'. The focal point was a White man directing a Black man operating a tractor, while four other Black men looked on. Are there no Black trainers in the 'Third World', and more specifically in Africa?

Furthermore, the distribution of questions and the allocation of marks in the 1982 examination on Section D – the most catholic of the five options – is instructive. This examination was divided into two papers, the first worth 40 per cent and the second 60 per cent. Paper 1 consisted of seven obligatory questions worth 100 marks, distributed as follows: Europe, 58 (continental Western Europe 26, Ulster [Northern Ireland] 15, other Great Britain 6, USSR and Eastern Europe 11); China, 18; USA, 7; superpowers, 6; the 'Third World', 5; other, 6. The question for which most marks (20) could be earned was one consisting of seven questions on the European Economic Community (EEC). Northern Ireland was approached entirely from a British establishment perspective. Although Britain in particular and Europe on the whole counted for such a large proportion of the marks, there were no questions on post-war labour migration, cultural diversity or 'race' relations. Africa counted for only two marks, and the Caribbean (i.e. a 'Cuban revolutionary') for exactly one. India did not feature.

Paper 2 provided a choice of 4 out of 14 questions – or 3 questions plus an individual assignment – each being worth 20 marks (i.e. 80 marks altogether). The marks were distributed as follows: Europe, 80; the whole 'Third World' – excluding the 'Middle East' – 80 (Africa 23, Cuba 20, India 20, Latin America 13, 'Third World' in general 12); the 'Middle East', 33 (Egypt *or* Arab–Israeli conflict 20, Persian Gulf 5, Khomeini 4, Gadafy 4); USA, 20; Vietnam War and USA, 20; post-war Japan, 20; international organizations, 20 (including optional sub-question on the Organization of African States 5, counted above); international affairs, 12 (including boycott of South Africa 4). (On account of forced alternatives, the sums do not all 'add up'). Concepts like 'Third World', 'Middle East' and even 'Africa' are problematical, yet seem to be used unquestioningly.

A candidate could, by answering four specific questions in Paper 2, have gained all marks there – plus more than half in Paper 1 – for knowledge of Europe. The marks linked to the 'Third World' by contrast, were spread over 5 questions, although only 4 questions were to be answered in the paper. Moreover, these questions on the 'Third World' tended to be 'problem' orientated and to assume a western, or superpowers, point of view. Cuba was again the only Caribbean country mentioned. Although Africa was all but absent from Paper 1, the 27 marks linked to Africa in Paper 2 were spread over 4 questions – Southern Africa and the Horn of Africa accounting for 14, and optional alternative sub-questions for the other 13. Any candidate with a special interest in Africa was thus disadvantaged. And, of course, any candidate with a special interest in the Caribbean was in a hopeless position.

The one question on India concerned the career of Mrs Indira Gandhi. The examination in which this question was asked took place five weeks after the 'Festival of India' opened at the Royal Festival Hall, London, in the presence of Prime Minister Mrs Thatcher and many other notables. The question, worth twenty marks, included a large portrait of Mrs Gandhi, and read in full as follows:

Describe the career of Mrs Indira Gandhi using the following headings:
   Modernization of India
   Emergency Powers
   Victory of Desai
   Re-election of Mrs Gandhi.

This question seems to highlight history through 'heroes' and the cult of personality, while at the same time invoking such concepts and issues as those of capital construction, civil war, and representative democracy. 'Modernization' tends to convey a particular version of India's history. What implicit assumptions are contained within this question concerning India's nationhood? Is the military history of India invoked in this question in relation to the carefully controlled regional and ethnic division of the Indian Army? In short, the question is at the least an oversimplification, and does not do full justice either to Britain's imperial domination of India or to Mrs Gandhi's resistance to such domination. Also, neo-colonialism is not even hinted at. Moreover, the pupils' experiences are left out. Perhaps, more importantly, we can ask whether Mrs Gandhi's career had its beginnings with the problem of the British partition of India in 1947 – a problem inherited from the British Raj – or with her election to office in 1966. Would 14–16-year-olds, using dated text-books, be considered able enough to describe how, during the most difficult periods of Mrs. Gandhi's career, British private investment in India was nearly 80 per cent of the total foreign investment, and what particular implications this had for policing and militarizing the area? Since partition in 1947, what role has Britain played in contributing to or stopping the three wars between India and Pakistan? In 1966, why was it that Britain suffered the diplomatic humiliation of being passed over as a conciliator between the warring parties in favour of the Soviet Union?

No mention is made, in the marking scheme to this question, of Mrs Gandhi's election to the leadership of the Congress Party in January 1966 when Morarji Desai was defeated. Nothing is said of Desai's followers, some say backed by the CIA, founding the dissident movement in November 1969, or of the charges of electoral corruption made against Mrs Gandhi after the March 1971 elections. The High Court at Allahabad declared Mrs Gandhi guilty in June 1975. The marking scheme is silent about the government's enforcement of the Maintenance of Internal Security Act, and the imprisonment of Desai's supporters. Civil War was threatened throughout 1976. Soon after this Mrs Gandhi was defeated at the ballot box, while the Desai dissidents gained a landslide victory over the official Congress candidates. But was it through sabotage or through legitimate opposition? Why did Mrs Gandhi resign from office on 22nd March 1977? It is interesting to note that during the last stages of Mrs Gandhi's defeat four history textbooks were requested by the Prime Minister's Office to be withdrawn. The grounds for this request were that the books contained controversial material (Abraham 1977: 10).

In the entire 1982 examinations it was the papers on Section D which provided the greatest scope – limited as it was – for candidates to gain marks for knowledge of India, Africa, the Caribbean or the 'Third World' in general. That is why we have given particular attention to them. However, there was also a sprinkling of questions on these areas in the papers on the other sections of the syllabus. Another example relating to India in the 1982 examinations comes from Paper 2 of Section B, and it reads in part as follows:

The sun never sets on the British Empire

(5 marks)   (a)   Why did Britain conquer and control her Empire during the nineteenth century?

(5 marks)   (b)   Explain why three of the following were important to the history of the British Empire [a list is then given, one item of which is:] The Indian Mutiny – 1857.

First of all, there is a clear disproportion in the allocation of marks. More basically, however, this question highlights the problem of trying to separate out an indisputable 'factual' content from the context of interpretation. Thus, given the context and content of this question there is no invitation to offer an answer which would allow the events of the 'Mutiny' to be described as the first major step in the struggle for self-determination *vis-à-vis* British domination – which is the context in which Asian children in particular might see this episode.

Overall, taking the five sections together, India, Africa and especially the Caribbean were only minimally represented in the 1982 examination papers. Moreover, to the extent that they did feature at all, they tended to be presented from a non-Indian, non-African and non-Caribbean point of view, for even the World History Sections C and D had a strong Western or superpowers bias. Thus, not only was world history misrepresented but important factors or dimensions of British history were left out or distorted. Yet they are necessary for Britain's understanding of itself, are specifically important for Black Britons, and are essential for understanding post-war developments in Britain – including post-war cultural diversity and racism. Here, then, is bias by omission, minimal treatment or restrictive and partial perspective.

The case of Ireland

Counting the number of questions and their constituent words, terms, phrases, concepts, ideas, topics, and content-components – in order to access the fairness or bias of the examination papers is a complex and difficult task. The results, like examination marks, can only be seen as approximations. Within these limitations, we consider here, by way of an example, the case of Ireland as seen in the 1978 papers. In this assessment we have read each 1978 examination paper and each question, asking ourselves: Is a history of Ireland given, or only a history of British colonization and settlement? Is a history of 800 years of subjugation, repression and coercion of Ireland given? Are economic exploitation and political segregation conceded? Are British military invasion and domination admitted? Are derogatory terms used in reference to Gaelic, Catholic, Republican and other Nationalist Irish people?

A limited number of questions referred to Irish history in the examination papers in three of the six options available at the time: mainly in Section C, 'British History *c.* 1760 to the Present Day'; to some extent in Section B, '*c.* 1450 to the End of the Eighteenth Century'; and to a lesser extent in Section F, 'British Social and Economic History from Mid Eighteenth Century'. In the examination papers on Section C there was one complete question (20 marks), seven sub-questions (18 marks in all) and two implied questions (? marks) relating to Irish history. Ireland was absent from Section A, 'Prehistoric Britain to *c.* 1500 AD'. The nature and culture of early Gaelic society, which has been described by some historians as truly multiethnic, was thus ignored. Ireland was similarly absent from Section D, 'Britain and the World 1789–1914', and from Section E, 'Britain and the World since 1900'.

Out of a total of 121 complete questions, and over several hundred sub-questions (parts of a question), Ireland appeared only twenty-two times. Only one of these questions wholly consisted of a specifically 'Irish' content. Many of the twenty-two questions on Ireland were allocated a low proportion of the overall marks given to the question. For example, a question might be allocated twenty marks, but in many cases only one or two of these marks were given to the Irish component of the question. None of the questions referred to the period before British settlement. Two-thirds of them used derogatory terms for Irish people, while relatively little reference was made to military invasion and domination, repression and coercion, or exploitation and discrimination (Table 8.1).

In the questions asked, the massive slaughter, torture, and massacre of Irish people thus tended to be ignored. The 800 years of subjugation and coercion can barely be traced in the pages of the examination papers. The year 1832 is hailed as a landmark in the development of British democracy but the Coercion Act of the same period, and later under Gladstone, is left out of account. The derogatory term 'potato famine' is repeatedly mentioned whilst the possibility of interpreting the same events as the 'Great Starvation' is beyond the normative prescription of history as contained in the examination papers.

In short, bias operated in the 1978 examination through omission, restriction, slanting and inexplicitness. Irish history appeared as a potted, selective series of ahistoric incidents seen from the dominant, establishment British point of view. Yet, the history of Ireland is a long

Table 8.1: A summary of bias in twenty-two examination questions on Ireland

Cultural bias criterion	Yes	No
History begins before British settlement	0	22
The use of repression and coercion conceded	9	13
Exploitation and discrimination referred to	10	12
Military invasion and domination admitted or provided for	7	15
Derogatory terms used for Irish people	7	15

and thoroughly documented one, documented not only by those on one side of the conflict (see, for example: Burns 1976; Chubb 1970; Coogan 1971; Curtis 1984; Farrell 1976; Jackson 1976; Kee 1972 and 1980, Kelly 1967; and Maguire 1973).

RECENT DEVELOPMENTS: THE GCSE

Since the research into the SREB CSE was carried out, important developments have taken place. The CSE has been phased out and so has the Ordinary level of the General Certificate of Education (the GCE 'O' level), which used also to be taken mainly at 16+. The General Certificate of Secondary Education (GCSE) has replaced the CSE and the GCE 'O' level. A major Education Act (1988) has been passed, which introduces a national curriculum and assessment at the 'key stages' of 7, 11, 14 and 16. Also, the Swann Report on 'Education for All' (DES 1985a) discussed in Chapter 4 above, has appeared. Furthermore, the Examination Boards have been reorganized and grouped together, so that the SREB now forms part of the Southern Examining Group. Have the common syllabuses and examination papers which this Group issues become any more appropriate to present-day multicultural Britain?

Both general and subject criteria have been issued for the GCSE (DES 1985b and c). Criterion 19 of the general criteria (DES 1985b, 3–4) lays down the following requirements for all subjects and syllabuses:

(h) *Avoidance of bias*
Every possible effort must be made to ensure that syllabuses and examinations are free of political, ethnic, gender and other forms of bias.

(i) *Recognition of cultural diversity*
In devising syllabuses and setting question papers Examining Groups should bear in mind the linguistic and cultural diversity of society. The value to all candidates of incorporating material which reflects this diversity should be recognised.

(j) *Language*
The language used in question papers (both rubrics and questions) must be clear, precise and intelligible to candidates throughout the range of entry for the examination. Examining Groups should consider whether they need to make special provision for candidates whose mother tongue is not English.

(k)   *Emphases to be encouraged in all subjects*
All syllabuses should be designed to help candidates to
understand the subject's relationship to other areas of study and
its reference to the candidates' own life. Awareness of
economic, political, social and environmental factors relevant
to the subject should be encouraged wherever appropriate.
Questions seeking to test this awareness should be in the
context of the subject concerned and not be independent of it.

The aims which the history criteria (DES 1985c) set out for the subject
include an understanding: 'of the nature and use of historical evidence';
'of the development over time of social and cultural values'; and of
'similarity and difference'. The objectives include: showing 'an ability to
look at events and issues from the perspective of people in the past'; and
showing:

the skills necessary to study a wide variety of historical evidence . . .
by interpreting and evaluating it – distinguishing between fact, opinion and judgement; pointing to deficiencies in the material as evidence, such as gaps and inconsistencies; [and] detecting bias.

The history criteria also highlight the need 'to study History in its varied
contexts', and the need for range and balance – as well as depth – in the
syllabus.

All of these aims, objectives and criteria are relevant to, and can be
promoted especially well through a multicultural, antiracist or world
approach to history. Such approaches for example provide a wide range
and variety of historical evidence, highlight its problematic nature, help
one to be sensitive to detecting bias and other deficiencies in the
evidence, and contribute to an awareness and understanding of similarity and difference. Furthermore, even within the context specifically
of British history, an understanding of the development of social and
cultural values in the past as well as in the contemporary era entails a
multicultural perspective. Again, looking at events and issues from the
perspective of people in the past – whether in the context of British or
world history – presupposes being able to take up a perspective
(cultural, social, etc.) different from that to which one is usually
accustomed.

How well do the syllabus and examination papers of the Southern
Group measure up to such criteria? It is not possible to answer this ques-
tion fully here. Only a preliminary investigation can be attempted. The
Southern Examining Group (1986) offered five GCSE syllabuses in
History for the first year of the examinations, 1988. These were as follows:

(I) British Social and Economic History since 1750; (II) World Powers since 1917; (III) British History, 1485–1714; (IV) British History, 1815–1983; (V) Britain, Europe, and the World, 1848–1980. In addition it offered a syllabus and examinations in the Schools History Project 13–16 which has four elements (i.e. a study each in: development; depth; modern world history; and history around us). The stated aims and objectives for all of these syllabuses conform closely to those set out in the National Criteria. The first thing to note about these syllabuses is that they have a strong British orientation. Of the five syllabuses (excluding for the moment the Schools History Project 13–16) only two – Syllabus II and Syllabus V – have a world history dimension. Of these, Syllabus II has a distinct superpowers orientation, while Syllabus V has very much a British and especially a European one.

However, the contents for all of these syllabuses are more fully stated than was the case for the SREB CSE syllabuses and there is, for example, a sub-topic on immigration and the multiethnic society in Syllabus I. In Syllabus II one of the three major themes is 'Imperialism, Decolonization and Post-Imperial Relationships'. In Syllabus III one of the eight main themes is 'Exploration and Colonization'. There are also sub-topics on such aspects as: the commercial and national significance of the navy in Elizabethan times; and Anglo-Spanish and Anglo-French 'rivalries' overseas between the latter part of the fifteenth and early part of the eighteen centuries. In Syllabus IV one of the eight main themes is 'The British Empire and Commonwealth'. Also, there is a sub-topic on 'education for a multicultural society'. Again, one of the eight main themes in Syllabus V is 'British Empire to Commonwealth, 1867–1980'. There are also sub-topics on: 'overseas and imperial policies' under Gladstone and Disraeli; 'immigration and a multiethnic society' after the Second World War; and the 'growth of nationalist consciousness among ex-colonial peoples' during the Second World War. All of these themes and sub-topics, however, are in optional parts of the various syllabuses, and, overall, there is again in these syllabuses no great attention given to the Indian sub-continent, less to Black Africa and less still to the Caribbean. There is barely a reference to the slave trade. The syllabus for the Schools History Project 13–16 permits a good deal of choice by pupils and teachers, especially in the elements on 'modern world history' and 'history around us'. But even in this syllabus the topics that are actually named include little or nothing on India, Africa or the Caribbean, and little of an overtly multicultural or antiracist nature.

Let us turn now to the first batch of papers actually set (summer 1988). There were papers for six syllabuses, plus for the Schools History Project. There is nothing of a specifically multicultural nature in either of the two papers for Syllabus I, 'British Social and Economic History since 1750'.

Between the two papers for Syllabus II 'World Powers since 1917', India, Africa and the Caribbean figure specifically only in Paper 1. All of the questions concerned are optional. The question on India is allocated 25 marks, as is a question primarily on South Africa. The only question which refers otherwise specifically to Africa is one on *de*coloniization, also worth 25 marks. There is also a question on 'Population increase and Third World cities', again allocated 25 marks. This could perhaps help to reinforce stereotypes of the 'Third World'. The only specific reference to the Caribbean in either of these two papers is, again, (as one of 15 possible topics) to 'the Cuban Crisis' in a question on 'Relations between the USA and the USSR since 1953'. The two papers for Syllabus III, 'British History, 1485–1714', make no explicit reference to the growing slave trade nor to the growing Black population in England – nor indeed to the early colonies in the Caribbean. Paper 1 of Syllabus IV, 'British History, 1815–1983', includes two questions on the British Empire and the Commonwealth. Each is allocated 25 marks, but only one or the other could be done, and neither is obligatory. Paper 2 focuses mainly on Europe and to a large extent on war.

Paper 1 of Syllabus V, 'Britain, Europe and the World, 1848–1980', includes two questions on the theme of 'British Empire to Commonwealth, 1867–1980'. As above, each is allocated 25 marks, neither is compulsory and only one or the other could be attempted. The first one is on the Rhodesian Federation and the establishment of Zimbabwe. The second is on the Indian sub-continent. Paper 2 includes an optional question on the Boer War, worth 30 marks. It would be possible to answer both this and the question above on the Rhodesian Federation and Zimbabwe. Thus Southern Africa is strongly represented. Yet, apart from these questions, a question on Palestine and Israel, and one on the United Nations, there is no other explicit mention of India or Africa – and the Caribbean does not feature at all. There is a question worth 30 marks in Paper 2 on 'great social changes in Britain after the Second World War, 1945–1974'. The candidates are expressly told, 'Your answer might include reference to: transport; fashion; entertainment; housing; education'. Yet immigration, 'race' relations and multiculturalism are not specifically mentioned. There is hardly anything of a multicultural nature in either of the two papers for Syllabus VI, 'A History of Medicine with Social Aspects'. There seems to be no mention, for instance, of Asian and Arab contributions.

Similarly, apart from Amerindians in the American West, and other than in a fairly narrow European context, there is very little of a multi-cultural nature in the two papers for the syllabus for the Schools History Project. The themes covered, in addition to 'the American West', are 'Medicine Through Time', 'Energy Through Time', 'Elizabethan England' and 'Britain 1815–1851'. There is also a special sheet on 'Guernica'. There is much mention of Greece in the sections on medicine and energy – but little or no mention of the Asians and Arabs, or anyone else. Furthermore, as already indicated, Elizabethan England saw the growth of the slave trade and of the Black population in England. Moreover, 1815–1851 immediately followed the Act for the Abolition of the Slave Trade (1807) and included the Emancipation Act (1833). This was a time of great debate about the related issues. Carlyle's infamous essay appeared in 1853. Besides, Blacks were active in the Chartist movement. But candidates are given little stimulus to develop or use any such knowledge.

A quick check of the illustrations in all fourteen papers gave the following results. Counting all illustrations, including maps, diagrams, graphs, posters, cartoons, pictures, etc., there was a total of 81 illustrations. Of these, over half (44) were of or included people. The great majority of these (35) were of Whites only. There was only one showing Black Africans only, and this was a caricature. There were two of Jews, one of which was a caricature. There was only one which depicted Africans, Asians and Europeans together: it was a cartoon (and was the only illustration in which anyone from the Indian sub-continent appeared). No 'non-white' Britons or 'non-white' Europeans featured in any of the illustrations. Of the 44 illustrations showing people, 21 were of males and females, 19 were of males only, but a mere 4 were of women only. There were 14 maps. Of these, as many as 8 were of Europe (including the UK), 2 were of India, one of Korea, one of Australasia, one of Southern Africa, (which as we have seen often features, and often with a high profile) and one of the world. There was not a single map specifically of the Caribbean, nor of the great African continent – apart from the one of Southern Africa.

From this preliminary review it seems clear that these GCSE examination papers are no more specifically multicultural, antiracist or world orientated than the CSE papers were. However, there are good features – such as the large amount of choice, the provision in many of the questions of a range of sources for the candidate to react to or reflect on, and the inviting of the candidate in many of the questions to try and adopt a variety of perspectives.

CONCLUSION

The SREB Mode 1 CSE History syllabuses and examinations, despite some advances, showed insufficient sensitivity to, and insufficient coming to grips with, pluralism, racism, and ethnic minority educational needs and rights in present-day Britain. Also, they had only just started moving towards a genuine world history approach. Similarly, the Southern Examining Group's 1988 GCSE syllabuses and examination papers were not very sensitive to multiculturalism, racism or ethnic minority educational needs and rights. Indeed, it may even be that the GCSE has overall less of a genuinely world history approach than the CSE had at the end.

It is necessary for all those concerned deliberately to seek to overcome ethnocentrism in the syllabuses and examinations. They also need to be sensitive to racism, to inequalities, and to the wide variety of experiences, cultural and historical heritages, values, points of view, needs and rights which obtain in Britain (and indeed in the world) today. Of course, the history syllabus and examinations must necessarily be selective. Some form of a paradigmatic approach seems necessary. But the selection must represent a range of points of view. Also of central importance are the criteria on which, and the points of view from which, the selection is made. Ultimately, what matters is who controls and whether the control is spread throughout the community rather than being narrowly concentrated. In view of the variety of cultural, social and historical perspectives, particular care needs to be taken to ensure that the processes of syllabus development and of setting and marking the examination papers are truly democratic, with an equitable input and influence from all of the various perspectives.

The task is not an easy one. Even File (1983), who himself observes that 'the assessment of history in a multicultural society is a complex undertaking', and who provides a useful and extensive agenda for discussion in Britain, including general principles and short-term, medium-term and long-term changes, seems to underplay some important dimensions. He recognizes that students should learn about the historical dimension of their own and other cultures, that the syllabus should integrate local, national and world history in a balanced way, and that it should incorporate a much wider perspective than simply a British or European one. He also stresses the social and economic importance for Britain of colonialism, slavery, empire and immigration. However, he does not expressly highlight the basic principles of equality, positive interaction and antiracism – especially at cultural, interpersonal, institutional and structural levels. He tends to speak in the individual and limited terms of 'reducing ignorance', of challenging 'stereotypes' and of developing 'tolerance' – all important, but not sufficient. Also he conceptualizes labour migrants into Europe in the dubious terms of 'guest' workers. Moreover, he does not give sufficient saliency to the long history of Black people in Britain nor to their social, economic and cultural contributions. Finally, he continues to highlight Cuba in the Caribbean, although he does recommend a widening of the Caribbean coverage. Specifically, he suggests the inclusion of two 'British West Indian' territories, and a topic on the 'breakup' of the Federation of the West Indies – which could seem a negative choice. Why not, instead, suggest a more positive topic to do with the *growth* of the modern West Indies (see, for example, Lewis 1968)? Any of the following could, among others, serve as possible Caribbean-wide topics: the Caribbean Economic Community (CARICOM); the development of the trade union movement; the development of the party political system; decolonization and political independence; multinationals and neocolonialism; Uncle Sam and the fragility of sovereignty; migration; cultural developments; the growth of the consciousness of the African heritage; the University of the West Indies.

Undoubtedly, despite his wide vision it is difficult for File to speak for the various minority ethnic groups. Appropriate structures and procedures are needed, as already indicated, to bring together, collaboratively, different interests and different ethnic backgrounds. Black people, perhaps especially those of Caribbean background – who on the whole are among those experiencing the greatest inequalities in Britain and finding themselves most commonly constructed as a 'problem' – must have an adequate role in the selection and formulation of the syllabuses and examinations. This is especially true at present when the massive changes ensuing on the Education Reform Act 1988 are still being defined, developed and introduced into practice.

National Curriculum History – in the procedures used to define it, the ground it covers, the perspectives it incorporates and the methods it adopts – cannot take a narrow, exclusivist or 'little England' approach if it is to be true to British history in all its complexity. British history is the history of Britain in interaction with Africa, India, the Caribbean and elsewhere. It is, too, the history of Britain in those places, as well as 'at home'. Moreover, British history 'at home' is also the history, not only of the Celts, Goths, Saxons, Normans and many other European groups, but also of Africans, Caribbeans and Asians – at least since the early sixteenth century, as already indicated. Britain in the past and today cannot be understood without understanding 'Empire'. That means understanding the history of colonization, exploitation and domination, and, inseparably, of prosperity and 'progress' – of the 'generation of wealth' and cultured leisure through enterprise, and the sweat and lives of slaves and the labouring classes. The parallel of England's dominance of the Irish, Welsh and Scots with Britain's dominance of India, the Caribbean and Africa is quite a good one. Indeed, J.S. Mill observed that 'the trade of the West Indies is hardly to be considered as external trade, but more resembles the traffic between town and country' (quoted by Rodney 1972: 93). Rodney (1972: 93) points out that 'by the phrase "trade of the West Indies" Mill meant the commerce between Africa, England and the West Indies'. In the case both of England's domination of the Celts and of Britain's domination of the Caribbean, Africa and India there was a history of colonization and exploitation. In both cases migration from these places into England – and out of England into these places – needs to be understood in relation to that domination. So too do the present relations in Britain with those regions, and especially the present relations within Britain among peoples of the different heritages concerned. British history is also at the same time – and often interactively – other things, other struggles, other developments, other complex interrelations over time. It is very much a history of structural inequality, including classism, sexism and racism; but it is also a history of culture contact, of a concern for human rights, and of the growth of parliamentary democracy. In brief, then, History in the National Curriculum cannot be a history exclusively of the 'left' or of the 'right' if it is to be an authentic and critical history.

In fact, several features of the Final Report of the National Curriculum History Working Group (Department of Education and Science – DES – 1990) are promising. In discussing the purposes of school history this report acknowledges the cultural diversity of Britain. It stresses the 'immense breadth' of history, pointing out that it 'draws on the record of the entire human past' (DES 1990: 1). Two of the attainment tasks which it formulates (DES 1990: 116) are: 'Understanding points of view and interpretations in history'; and, 'Acquiring and evaluating historical information'. In discussing cross-curricular dimensions, it sees history as supporting 'the values of democratic societies: open-mindedness; respect for a range of possible interpretations based on evidence; objectivity' (DES 1990: 183). It also expressly addresses the issues of equal opportunities and multicultural education, and it states that historical skills 'should assist in identifying, and thus combatting, racial and other forms of prejudice and stereotypical thinking' (DES 1990: 184). Moreover, the core unit at Key

Stage 4 entitled, 'Britain: in the twentieth century', as exemplified in Annex A to chapter 6, attempts to take on board post-war immigration; 'race' relations legislation; Irish nationalism; and linkages with the rest of Europe and the Commonwealth. Also, the provision for schools in Key Stages 2 and 3 to design some units of their own, the 'School Designed Themes', and the encouragement for them to make use of a local history approach where appropriate, offer great opportunities for work informed by multicultural and antiracist principles to be developed.

Nevertheless, despite all this, many question-marks and problems remain. India, Africa (except for ancient Egypt, which never seems to be defined as part of Africa), Islam and the slave trade are mentioned only in the optional parts of the syllabus. Besides, Africa features only within a post-1945 context, and South Africa is highlighted (DES 1990: 108–9). The Caribbean is only mentioned in an optional unit at Key Stage 3 on 'Black peoples of the Americas: C16th to early C20th' (DES 1990: 90–1). One could also get the impression that there was no significant presence of Black people in Britain before post-war immigration. Only one mention of antiracism is made – quoted above – and it is in terms of prejudice and stereotypes, not referring to discrimination nor cultural, institutional or structural racism (see DES 1990: 184). Also, the at best ambiguous concept of 'racial' is unquestioningly used. Overall, the focus still seems to remain a British one in a narrow sense. The enigmatic statement is made that 'an ethnically diverse population strengthens rather than weakens the argument for including a substantial element of British history within the school curriculum' (DES 1990: 184). Is the rationale behind this assimilationist? Is 'British' to be read exclusively or inclusively? The history of Black people (in the widest sense) in Britain over many centuries is an integral part of British history. The lucrative transatlantic slave trade and the immense Black British Empire were crucial stages in British history.

In conclusion, more research is needed, in particular to scrutinize the actual teaching of history for the GCSE, and more generally the teaching of history within the National Curriculum. To what extent does this teaching engage the various ethnic minority pupils? Does it seem in any way to put them at a disadvantage? In general, how are they situated in relation to it, and does it help them to understand themselves and their society (i.e. Britain) today? Moreover, and of central importance, what messages do the teaching, the syllabuses, the examination papers and, in general, the assessment procedures, convey explicitly or implicitly to the White majority? What different messages, under-standings, frames of reference or skills are transmitted to, or facilitated for, the whole range of pupils? Are all pupils helped to become aware of, understand and relate constructively to (or rather within) the diverse and unequal reality that has been and is Britain – and the 'global village' in which we all live? Furthermore, the assessment of ethnic minority pupils – whether internal or external – needs to be monitored carefully. Is it unbiased? In its wider messages and effects is it educational rather than miseducational? In particular, one needs to scrutinize the GCSE examination scripts and project work of ethnic minority candidates, their grades, the questions, topics or investigations they opt for, how they deal with them, and how their work or scripts are marked. What are the areas, perhaps so far unrecognized, of strengths, and what are the difficulties encountered? Are candidates whose first language is not standard British English, or who write from a minority ethnic or a 'Black' perspective, in any way penalized (even if quite unintentionally)? All must be done to try and ensure equality *and* quality, in education and beyond.

NOTE

* The first part of this chapter has been written jointly by Peter Figueroa and Lionel Vida. It reports on part of a project initiated by Figueroa, and directed by himself and Roger J.L. Murphy. Vida was one of the research assistants. In preparing this chapter Figueroa has drawn on Figueroa and Vida 1984 and Vida 1982, and has also gone back to the primary documents.

9 White schools – black marks
Constructed 'underachievement'

INTRODUCTION

It is often asserted that 'Afro-Caribbean' or 'West-Indian' children 'underachieve' in British schools while 'Asian' children do well or even 'overachieve'. Such statements are misleading and are part and parcel of the social construction of 'race'. They are myths which are constantly sustained through social arrangements, processes, behaviour and discourse. Rather, minority ethnic pupils, in particular 'Asians' and especially 'Caribbeans' are *unequally* placed within the British education system. This educational inequality is itself a social construction, not however in the sense of being a socially generated and sustained *myth*, but in so far as it is largely a function and consequence of social arrangements, processes and behaviour.

Schools, and more widely the education system, can play a part in contributing to and maintaining this inequality, as some of the preceding chapters have indicated. Alternatively, schools and the whole education system can help to dismantle this inequality by carefully addressing the specific rights and needs of minority ethnic pupils, by seeking to open everyone to the realities and riches of pluralism and by fighting institutional racism as well as the racist frames of reference and attitudes of the majority.

In previous papers (Figueroa 1984b and 1984c) I reviewed some of the main studies up to the early 1980s on the educational achievement of pupils of Caribbean and South Asian background in Britain. I pointed out that many of these studies were open to serious criticism; and concluded that these pupils, and especially the Caribbeans, were in an unequal position in the British education system, and that this system was failing them. In this chapter I will discuss critically some of the more recent studies on ethnic minority educational 'achievement' – though reference will also be made to some of the earlier studies. The aim is not to provide a comprehensive review – especially since such reviews exist (for example, Taylor 1981, 1987, 1988, and Taylor with Hegarty 1985) – but to show why common assumptions about 'West Indian' under-achievement and 'Asian' achievement must be questioned, and how the findings and issues might be reformulated.

The most extensive review of research relating to Caribbean heritage children in British schools was undertaken by Monica Taylor (1981) for the National Foundation for Educational Research. This was commissioned by the Committee of Inquiry into the Education of Children from Ethnic Minority Groups. The brief set by the Committee was formulated specifically in terms of the 'underachievement of West Indian Children in schools in Britain' (Taylor 1981: 3). Taylor concentrated on research from about 1965 to 1980. She concluded that 'there is an overwhelming consensus: that research evidence shows a strong trend to underachievement of pupils of West Indian origin' (Taylor 1981: 216). This bald and unqualified statement is made notwithstanding her acknowledgement that 'the picture is complex, with minor incon-sistencies, more important ambiguities and even contradictions at almost every turn'. These, however, she dismisses as 'niceties'.

She gives a good deal of importance to alleged problems of self-identity and self-esteem among West Indians, asserting that 'self-esteem' (in this context, problems with self-esteem) 'is obviously [sic] a crucial and pivotal concept in understanding the position of pupils of West Indian origin in schools' (Taylor 1981: 207). Although she lists Stone (1981) in her bibliography, she does not consider Stone's arguments against this view. Similarly, although she summarizes (Taylor 1981: 181–2) some aspects of Figueroa (1974, 1976), she does not mention that I found evidence of positive self-image among the West Indians of school-leaving age I studied (Figueroa 1974: 386–92). Nor does she seem aware of the reservations that can be made about the mechanistic way in which the development of self-concept and its relation to achievement have often been understood. For instance, I have written:

> It would . . . be unwarranted to assume that a subordinated group would necessarily have a thoroughly negative group-self-image . . . the subordinate group's image of itself . . . will also depend on the dynamics within the group. . . . Of course, the inter- and the intra-group dynamics which influence [note: not 'determine'] the self-image and the image of the other are themselves closely interrelated.
> (Figueroa 1974: 387–8)

Taylor does consider the issue of institutionalized racism – but this is the only factor she presents with a query point. Furthermore, she discusses in some detail the problematic nature of the concepts and measures of ability and achievement; yet she proceeds to treat at face value many of the studies which are conceptually and methodically problematical in precisely such terms – except, in particular, when discussing evidence of teacher racism. Thus, after reviewing evidence of teachers' negative stereotypes and attitudes regarding West Indians, she grants that 'it appears from research evidence that the attitudes of teachers, and hence probably their expectations, are likely to be of considerable influence on the performance of children of West Indian origin' (Taylor 1981: 206). But she hastens to stress 'that many of the research studies reviewed here tap only crude measures of teachers' attitudes' (Taylor 1981: 206). She thus proffers, instead, the unsubstantiated opinions that the reservations of many of the teachers about 'a multicultural curriculum *may well* be for professional . . . reasons' (Taylor 1981: 206, my italics) and, 'it is by no means to be assumed that they are racialist.' Yet, no reservations are expressed when she claims, on very slim evidence, that 'the general trend of this review would suggest that . . . the attitudes of white children to their black peers . . . and their behaviour especially towards West Indians . . . seems generally to be favourable' (Taylor 1981: 193).

The Rampton Report (DES 1981), which is the interim report of the Committee of Inquiry into the Education of Children from Ethnic Minority Groups, dealt specifically with pupils of Caribbean background, and focused very much on their 'underachievement'. It concluded (DES 1981: 70) that, 'West Indian children as a group are underachieving in our [sic] education system'.

Tomlinson (1983: 130), also in a review of the literature focusing on pupils of 'West Indian' and 'Asian' origin, points out that the dominant issue in the debate on multiethnic education in Britain 'has been concern with achievement'. She concludes (Tomlinson 1983: 44) that 'children of West Indian origin . . . do underperform and under-achieve in comparison with "white" and "Asian" minority groups'. Again, this unambiguous statement is made – even though she does point to some of the limitations of the research and to the complexity of the issues involved. She further concludes (Tomlinson 1983: 58) that 'Asian pupils have tended to score lower than their white peers on tests of ability and attainment, but Asian performance has improved with . . . length of schooling in Britain'. She also highlights (Tomlinson 1983: 58) that in 'selected urban areas with large numbers of ethnic minority people, Asian pupils achieve school-leaving qualifications on a par with their white peers'.

The Swann Report (DES 1985a), too, gives a good deal of attention to the 'underachievement' of pupils of Caribbean background, and confirms the finding of the Rampton Report. Thus the Swann Report concludes that:

> there is no doubt that West Indian children, as a group, and on aver-
> age, are underachieving, both by comparison with their school fel-
> lows in the White majority, as well as in terms of their potential,
> notwithstanding that some are doing well.

(DES 1985a: 81)

This stark insistence, however well intentioned, on 'West Indian underachievement' is misleading on both conceptual and empirical grounds, as I will argue below. It may itself contribute to the stereotyping of Caribbean pupils as being low academic performers, thereby possibly further contributing to pupils of Caribbean background being poorly placed within the British education system.

The most extensive review of research relating to South Asian children in British schools was, like that concerning Caribbean pupils, commissioned by the Committee of Inquiry into the Education of Children from Ethnic Minority groups. It was undertaken by Monica Taylor and Seamus Hegarty (1985) for the NFER, and reviewed research carried out over some 20 years.

The conclusions (Taylor with Hegarty 1985: 542–65) stress diversity among the Asians – 'diversity of performance . . . diversity in their school experiences, and diversity in their perceptions of the differences between their home and school lives' – and hence the difficulty of making generalizations. Nevertheless, except in English, Asian pupils tended, according to this review, to perform comparably with their local peers in school-leaving examinations. Indeed, they tended to do better than other ethnic minority pupils (Taylor with Hegarty 1985: 546–7). Compared with national standards, however, they 'are not performing so highly' (Taylor with Hegarty 1985: 542, 548–9). 'Generally . . . there is an increase in performance . . . with age and experience of schooling' (Taylor with Hegarty 1985: 550). However, although South Asians tended to stay in full-time education longer than other pupils, they experienced, like West Indians, 'inequalities of opportunity in the job market' (Taylor with Hegarty 1985: 543).

There was 'differential performance across subject areas' (Taylor with Hegarty 1985: 544) and across Asian sub-groups. Higher performance was associated with urban origin, middle class and professional background and East African origin, while lower performance was associated with rural origin, disadvantaged backgrounds and low caste (Taylor with Hegarty 1985: 545–6). To such factors, the review points out, must be added other influences, such as: English language competences; home-school relations; school factors, including teachers' expectations, the curriculum and ethos of the school and peer interaction; and societal discrimination and racial prejudice. The issues are far from simple, and 'there is an interactive complex of educational and social factors which has to be brought to bear on any attempt at explanation of performance' (Taylor with Hegarty 1985: 558).

Monica Taylor (1987, 1988) has also produced two other reviews of research for the Swann Committee. The first of these deals with pupils of Chinese origin, who 'form the third largest group of ethnic minority pupils in British schools', but who have received little attention (Taylor 1987: 1). Much of the limited research was of low quality (Taylor 1987: 300). The population of Chinese origin comprised several sub-groups (Taylor 1987: 310), and was largely dispersed throughout the country. Some evidence suggested that one should not be complacent 'with respect to the educational performance of Chinese pupils and their adaptation within the school environment' (Taylor 1987: 305). Also 'there may well be some grounds for claiming that in various degrees the educational system is guilty of covert institutional racism, through omission, with respect to pupils of Chinese origin' (Taylor 1987: 313).

Monica Taylor's final review of research (1988) deals with pupils of Cypriot, Italian, Ukranian and Vietnamese origin and with Gypsies and Liverpool Blacks. The relevant research was limited, and hardly permitted any conclusions on the educational 'achievement' of the Italian – and Ukranian – heritage pupils (Taylor 1988: 287–90, 325). As far as the Cypriot group is concerned Taylor (1988: 129, 133) concluded that their performance on English verbal reasoning and mathematics was not very good. Turkish-speaking Cypriots often tended to do worse than Greek-speaking Cypriots. The Liverpool Blacks consist of a long-standing population going back through at least the seventeenth, eighteenth and nineteenth centuries. Supplemented by immigration in this century, they have roots in Africa, the West Indies, the Middle East, the Far East and the local White community. The children of the Liverpool Blacks seemed to be at a great disadvantage in school (Taylor 1988: 344, 347, 348, 352). In general, the Liverpool Blacks suffered from 'a cycle of urban deprivation and institutional discrimination in terms of employment, housing and health' (Taylor 1988: 349).

The gypsies, 'an ethnically diverse group', are 'an amalgam of . . . Indian/Romany, Irish and indigenous' people (Taylor 1988: 355, 354). Their 'educational situation . . . is extremely unsatisfactory' (Taylor 1988: 355). In the words of the Plowden Report (DES 1967, vol. 1: 59), gypsy children are 'probably the most severely deprived children in the country' (Taylor 1988: 355). They often received no education at all (Taylor 1988: 355–6). Their experience of schooling was often negative due to an incongruence of 'cultural norms, expectations and skills', as well as 'prejudice and hostility . . . regularly encountered from both teachers and other pupils' (Taylor 1988: 361). Not surprisingly, perhaps, the limited research indicated educational 'underachievement on the part of Gypsy children' (Taylor 1988: 362). In conclusion, 'there has been a substantial failure to meet the educational needs of Gypsy children' (Taylor 1988: 364).

This last point it seems to me can to varying degrees be made with reference to ethnic minority children generally. Despite the tendency in the literature to use the constructs of 'achievement', 'underachievement' and even 'overachievement', the crux of the matter is that the educational system has often not met the educational needs of the Black ethnic minority children – and indeed has sometimes actually worked to the disadvantage of these children.

The following more detailed discussion – mainly of some of the more recent research findings – will highlight the unequal location of Black ethnic minority children in the education system and the problematical nature of the constructs such as 'achievement', 'overachievement' and especially 'underachievement'. Reference will be made mainly to research concerning the two largest Black ethnic minority groups, those of South Asian and Caribbean backgrounds. I shall focus especially on the latter, about whose supposed 'underachievement' so much has been written. It is my view that, although the issues are complex and many factors interact, much more focused attention needs to be given to school processes, to racism, ethnicism and ethnocentrism within the education system and to multicultural, nonracist and antiracist educational provision.

BLACK 'ACHIEVEMENT'

Inner London Education Authority, 1966

An early study which deserves to be briefly considered because it was very influential is that undertaken in 1966 by the Inner London Education Authority (ILEA 1968). This was concerned with 11 + transfer in fifty-two ILEA primary schools with a high proportion of 'immigrants'. The 'immigrant' pupils transferring from these schools numbered 1,068, over half of whom were Caribbean. This is the study that Tomlinson (1983: 29) considers 'probably had most impact on practitioners and on general beliefs about the educational underperformance of some minority groups' – in particular the Caribbeans, whom the study found came out the worst of all groups when scores for English, Mathematics, and verbal reasoning were combined. Its methodology was criticized by Bagley (1968). Yet it continues to be cited as one of the authoritative large-scale studies claiming to show Caribbean 'underachievement'. One must wonder to what extent, in Bagley's (1968) words, it bolstered 'the ideology that coloured children are intellectually inferior', and thereby, at least indirectly, itself contributed – through, for instance, teacher expectation – to the educational downgrading of Caribbean pupils.

Whereas half of the White British pupils in this study were rated as below average, as one would expect on a normal distribution, *four-fifths* of the 'immigrant' children were so rated – and the Caribbean children specifically were rated even somewhat worse. However, all three measures used in this study were, at the least, problematical, as Figueroa (1984b: 123) has commented. The scores for English and Mathematics were based on teachers' assessment. But as this study itself showed, the teachers perceived the 'immigrant' children as culturally disadvantaged, strange and having 'linguistic' problems – whereas of course they were strange only to the teachers, were culturally *different*, and spoke languages other than standard British English. Caribbean pupils in particular, many of whom, especially in the mid to late 1960s, would have spoken an English-based Creole, would no doubt have been seen by many of the teachers as speaking 'bad' English because the teachers were ignorant about Creole. Creole is a separate language (Bailey 1966, Le Page 1981), the power of which moreover has been amply demonstrated by outstanding West Indian poets and novelists such as Derek Walcott, Dennis Scott, Edward Kamau Brathwaite and V.S. Naipaul (see Figueroa 1982, and Herdeck *et al.* 1979).

More recent studies: 1979–81

Several studies, some large-scale, were carried out in the late 1970s and in the 1980s, although they are also subject to many of the limitations of the earlier studies. Craft and Craft (1983) carried out a study in 1979 of all fifth-formers and second-year sixth-formers in an Outer London borough with a high concentration of ethnic minority pupils. Of a total of almost 3,000 children, the sample included 568 Asian and 248 Caribbean fifth-formers, and 135 Asian but only 9 Caribbean second-year sixth-formers. The researchers found (Craft and Craft 1983: Table 6) that the Asians did less well than the White British at 'A' level, even when social class was controlled for, but better than the Caribbeans (although *their* sixth-form numbers were so very small that this finding is inconclusive). It would seem (Craft and Craft 1983: Table 5) that a much larger proportion of the Caribbean than of the White British or Asian fifth-formers went on to further education, rather than into the sixth-form, even controlling for social class and level of GCE 'O' level performance. Unfortunately, no information is available about their performance there, for further education certainly acts as an alternative route to university for some Caribbeans, and most of these pupils had achieved good levels in GCE/CSE. The GCE/CSE 'O' level results of the Asian fifth-formers, controlling for social class, were very similar to those of the White British, while those of the Caribbeans were poorer (Craft and Craft 1983: Table 2). None of the nine Caribbean second-year sixth-formers went on to a university or a polytechnic, and Asians were rather less likely than the White British to go into higher education, and in particular to a university (Craft and Craft 1983: Table 9).

Another study dating from the early 1980s was that carried out by Scarr and colleagues (1983) in 1980. It was concerned with the comparative development and educational 'achievement' of 'Indian', 'West Indian' and 'Pakistani' pupils compared with their White peers in one West Midlands Town (Roberts 1988: 100 – see also Taylor with Hegarty 1985: 130, 138, 262, 295 and 297). The data were partly longitudinal and partly cross-sectional. The measures used included the Young Non-Readers' IQ test, a standardized group test administered orally by teachers; NFER verbal reasoning tests; an NFER non-verbal test of abstract, figural reasoning; various reading tests between 5 and 12; selective school placement; setting; and entry to and grades in school-leaving examinations. Health visitors' ratings and head teachers' assessments were also used. Numbers varied for different measures and at different ages.

Table 9.1 Percentage of pupils in a West Midlands town obtaining higher grade GCE 'O' level or CSE results, 1980

	'O' level grades A–C and CSE grade 1		'O' level grades A and B		
	English language	*Mathematics*	*English language*	*Mathematics*	*(n)*
West Indian	8	16	1	2	(8)
Indian	32	49	6	25	(114)
White	35	37	19	20	(158)

Source: Roberts 1988: 104, Table 9.

Table 9.2 Percentage of pupils in a West Midlands town entered for GCE 'O' level examinations, 1980

	Any subject	English language	Mathematics	(n)
West Indian	9	1	7	(88)
Indian	42	23	37	(114)
White	42	34	27	(158)

Source: Roberts 1988: 104, Table 8.

Roberts (1988: 104), reporting on a selection of Scarr's findings, sets out GCE 'O' level entry and some 'O' level and CSE results for 88 West Indians, 114 Indians and 158 Whites. The higher grade results for these examinations are shown in Table 9.1. It appears that the Indians were doing very well in Mathematics and quite well in English Language. But the West Indians were doing poorly, and, remarkably, especially so in English Language.

However, these figures do not indicate what proportions of the base numbers had taken the 'O' level or the CSE examinations – or neither. In fact Roberts (1988: 104) sets out separately the entry percentages only for the GCE 'O' level examinations. These are shown in Table 9.2. It is nothing short of scandalous that only 9 per cent of West Indians were entered for GCE 'O' level examinations overall, compared with over 40 per cent of the Indians and Whites. It is especially scandalous that only 1 out of the 88 West Indians was entered for the English Language 'O' level examination, compared with almost 1 out of 4 of the Indians and over 1 out of 3 of the Whites. This is particularly scandalous since the mother tongue of the majority of these Caribbean-heritage pupils was undoubtedly a dialect of English, and especially since at age 12 their mean reading age was actually marginally higher than that of the Indians: 11.5 versus 11.4, compared with 12.2 for the Whites (Roberts 1988: 103). When one looks at the top-grade pass rates of those who actually took the 'O' level examinations, the picture is substantially qualified (Table 9.3) and appears much better for West Indians than suggested by the earlier figures. Of course, the numbers for West Indians is extremely small here. It also becomes apparent that it would be a mistake to be too complacent even about the performance of the Indians.

Scarr *et al.* (1983) and Roberts (1988: 103) also show that Caribbean-heritage pupils were much less likely than the others to be selected for grammar school or grammar stream placement. Compared with almost

Table 9.3 Percentage of GCE 'O' level candidates in a West Midlands town who obtained top level grades, 1980.

Grades A and B	West Indian	Indian	White
English Language	100	27	57
(n)	(1)	(26)	(53)
Mathematics	33	67	71
(n)	(6)	(42)	(45)

Source: Adapted from Roberts 1988: 104, Tables 8 and 9.

one third of Whites (30.1 per cent), only 17.5 per cent of Indians, 6.8 per cent of Pakistanis and a mere 2.5 per cent of West Indians were in grammar schools or grammar streams. Can it be surprising then that West Indians do so badly when it comes to 'O' levels? Yet, as already remarked, at age 12 their reading age was actually marginally higher than that of the Indians. Furthermore, at age 8 their Young Non-readers' IQ score was, if anything, also marginally higher than that of the Indians: 98.1 versus 97.9 compared with just over 106 for the Whites and about 95 for the Pakistani pupils (Roberts 1988: 102, and Taylor 1985: 130). These data suggest a massive failure of the education system *vis-à-vis* the Caribbean heritage pupils – at least in this one town.

In a national study at about the time of Scarr's study, the Child Health and Education Study (reanalysis by Mackintosh *et al.* 1988: 90), some 15,000 children born in one week in 1970 were given various tests when aged 10 in 1980. It was similarly found that 10-year-old 'West Indians' obtained somewhat higher IQ scores than 'Pakistanis' and 'Indians', but had reading scores intermediate between theirs, and also had lower mathematics scores (Table 9.4). This was a study similar to the National Child Development Study (Davie *et al.* 1972), and, as with it, the representativeness of the Black minority ethnic respondents should not be taken for granted.

Table 9.4 IQ, reading and mathematics scores of children aged 10 in 1980, drawn from the Child Health and Education Study

	West Indian	Indian	Pakistani	White
IQ	92.3	91.9	89.3	100.4
Reading	90.3	93.1	88.6	100.8
Mathematics	88.1	93.0	89.5	100.8
(n)	(125)	(170)	(91)	(10812)

Source: Mackintosh *et al.* 1988: 90.

Another large-scale study, but a cross-sectional one, also showed Caribbean-heritage pupils doing badly. This study was carried out by Dawson (1988) in a north-western city, apparently in the inner-city area. She studied 526 'Asian', 566 'Afro-Caribbean' and 3,407 'European' 12–16 year old pupils in, it would seem, 1981. There was a strong focus on home 'background' data. Measures were also obtained of 12 + attainment and ability. Dawson (1988: 145) found that Caribbean pupils had 'the lowest mean score on all three of the measures used' (tests of mathematics, reading and non-verbal reasoning) and that White pupils had the highest. She seeks to account for this with a deficit and pathological model.

Her measures of 'ethnicity' and of 'disadvantage' in home background are open to criticism. 'Ethnicity' (Dawson 1988: 133–4) was based on whether the respondent felt 'they belonged to a country other that England, belonged to a special group, used a home language other than English and/or had a particular religious affiliation'. In addition the pupil's report of their own physical appearance, and their name was taken into account. The researcher ended up with the broad categories of Whites (72.6 per cent), Afro-Caribbeans (12.5 per cent) and the Asians (12.2 per cent). It was not clear, for instance, how any Caribbeans of Indian subcontinent background would have been classified. Also, why were Africans and Caribbeans grouped together? Was it purely because of their 'race'? Or was it because of their socio-political location within the society? Culturally, they would be very different.

On home background, Dawson (1988: 145) simply assumes – contrary for example to Kerr and Desforges (1988: 36) and to Saunders (undated: 16–22) – that speaking a home language other than English would inherently be an educational handicap. She also assumes that Asian women's staying at home is a valid index of disadvantage; but developmentally and educationally it might well be the opposite. She takes it for granted that social indicators (such as family size) which may work for the majority population, will automatically have the same (negative) social, developmental and educational implications for minority ethnic groups. Finally, like many other researchers she takes (Dawson 1988: 141) as unproblematic the assumption that 'tests of reading and mathematics are . . . valid indicators of in-school attainments . . . measures of the concepts and skills which depend upon direct instruction and on the child's interest and industriousness'. Yet, such tests might well be culturally biased, and the instruction the child receives would be a function of the teacher's cross-cultural awareness and competence, the resources of the school and the extent to which its ethos is not ethnocentric. Schools in the more deprived inner-city areas, where the Black population often lives, may well be underresourced and may be unpopular with teachers who can get jobs elsewhere.

Swann data (1979–82)

Another of the more recent sets of information available appeared in the Swann Report, and is based on the DES 1978/1979 and 1981/1982 school-leavers surveys in five selected local education authorities (DES 1981 and 1985a). The data consist mainly of CSE and GCE examination results, and are summarized in Tables 9.5 and 9.6. First, these data suggest that, although the 'Asians' are doing relatively well, their examination results are less good than the national results across the board, and especially in English. Second, the results for the 'West Indians' on the lower grades at CSE and GCE 'O' levels are quite good; but they are well below average on the higher grades. With such CSE and GCE 'O' level results it was not surprising that the Caribbean 'A' level results were also well below average. Furthermore, since only a small proportion of Caribbeans were being funnelled through to success at 'A' level, it was also not surprising that such a small proportion seemed to be going on to university.

However, although it is clear that a very large proportion of the Caribbean pupils take *some* school-leaving examination (and obtain some graded results), the Swann Report does not make it clear to what extent Caribbean pupils are entered for the high status GCE 'O' or 'A' level examinations. It is not therefore clear whether the low proportion of 'O' level higher grades and of 'A' level passes is mainly a function of the Caribbeans who take these examinations not doing very well, or of only a small proportion of Caribbean pupils being entered for these examinations at all.

In any case one must be wary about taking the Swann data at face value. First, bearing in mind the findings of Chapter 8 above, questions could be raised about linguistic and cultural bias in the examinations. Second, the representativeness of the Swann data should not be taken for granted. The five LEAs studied all contained high concentrations of 'Asian' and 'West Indian' pupils, probably accounting for something under half of all Black minority ethnic school leavers. But it may well be that the more dispersed middle class Black population was under-represented.

Besides, the ethnic categorization of the pupils in the study was based on teacher assessment – and that carried out in many cases 'several months' (DES 1985a: 61) after the pupils concerned had left school. Hence, the accuracy of this categorization could be brought into question. Furthermore, the broad categories actually used in presenting the data – 'Asian', 'West Indian', and 'all other leavers' – are not unproblematic. First, 'Asians' include 'other Asians' – i.e. 'children for whom a more precise category was either not appropriate or was not known' (DES 1985a: 110). What does this mean? Vietnamese? Chinese? Above all might these 'other Asians' also include Indo-Caribbeans, – i.e. those Caribbeans whose origins lie at least partly in the Indian sub-continent? (About half of all Trinidadians and about half of all Guianese are Indo-Caribbeans). Second, 'the small numbers of African or undifferentiated West Indian/African leavers' (DES 1985a: 110) were added to the category of 'all other leavers'. Third, it would seem that many in this last category were not assigned to it by positive identification, but consisted of 'leavers whose ethnicity was not recorded' (DES 1985a: 110). One must wonder therefore in view of these three procedures how many unidentified Caribbean pupils – how many Caribbean pupils that *do not fit the usual stereotypes* – were excluded from the 'West Indian' category and included in either of the other two categories. It is relevant to mention here that Smith and Tomlinson (1989: 236 – see below) have found that teachers' assessment of ethnicity (as defined by family's country of origin) was very inaccurate, especially where Caribbean pupils and pupils of mixed or 'other' origins were concerned. Comparing teachers' categorizations with information from parents themselves, they found that 91 per cent of teachers got UK origins correct, 88 per cent South Asian origins, only 56 per cent West Indian origins and a mere 18 per cent mixed or 'other' origins.

A third important limiting point about the Swann data is that they are presented in very broad, undifferentiated categories without any account being taken of cultural diversity *within* these broad categories. Nor is any account taken of social class and socio-economic circumstances, or of quality of education received. Parekh (1988: 65), for example, states that 'Indian children ... tend to achieve better than their Pakistani counterparts, whereas the Bangladeshi children perform little better than the West Indian'. As Verma (1987: 19) points out there are 'widely differing linguistic, social, religious and cultural traditions and experiences of the Asian sub-groups'. He also points to the importance of urban versus rural background (Verma 1987: 20). What is perhaps not so often appreciated – although Verma (1987: 19) does also recognize this – is that there is similarly an amazing diversity of religion, language, culture, phenotype, and social circumstance and experience among the 'West Indians', some of whom originate from the South – or Central – American continent, and others from islands thousands of miles apart, while some can trace several generations in Britain. The

Table 9.5 CSE and GCE 'O' level results of school leavers in five LEAs and in England as a whole 1978/9 and 1981/2 (in percentages)

| | English | | | Mathematics | | | All examinations | | | |
	U/NT	LG	HG	U/NT	LG	HG	U/NT	Less than five HG	Five or more HG	(Base Numbers)
Asians										
1979	31	47	22	38	41	21	20	63	17	(466)
1982	28	51	21	33	46	21	19	64	17	(571)
Caribbeans										
1979	31	61	9	47	47	5	17	80	3	(718)
1982	25	60	15	45	47	8	19	75	6	(653)
Others										
1979	30	41	29	40	42	19	22	62	16	(5,012)
1982	25	46	29	32	47	21	19	62	19	(4,718)
Totals in the five LEAs										
1979	30	44	26	40	42	17	21	64	15	(6,196)
1982	25	48	26	34	46	20	19	63	18	(5,942)
Totals for England										
1979	21	45	34	32	45	23	14	66	21	(693,840)
1982	18	47	36	27	45	26	11	66	23	(706,690)

Source: Adapted from DES 1985a: 114–15, Tables 4, 5 and 6
Notes: U/NT = Ungraded/Not taken; LG = Lower grades; HG = Higher grades (i.e. grades A–C at GCE 'O' level and grade 1 at CSE).
These figures are based on a 10 per cent sample and all refer to maintained schools

Table 9.6 GCE 'A' level results and destinations of school leavers in five LEAs and in England as a whole 1978/9 and 1981/2 (in percentages)

	'A' LEVEL RESULTS		DESTINATION				(Base numbers)
	No pass/ Not taken	At least one pass	University	Other full-time FE	Employment	Not known	
Asians							
1979	88	12	3	17	55	25	466
1982	87	13	4	30	39	28	571
Caribbeans							
1979	98	2	–	16	66	18	718
1982	95	5	1	27	51	22	653
Others							
1979	88	12	3	9	76	12	5,012
1982	87	13	4	14	64	18	4,718
Totals in the five LEAs							
1979	90	10	3	11	73	13	6,196
1982	88	12	4	17	60	20	5,942
Totals for England							
1979	87	13	5	14	73	8	693,840
1982	86	14	4	21	64	11	706,690

Source: Adapted from DES 1985a: 113, Table 2; and 116, Table 7
Notes: FE = further education; – = less than half a percentage
These figures are based on a 10 per cent sample and all refer to maintained schools; presumably 'Not known' includes the unemployed.

Caribbean basin itself has historically been a great meeting ground of peoples from all over the world.

About the 'Asians', Parekh (1988: 65–6) also says that the relatively good Indian performance stems from the Indians' having 'a higher than average proportion of the middle classes . . . and conceals the fact that the educational performance of their working class compatriots falls far below the national average'. Other authors also indicate the importance of social class and socio-economic circumstances for educational 'achievement' (see, for example, Mackintosh and Mascie-Taylor 1985: 134 and 139; Mackintosh *et al.* 1988: 96–8; and Maughan and Dunn 1988: 117–8). Likewise there seems to be some evidence to suggest that Black pupils tend to perform similarly to their school peers so that they tend to do well in 'good' schools, and badly in 'bad' schools – but that they are overrepresented in the latter (see Newsam 1988: 79; Maughan and Dunn 1988: 119–120; and Barrow 1988: 170).

The Townview case study (1980–83)

The Townview case study reported in Chapter 7 also provides some information on the educational situation and 'achievement' of Black pupils. As stated in Chapter 7, this study was carried out mainly in 1982, but Figueroa subsequently obtained results for school-leaving examinations for 1980–83.

The Cognitive Abilities Test (CAT) scores for the 1982 fourth-year pupils – all of whom were covered by the case study – are shown in Table 9.7. The one 'other' fourth-year pupil, a Fijian girl, has been omitted. Also, six Whites, six South Asians and one Chinese have had to be excluded as data were missing for them. The CAT had three components: the verbal (V), the quantitative (Q) and the non-verbal (NV).

The small Chinese and Vietnamese group scored best of all on the non-verbal and especially on the quantitative measures, but worst of all

Table 9.7 Mean verbal (V), quantitative (Q) and non-verbal (NV) scores for the 1982 fourth-year pupils at Townview School, by ethnic group

	V	Q	NV	*(n)*
Whites	97	100	99	(27)
South Asians	90	94	92	(35)
Chinese and Vietnamese	81	106	102	(5)
Caribbeans	95	97	94	(4)
All these pupils	92	98	96	(71)

Table 9.8 Distribution of fourth-year pupils at Townview School, by ethnic group, 1982

	Whites		South Asians		Chinese and Vietnamese		Caribbeans		Total	
	n	*%*	*n*	*%*	*n*	*%*	*n*	*%*	*n*	*%*
4A₁	12	36	11	27	2	33	1	25	26	31
4A₂	10	30	11	27	4	67	1	25	26	31
4B	7	21	11	27	0	0	2	50	20	24
4C	4	12	8	20	0	0	0	0	12	14
Total	33	99	41	101	6	100	4	100	84	100

on the verbal measure. Their scores suggest that this latter measure at least was linguistically or culturally biased against them. The mean non-verbal and quantitative scores of the South Asians were the worst of all, and their verbal score was better only than that of the Chinese and Vietnamese. Again, it may well be that the tests, especially the verbal test, were linguistically or culturally biased against the South Asians – and indeed against the Caribbean pupils. Even the White pupils, who were mostly of working-class background, did best on the quantitative test and worst on the verbal one. Compared with the group as a whole, the small group of four Caribbeans were above average on the verbal test, near average on the quantitative, and just a little below average on the non-verbal. They scored better than the South Asians on all three measures.

In terms of distribution across the streams in the fourth year, the Chinese and Vietnamese were located entirely in the two top streams, while the Whites were also a little overrepresented there, but the South Asians and Caribbeans were somewhat underrepresented (Table 9.8). Furthermore, the South Asians were overrepresented in the C stream (i.e. the remedial/English-as-a-second language stream). Of course, the numbers here are very small, especially for the Chinese, Vietnamese, and Caribbean pupils.

How were these pupils 'performing'? Let us look first of all at internal examinations (Table 9.9). In the two top fourth-year streams combined, the Chinese and Vietnamese – all six of whom were to be found in these two streams – had obtained the lowest average mark of all groups in English Language, but the best in Mathematics in the school's internal examinations. This again suggests that their English Language competence was a handicap. The two Caribbeans in these two top streams between them had averaged the best English Language mark of all

Table 9.9 English language and mathematics scores in internal examinations for 4A$_1$, 4A$_2$ and 4B at Townview School, by ethnic group, 1982

	4A$_1$ and 4A$_2$ English Language	Mathematics	(n)	4B English language	Mathematics	(n)
Whites	50	24	(22)	32	58	(6)
South Asians	45	25	(22)	26	47	(10)
Chinese and Vietnamese	34	35	(5)	–	–	–
Caribbeans	52	24	(2)	26	62	(2)
All these pupils	46	26	(51)	28	52	(18)

Notes: Omitted from this table are: one Chinese 4A$_2$ boy, one South Asian 4B girl and one White 4B girl, for all of whom data were missing. One Fijian girl is also omitted from 4A$_2$.

groups. However, their Mathematics average was, along with that of the Whites, the lowest – although nevertheless only two marks below the overall Mathematics average for 4A$_1$ and 4A$_2$ together. The South Asians were just below average on both English Language and Mathematics. Unlike the two Caribbeans in 4A$_1$ and 4A$_2$, the two in 4B had the best average of the three 4B groups in Mathematics, but, along with the South Asians, the worst in English Language – although this was only two marks below the 4B English Language average. The Whites did best in English Language here, and again the South Asians had averages in both English language and Mathematics which were below the 4B averages. Again the very small number of respondents, especially of Caribbean pupils, means that these findings must be treated with caution.

Let us now look at school-leaving examinations, that is at CSE and GCE 'O' level examinations, for which figures were available for the years 1980–83 inclusive. Over these 4 years nearly 78 per cent of all of the fifth-year group took at least some CSE or GCE examination. Over this period 100 per cent of the Chinese and Vietnamese group had done so (that is fifteen out of fifteen). The entry rate was above average for the 'others' (90 per cent) and for the Caribbeans (81 per cent). The South Asian entry rate at 79 per cent was just above the average. Only for the White group therefore was the participation rate – at 73 per cent – in CSE and/or GCE examinations below the average. A larger proportion of South Asian boys than girls had taken some examination, but a much larger proportion of Caribbean – and 'other' – girls than boys had done so.

Focusing now only on entry to the higher-status GCE 'O' level examinations, I found that overall only 30 per cent of the pupils had been entered over the 4-year period for at least some GCE examination. The highest entry rate was among the Chinese and Vietnamese, almost 90 per cent of whom had been put in for the GCE. At the other extreme none of the seven 'other' pupils (one Brazilian, one Fijian, one Greek and four Italians) had taken any GCE examination. The percentage of Caribbean pupils, especially the boys, who had been entered for these higher-status examinations was well below average. Fourteen out of the sixteen Caribbean boys (almost 90 per cent, against 75 per cent of the girls) had *not* been entered for them. The *entry* rate for White pupils (26 per cent) was also below average, while that for the South Asian pupils (32 per cent) was just above average. Why was the school failing the Caribbean boys to such an extent?

I also found that the one Caribbean boy in $4A_1$ had been allocated to the CSE rather than the GCE set in Mathematics although he had obtained higher marks in the relevant internal examination than three Whites, one Chinese and one 'Asian' who had been placed in the GCE set. Moreover, this Caribbean boy had received some of the highest CAT scores ($V = 120$, $Q = 114$ and $NV = 106$). However, there were also two Whites and three 'Asians' with the same or higher marks in Mathematics who had likewise been placed in the CSE set. The one $4A_2$ Caribbean boy had obtained one of the highest scores on the relevant internal English examination, but had been placed in the English CSE set, while three Whites and three Asians with lower marks had been allocated to the GCE set. Again, however, two Whites and three Asians with the same or higher marks had also been placed in the CSE set. It was not possible to establish whether these discrepancies were due to the use of behavioural as against academic criteria or to the operation of stereotypes or particular frames of reference. It is interesting to note, however, that Smith and Tomlinson (1989: 303, 302 – see below) have concluded in their study of urban 'multiracial' comprehensives that: 'there was a tendency to allocate children to course levels partly on the basis of social class (after taking account of attainment)'; there were 'wide variations between the schools in the extent to which they make the allocation on the basis of attainment, rather than . . . of other (generally irrelevant) factors'; and 'the academic level at which a child is expected to compete is more a function of school policies and practices than of the individual qualities of the child'.

Overall, almost three-quarters of the GCE 'O' level candidates at Townview during 1980–83 obtained at least one higher grade pass – i.e. A, B or C (Table 9.10). The White candidates did the best with an 80 per cent pass rate at this level, while the Vietnamese and Chinese were close

Table 9.10 Percentage of 1980–3 Townview School GCE 'O' level candidates obtaining at least one Grade A, B, or C, by ethnic group

| | Percentages of each group receiving: | | | | | | Numbers in each group | | |
| | Less than one A, B or C | | | At least one A, B or C | | | | | |
	G	B	Total	G	B	Total	G	B	Total
Whites	26	13	20	74	80	80	27	24	51
South Asians	29	31	30	71	69	70	21	32	53
Chinese and Vietnamese	25	22	23	75	78	77	4	9	13
Caribbeans	50	50	50	50	50	40	4	2	6
All Groups	29	24	26	71	76	74	56	67	123

Note: The 1982 fourth-form members have been used as the base numbers for the 1983 fifth-year group
G = girl; B = boy.

Table 9.11 Percentage of 1980–3 Townview School CSE candidates obtaining at least one Grade 1 pass, by ethnic group

| | Percentages of each group receiving: | | | | | | Numbers in each group | | |
| | Less than one Grade1 | | | At least one Grade1 | | | | | |
	G	B	Total	G	B	Total	G	B	Total
Whites	70	75	72	30	25	28	69	72	141
South Asians	80	72	76	20	28	25	54	76	130
Chinese and Vietnamese	50	55	53	50	45	47	4	11	15
Caribbeans	93	91	92	7	9	8	15	11	26
Others	100	50	78	0	50	22	5	4	9
All Groups	76	73	74	24	27	26	147	174	321

Note: See note to Table 9.10.

behind. The South Asians performed just below the average, but the Caribbeans did the least well with only a 50 per cent pass rate at this level. A much smaller proportion (only 26 per cent) of the much larger numbers taking CSE obtained at least one higher grade pass – i.e. a Grade 1 pass (Table 9.11). The Chinese and Vietnamese did best with almost half passing at this level. Next came the Whites, performing just above average in this respect. The South Asians again performed just below average with a 25 per cent pass rate at this level. And again the Caribbeans performed worst overall, with a mere 8 per cent of Caribbean CSE candidates obtaining at least one Grade 1 pass.

The conclusions from these data do not seem entirely straight-forward. First, numbers are small except for South Asian pupils and Whites. Second, it has not been possible to control for social class and other factors that are undoubtedly of great importance. Third, broad categories have had to be used. For example, 'South Asian' includes Sikhs, Muslims and Hindus, people of Indian, Pakistani, Bangladeshi and East African backgrounds, and people of varying language backgrounds, in particular Punjabi, Gujerati and Urdu – although Punjabi was the commonest South Asian language among the sample studied. Fourth, the measures used may well be biased linguistically if not in other ways. Finally, the information on streaming, CAT scores and internal examinations was available only for the 1982 group, whereas results for school-leaving examinations were available for four years, 1980–3 inclusive. Thus, direct comparisons cannot be drawn between these two sets of data.

Nevertheless, it would seem that the Chinese and Vietnamese, despite some English Language problems, are regularly placed in the higher streams and frequently entered for the higher status GCE examination. And they get good results. The South Asians tend to score on average below the mean on IQ tests (is this a language problem?), tend to be somewhat overrepresented in the lower streams and tend to do below or about average on the internal and school-leaving examin-ations, for which their entry rate is about average.

For the Caribbeans, who were a rather small group, the results were more mixed. Although their CAT scores were above average, and they had some good – and some bad – results on the internal examinations, they were overrepresented in the lower streams, underrepresented especially in the top examination classes, underrepresented among GCE candidates (but high on entry to CSE), and did badly in the school-leaving examinations. Are such findings largely to be explained by biases in the selection and allocation processes, by unequal educational treatment and by negative school experiences? Perhaps larger scale data would help to answer some of the questions these data raise.

ILEA CSE and GCE 'O' level data: 1985

A large-scale set of information on examination results is discussed by Kysel (1988). These results relate to CSE and GCE 'O' level examinations in summer 1985. However, they refer only to the ILEA, and only to 72 per cent of the secondary maintained schools there. Table 9.12 shows the percentage of pupils, by ethnic groups, who attempted CSE or GCE 'O' level examinations and who were successful at various levels. Table 9.13 shows the average performance scores for each of the groups. These scores were calculated by awarding points as follows:

'O' level	CSE	Points
A		7
B		6
C	1	5
D	2	4
E	3	3
	4	2
	5	1
Ungraded	Ungraded	0

Although this was not made explicit, it seems as though those who had attempted neither CSE nor GCE 'O' levels were included in these calculations and assigned zero points.

In the top band of grades (five or more passes at grade one CSE or at grades A, B or C of the GCE 'O' level) the Indian pupils had the best results of all groups, and after them came the African Asians (Table 9.12). In these grades the Pakistanis also performed well above average, although a good deal less well than the Indians and African Asians. It was also among these three Asian groups that the highest proportion of pupils took at least some CSE or GCE 'O' level examinations (Table 9.12). At the other extreme, however, it was the Bangladeshi who were least likely of all of the groups to attempt any papers in either of these examinations. No doubt partly as a result of this, they also had the worst overall average performance score (Table 9.13). Their results in the top band of grades were also among the worst (Table 9.12). These results confirm that the 'Asians' *overall* were doing well compared with their *local* peers, but that there was a great deal of difference in the performance of different Asian groups.

In the top band of grades the White British performed at about

Table 9.12 CSE and GCE 'O' level entry and results among ILEA fifth-formers, summer 1985 (percentage of pupils by ethnic group)

	No exams taken	No grade	One or more CSE 4/5	One or more CSE 2/3 or GCE D/E	One to four CSE1 or GCE A–C	Five or more CSE 1 or GCE A–C	Total number of pupils
Bangladeshi	35.7	6.0	12.0	24.3	17.7	4.2	333
White British	21.8	3.5	8.8	26.9	28.7	10.3	10,685
Turkish	21.3	4.1	10.8	29.5	31.7	2.6	268
Arab	16.5	7.7	7.7	30.8	30.8	6.6	91
African	15.5	1.2	9.9	32.4	30.8	10.3	426
SE Asian	15.0	2.0	5.3	21.7	39.0	17.0	300
Caribbean	13.8	3.0	13.4	37.9	27.3	4.6	2,981
Greek	13.2	2.1	11.9	28.0	33.3	11.5	243
'Others'	11.0	2.6	5.0	23.2	40.3	18.0	940
African Asian	10.5	0.6	3.7	27.2	33.3	24.7	162
Pakistani	8.7	0.9	8.7	26.4	37.7	17.7	231
Indian	6.3	0.8	5.3	26.4	34.9	26.4	398
All	19.0	3.2	9.3	28.7	29.5	10.2	17,058

Source: Adapted from Kysel 1988: Table 1.

Table 9.13 Average performance scores of ILEA fifth-formers in CSE and GCE 'O' level examinations, summer 1985, by ethnic group

	Score	n
Bangladeshi	8.7	333
Turkish	11.9	268
Caribbean	13.6	2,981
Arab	14.0	91
White British	15.2	10,685
African	16.9	426
Greek	17.6	243
South East Asian	19.1	300
Pakistani	21.3	231
'Others'	21.3	940
African Asian	22.7	162
Indian	24.5	398
All	15.6	17,058

Source: Adapted from Kysel 1988: Table 2.

average – in other words well below the level of the Pakistanis, the African Asians and especially the Indians. Similarly, their average performance score was about the general average. However, these statistics somewhat understate the performance of the White British among those who took some CSE or GCE 'O' level examinations, for a very high proportion (almost 22 per cent) of the White British took neither examination.

The results for the Caribbean-heritage pupils in the top band of grades are among the worst, and their overall performance score is below average. However, they did well in the middle band of grades, and the proportion of Caribbean pupils who obtained no graded results at all was a little *below* the average.

Kysel (1988: 86, Table 4) also shows that, at the time of their transfer from primary to secondary school, a larger proportion of the Caribbean pupils than of the group as a whole had been considered by their primary head teachers as below average on verbal reasoning. He also found (Kysel 1988: 87) that the Caribbean performance as measured by combining the CSE and 'O' level results matched quite closely the performance that one would expect on the basis of the depressed verbal-reasoning categories they had been placed in. Indeed, this categorization, which was based on teacher assessment, corresponded more closely with the Caribbean average performance score than did the results from tests of reading and mathematics, which would have led one to expect a better performance than actually obtained (Kysel 1988: 88).

Kysel (1988: 88) concludes that the verbal-reasoning categorization by teachers 'does provide a useful measure of primary attainment against which examination results can be assessed'. However this loses sight of two other possibilities. The first is that it might, at least in part, be the placement in the lower verbal-reasoning categories in the first place which leads to the depressed examination results for Caribbean pupils. The other is that both the depressed verbal-reasoning categorization *and* the depressed examination results might each partly be a function of stereotypes and expectations about Caribbean pupils and of negative judgements about Caribbean speech. These two possibilities are not mutually exclusive; and indeed might reinforce each other. Furthermore, it might also be that the tests of reading and mathematics are themselves *de facto*, overtly or covertly, biased against the Caribbean-heritage pupils, because of cultural, linguistic or other reasons.

A comparison of actual average performance scores with the 'predicted scores' (i.e. with what could have been expected on the basis of the primary head teacher's assessment of verbal reasoning, taking separate account of boys and girls) suggested that teacher assessment

Table 9.14 Actual and predicted performance scores of ILEA fifth-formers relating to CSE and GCE 'O' level examinations, summer 1985, by ethnic group

| Ethnic group | Average performance score | | Difference |
	Actual	Predicted	
Indian	25.3	16.3	+9.0
African Asian	23.0	15.7	+7.3
Pakistani	22.0	15.9	+6.1
South East Asian	22.9	17.5	+5.4
'Others'	21.1	16.5	+4.6
African	19.2	15.3	+3.9
Greek	17.7	14.3	+3.4
Arab	15.4	12.9	+2.5
Bangladeshi	12.8	10.8	+2.0
Turkish	12.4	11.6	+0.8
Caribbean	13.9	14.2	– 0.3
White British	15.4	16.6	– 1.2
All (n = 14,501 pupils)	15.9	15.9	

Source: Adapted from Kysel 1988: Table 5
Note: The 'predicted performance scores' were obtained as follows. First, the actual mean performance scores were calculated separately for girls and boys within each of the three verbal reasoning categories used by primary heads. The appropriate mean was then assigned to each pupil depending on sex and verbal reasoning category. Finally, from this, the mean 'predicted score' for each ethnic group was calculated.

did tend to be biased against ethnic minority pupils generally, and marginally in favour of White British pupils. Thus, while the actual performance score of the White British was worse than their 'predicted score', it was better for every single ethnic minority group except for the Caribbeans, for whom the two scores were about the same (Table 9.14).

The position of the Caribbeans could plausibly be explained in part by their specific, negatively perceived linguistic situation – that is, that they may often speak, and are often seen as speaking, low status Creole or low status Black British English (see Taylor 1981: 202–3). Their linguistic situation, however, is often negatively perceived, not only in the sense that they are perceived as speaking these low level status languages, which tend to be equated with 'bad English', but also in the sense that they are perceived plain and simply as being linguistically deficient since such 'bad English' is perceived as their only language. 'Asians' too are often thought of as speaking 'bad English'. The difference, however, is that this is seen as a second language for them, and language provisions are often made for them, but not for Caribbeans (Taylor 1981: 76–7, 82). It might be, then, that neither the verbal reasoning assessment of the Caribbeans, nor their scores on the tests of reading and Mathematics, nor their examination results do them justice.

Of course, many other and interrelated factors, besides language and the way the Caribbeans' language is perceived, are important. Kysel's data do not, however, permit us to relate performance to such factors (social class or racism for instance) any more than they do to language or to the perceptions of and assumptions about the language of the Caribbean-heritage pupils. In general, many of the problems that have been noted with other studies also apply to Kysel's data. For example, little information is given about how pupils were identified as belonging to the different ethnic groups. Also, as indicated above, the various measures used may well be open to bias. Furthermore, the data refer only to the ILEA and cannot therefore be taken as generally represent-ative. It seems clear, however, from Kysel's data that the ILEA education system, for whatever reasons, was seriously failing a large proportion of its Caribbean-heritage children, and also of some other minority ethnic children, notably the Turkish, the Bangladeshi and the Arabs.

Urban comprehensives: 1981–86

Smith and Tomlinson (1989) carried out a study between 1981 and 1986 of nineteen multiracial urban comprehensives in four local education authorities in different parts of England. They found that performance varied more across schools than across ethnic groups within schools (Smith and Tomlinson 1989: 281 and 305). In schools where 'Whites' did well, so too did ethnic minority pupils on the whole. They found (Smith and Tomlinson 1989: 136 and 142) that among the 'Asians' in the first year of secondary schooling the 'Bangladeshi' children had the lowest level of initial performance, followed by the 'Pakistanis', then by the 'Indians' and other 'South Asians', with the 'African Asians' doing best, although even they achieved just below the average. The 'West Indian' children at this stage achieved overall a little above the 'Indians' in reading, but below them (although distinctly better than the 'Bangla-deshis' and 'Pakistanis') in mathematics. However, the 'West Indian' girls performed consistently better than the 'West Indian' boys.

When it came to GCE 'O' Level and CSE results, Smith and Tomlinson (1989: 245 and 253) found that 21 per cent of Whites had three or more higher grade passes compared with 19 per cent of the West Indians and 18 per cent of the South Asians. In English language the West Indians, with 26 per cent receiving higher grades, did better than both the Whites (23 per cent) and the South Asians (18 per cent) (Smith and Tomlinson 1989: 248 and 261). But in mathematics things were different: 18 per cent of Whites obtained higher grades compared with 15 per cent of South Asians and 11 per cent of West Indians (Smith and Tomlinson 1989: 248 and 261). In science the percentages were: South Asians 15; Whites 14; West Indians 11 (Smith and Tomlinson (1989: 261).

Smith and Tomlinson (1989: 306) enunciate the somewhat ambiguous 'conclusion' that 'school effectiveness is an issue for racial [sic] minorities in much the same way that it is for everyone else'. Yet they go on to speak of some of the specific needs of 'cultural minorities' (Smith and Tomlinson 1989: 306–7). They also make the undocumented claim that 'overt racism' is not a 'serious problem in multi-ethnic schools' (Smith and Tomlinson 1989: 306). The findings and the literature referred to in the present book must at least bring that claim into question. Moreover, they remain silent about covert racism – and its likely consequences and perpetuation (not only in multiethnic but also in all-White schools). Their bald claim is all the more remarkable in view of the difficulties they faced (Smith and Tomlinson 1989: 30–1) in finding local education authorities and schools to take part in the project and especially in view of the defensiveness of the teachers, who held the misguided belief that 'the enlightened are "colour-blind"', and who were hypersensitive about any enquiry into the performance of ethnic minorities, especially West Indians, and even more about any enquiry into racism. In view of these difficulties, of the purposive nature of the sampling, and of the identified inaccuracy of teachers' assessment of the ethnicity of pupils other than the White British and the South Asians (Smith and Tomlinson 1989: 236), it cannot be assumed that Smith and Tomlinson's findings are representative even of multiethnic schools in urban areas – let alone more widely. The fact that the findings did not highlight racism, either overt or covert, very possibly has much to do with the difficulties faced and especially the methods used – in particular the areas investigated and those left unexplored, the questions asked and those left unasked.

RESEARCH LIMITATIONS

I have indicated from time to time that the various studies finding that Caribbean pupils are poorly placed suffer from certain shortcomings and limitations. I shall now focus further on such limitations.

Despite Tomlinson's claims (1983: 130), a good deal of the research on Caribbean pupils – and indeed on other ethnic minority pupils – is small-scale. Her tally (Tomlinson 1983: 28) of 'large-scale', 'medium-scale' and 'small-scale' studies is misleading since it omits many of the 'smaller-scale' studies, including Figueroa 1974, Stone 1981, Watson 1973 and Wiles 1968. It also lists several studies as large-scale where the Caribbean component is small – and in some cases very small indeed. Clearly, it is the size – and representativeness – of the Caribbean sub-sample that is important if one is drawing conclusions specifically about Caribbean pupils. There is also some 'double-counting' as far as the 'large-scale' studies are concerned.

Another limitation of many of the studies on Caribbean – and other ethnic minority – pupils is that they often (including many of the larger-scale studies) relate to conurbations and inner-city areas with substantial ethnic minority populations. These are often deprived areas where the mean performance in school often tends to fall below the national average. Many of the studies were carried out in London, especially in Inner London. Yet, almost half of the Caribbean population and more than half of the Asian population live outside Greater london (CRE 1978, Taylor with Hegarty 1985: 49). Furthermore, many of the studies rely on 'opportunity samples'. One cannot therefore assume the representative nature of the findings.

Perhaps an even more serious limitation, related to this last point, is that adequate controls are seldom introduced in the research to ensure that in comparisons between Caribbean, Asian, other ethnic minority and White pupils, like is being compared with like – in terms, for instance of social class or learning opportunities. When in fact Bagley (1971) carefully matched 50 Caribbean and 50 White primary school children on a range of factors he found that the Caribbeans had a mean IQ of 105.7 compared with the White score of 103.2 – though this difference was not statistically significant.

Yet another problem with the measures and instruments used in many of the studies, is the reliance on teacher assessment (or on reports by head teachers or other professionals) in the categorization of pupils as 'West Indian', 'Asian' or otherwise, and in the measurement of attainment, linguistic competence, 'adjustment' or the like. But in view of the stereotypes, ignorance, confusion and even prejudice and racism on the part of many teachers and other professionals – see, for example, Coard (1971), Green (1972), Rutter *et al.* (1974), Allen and Smith (1975), Brittan (1976), Driver (1977), Edwards (1978), Mabey (1981), Tomlinson (1982), Carrington (1983), Wright (1986), and Chapters 6 and 7 above – the use of teacher assessment (or assessment by other personnel) must raise serious doubts about the reliability and especially the validity of the resulting data. This is underlined by Smith and Tomlinson's finding (1989: 236) referred to earlier.

A related point is the odd definition of 'immigrant' pupils which the

DES previously used. 'Immigrant' pupils included children born in the UK (!) to parents who had come to Britain not more than 10 years previously (!!) – thus excluding increasingly more and more Black English children as the years passed. Moreover, in practice this definition may well have resulted in a good deal of unreliability in the returns made by head teachers. For instance, did they always have or seek reliable information on the place of birth and date of parents' arrival in the UK? The net effect may well have been to exclude from these statistics a good many children who were quite well placed educationally. Perhaps this affected Caribbean pupils in particular, because of the specific stereotypes held of them, because their names are often not distinctive (or may even be Asian) and since the Caribbean post-war migration predated that from the Indian subcontinent and especially the more middle-class migration of Indians and East African 'Asians'. Such points are relevant, not only to the DES definition of 'immigrant', but to any study using teacher assessment of ethnicity, as indicated above in relation to the Swann Report.

One particular aspect of teacher assessment of ethnicity already alluded to that has so far received little attention has to do with how teachers categorize Caribbeans who are not 'Afro', and especially Indo-Caribbeans. It does not seem to be generally realized that a large proportion of people from the Caribbean do not fit the usual image in Britain of the 'Jamaican' or the 'West Indian', and indeed that a substantial proportion of Caribbean people are not 'Afro' at all.

Another basic problem with measures in many of the studies is that of using an instrument in Standard British English with children who are not fluent in that dialect. It is well established (see, for example, Alleyne 1962, Vernon 1969, Houghton 1970, McFie and Thompson 1970, Hudson 1971, Karier 1976 and Kamin 1977) that 'intelligence' tests, and perhaps especially verbal tests (certainly if not given in the testee's mother tongue) tend to be culturally, ideologically and socially biased. To administer a verbal reasoning test in Standard British English to non-standard British English speakers is to measure the level of their *Standard British English* competence more than that of their *verbal reasoning*. Not surprisingly the first large-scale study by the ILEA (1968) found that the performance of 'immigrants' related to their knowledge of Standard British English.

Of course, a sound knowledge of Standard British English is necessary in British society. But that is a different point; and does not justify taking a score, that must largely be a function of Standard British English competence, as an unproblematic measure of 'verbal ability' – and even less of 'general ability'. The verbal ability of children for whom

Standard British English is a second language – or dialect – and who score low in a verbal ability test in the medium of Standard British English, might in fact be very high in their own first language or dialect whether that is a Creole, an Indian language, some other language, or indeed a non-standard dialect of English. And their verbal ability might also be high in more than one other language – and that might go entirely unrecognized.

Furthermore, many of the studies use CSE or GCE examination results as a major measure of achievement, but these school-leaving examinations, like most other tests of attainment in Britain, and like the tests of 'ability' mentioned above, also assume competence in Standard British English – as well as familiarity with many cultural phenomena or contexts that might be foreign to many ethnic minority pupils (see Chapters 7 and 8). It is therefore difficult to know, as far as minority ethnic children are concerned, to what extent these examinations measure particular bodies of knowledge and particular related skills or competence in Standard British English and, more generally, in a particular (British) culture. It is, of course, important in many walks of life in Britain to do well in these examinations, but one should be wary of the inferences that are drawn relating to those who do badly in them and of the assumptions that are built into those inferences.

CARIBBEAN PUPILS: HIGH ACHIEVEMENT?

What seems clear in general, however, is that whatever the limitations of the available research, much of it suggests that many Black minority ethnic pupils and especially those of Caribbean background overall often receive relatively poor results and are often badly placed within the British education system. However, not all of the findings we have seen support the common view of 'overachievement' by Asians and 'underachievement' by Caribbeans. There is also some other evidence of good performance by Caribbean pupils on various ability and attainment tests, although the studies concerned have their limitations too.

Bagley (1982) in a re-analysis of the National Child Development Study (Davie *et al.* 1972), found that some Caribbean pupils came out very well on the Draw-a-Man test used to identify gifted children. In 1965, when the children were 7 years old, a higher proportion (4 per cent) of the Caribbean pupils than of pupils in any of the other ethnic groups, including the White British, fell in the highly gifted group. Stones (1979) carried out a study of thirty Caribbean and thirty White British children in a Midlands inner-city school. When they were taught in ways consistent with the principles contained in the Raven's Progressive Matrices Test, he found little difference in the performance on this test of the Caribbean and White British pupils. Mackintosh *et al.* (1988: 91) in a study of 7-, 9- and 11-year-old children in three south-east Midlands towns found that in 1985/6 West Indians performed better than Indians and Pakistanis, but somewhat less well than White pupils on tests of vocabulary, non-verbal reasoning, reading and mathematics.

Some studies, again limited, also produce some evidence of good performance by Caribbeans on school-leaving examinations. Rutter (1982) reported CSE and GCE results for examinations taken in the fifth and up to the end of the sixth form between 1976 and 1978 by pupils in twelve non-selective Inner London schools, a subset of a cohort of pupils who were originally studied at age 10 (Yule *et al.* 1975). Rutter found that, altogether, the Caribbeans did slightly better than Whites:

> 26 per cent had 1 to 4 'O' levels compared with 24 per cent of whites, and a further 19 per cent had 5 or more 'O' levels compared with 11 per cent of whites . . . only 18 per cent of blacks left school without any graded passes in CSE or 'O' levels, compared with 34 per cent of whites.
>
> (Rutter 1982)

But the best known study showing good achievement in GCE 'O' level and CSE examinations is that by Driver (1980). He investigated combined GCE 'O' level and CSE examination results in 1975–7 of 2,310 16-year-old school-leavers from five inner city schools. Of these school-leavers 590 were Caribbean. Driver found that these, especially the girls, on the whole did somewhat better than their White British school peers.

It must be noted, however, not only that Driver's sample cannot be taken as representative – like a number of other samples on the basis of which claims about Caribbean 'underachievement' are made; but also that the unit system he used to score various levels of passes probably tended to inflate the value of lower level results and to deflate that of the higher level passes. In any case, even though these Caribbean leavers as a whole may be doing somewhat better than their White British school peers locally, their performance was still not as good as their peers nationally (Taylor 1981: 21). It is interesting, however, that Driver's study is the only one which Taylor (1981: 113-122) subjects to a minute and searching critical analysis. Still, she concludes that: 'it is clear that not all pupils of West Indian origin are under-achieving and . . . some are indeed attaining relatively high results' (Taylor 1981: 122).

Driver's study does remind us that even if *generally* and on *average* the situation of Caribbean pupils in Britain is not very good, the matter is complex and it is difficult to discuss it without oversimplifying and falling into stereotypes.

CONCLUSIONS: EDUCATIONAL INEQUALITY

'Underachievement' and the pathological model

The notion of 'underachievement', as we have seen, is salient in reports and reviews on Caribbean-heritage pupils in British schools. But this common conceptualization is misleading. First of all, many Caribbeans do well in the British education system – and more widely in society; but one seldom focuses on them. The Caribbean as problem seems to fit the dominant assumptions better.

This notion of 'underachievement' in fact tends to be used within an atomistic and pathological frame of reference. The large range of factors considered in the literature in seeking to account for Caribbean – and more widely ethnic minority – 'underachievement' tends to be treated atomistically in two senses. First, the factors have often been treated as isolable and as functioning independently, rather than in an interactive way. Second, there has been a stress on supposed individual characteristics and background. Moreover, these various factors tend to be viewed within a pathological perspective in so far as there has tended to be a search for what might be 'wrong' with, or 'problematical', 'deficient' or 'deviant' about, ethnic minority children, and their backgrounds. This has perhaps been particularly the case in views about the Caribbeans (see, for example, Taylor 1981, 1987 and 1988, and Taylor with Hegarty 1985; see also Troyna 1988 for a critique of 'cultural deficit' perspectives).

Thus, Caribbean pupils' supposed identity, self-concept and self-esteem problems have been much emphasized. So has the question about whether they might be of below average intelligence – a question about a whole, diverse group which is only plausible within a racist frame of reference. Supposed problems in motivation and cultural factors have also been highlighted. Attention has been focused, too, on 'migration shock', 'culture shock', degree of identification with the 'host' community, child-minding patterns, 'female dominance', and other aspects of family life and family organization – often within a 'problem' orientation. Parents' and pupils' attitudes towards education have sometimes been thought to be negative or inadequate, although evidence to the contrary has been provided by Hill (1968), Evans (1972), Figueroa (1974), Jelinek (1977), Dawson (1978), Rex and Tomlinson

(1979), Stone (1981), Rutter (1982), Smith and Tomlinson (1989: 91) and others. Sometimes the focus has been on the 'problems' of adjustment to British educational practices, differences between home and school (especially with respect to discipline), parents' educational background, pupils' early education, length of education in Britain, and length of stay in Britain. Supposed 'language problems' and 'linguistic deprivation' have also received attention. Socio-economic background has been considered too, but mainly within the context of social disadvantage and along with related factors such as quality of accommodation.

Some recent examples of a pathological perspective are to be found in Roberts (1988) and Dawson (1988). As we have seen above, the research findings discussed by Roberts (1988) could lead one to ask whether it might be the education system which is failing the Caribbean heritage pupils. Yet many of the initiatives undertaken following on from the study (Roberts 1988: 106–110) seemed to assume that the problems lay in the culture, language, family background or individual characteristics of the minority ethnic pupils. Scarr had indeed been asked to investigate such matters; but *not* teacher attitudes – nor, presumably, institutional racism. The initiatives undertaken did not include any searching review of the education service nor of the curriculum, organization, practices and procedures of the schools. Admittedly, an Adviser for Multicultural Education was appointed, and he has developed an Intercultural Support Service. The question remains about the frame of reference within which it works, and about what impact it can have on the mainline service.

The study by Dawson (1988) reported on above also did not include any data on the curriculum, teacher expectations, educational practices, processes or structures – none on discrimination or racism in any sense. Dawson (1988: 145) admittedly takes the view that her findings are not to be seen as 'measures of innate ability or "intelligence"' – though it is significant that it should even be thought necessary to state this. However, she is instead inclined to consider that:

> differences in cultural background and language, together with the socioeconomic deprivation common to most ethnic minority groups contribute to a large extent to the basic 'underpreparedness' of minority children for English education.
>
> (Dawson 1988: 143)

It could be argued equally that English education is 'unprepared' for ethnic minority children, especially Black and in particular Caribbean-heritage children – although it is its duty so to be prepared, and it has had at least three decades to start adjusting.

An example of how subtly the pathological view of Caribbeans – and the broader frame of reference in which they and other minority ethnic groups are seen – can operate is provided in the paper by Baynes (1983) on 'multicultural education as exemplified in the Stationers' Company's School', North London. This is the same school, a boys' school, in which I had some 20 years ago the experiences I referred to in the introduction – although, of course, a very great deal has changed since then. Baynes points out that in 1979 only 5 per cent of Caribbeans, compared with 30 per cent of the White British, 27 per cent of the 'Cypriots' and 23 per cent of 'Asians' had entered university from the school. (He lists what I take to be the White British under the rubric of the 'British Isles' – as though most of the ethnic minority pupils are not themselves from the British Isles. Similarly, he lists the Caribbeans under 'West Indies', the Cypriots under 'Cyprus' and the 'Asians' under 'Asia' – as though these pupils were all born in those places rather than in Britain.) He also indicates that some Caribbean boys do very well, one of them having obtained the best 'O' level result in the school in 1980. He then says 'I should dearly like to see a boy from the Caribbean win an open scholarship for Oxford or Cambridge, since I believe this will do more than anything else for the confidence of his community'. But what evidence *is* there that 'his community' lacks confidence? Why the regret (Baynes 1983: 72–3) that Caribbeans do not seem to form one close-knit community? They have their roots after all in several different nation states. Baynes (1983: 75) also implies that minority ethnic people are somehow 'beset by problems of identity'. He suggests too, without providing any evidence, that the single parent family is a major explanation of poor educational performance, and implies that this affects especially the Caribbean boys. On the contrary, Smith and Tomlinson (1989: 137, 144, 148) have reported findings which indicate that there is no association between the achievement of the Caribbeans and single parent households. Finally, Baynes (1983: 75) stresses that 'the indigenous [sic] are in ... a minority of 25%' in the school. Actually, the table on page 67 of Baynes 1983 shows that in 1979 the White British at 31 per cent of the school roll constituted the largest ethnic 'group' in the school. Why put all the other ethnic groupings together as 'non-indigenous', and suggest they are in the majority when they are made up of boys from such diverse backgrounds? The two next largest groupings were those with roots in the 'West Indies' at 22 per cent and those of Cypriot origin at 20 per cent. Again, this 'West Indian' grouping is itself something of a construction. Baynes (1983: 73) himself indicates that 'their' Caribbean families came from '11 separate islands, and Guyana'.

Instead of focusing just on individual characteristics in isolation from each other and interpreting them pathologically, one needs to look at the context, at how different factors interact and at relationships – especially human relationships involving mutual interpretations. In so far as contexts have been considered, they have often tended to be home contexts and the contexts of ethnic minority cultures; but the context of the school, of the education system and the wider social context must be taken centrally into account. To make a fair comparison of what two people have learned, one should ensure that they have had similar or comparable learning opportunities and experiences. One must ensure that they have both been equitably treated in educational and related terms. One must also ensure that the tests of ability and attainment used are valid and culture-fair. But the common conceptualization in terms of 'underachievement' often tends simply to take it for granted that this is so.

The discourse of 'underachievement' also tends to assume as unproblematic, or at least as valid, the key concepts built into it. Yet, the very notion of fixed and determinable levels of ability and, in particular, of 'general intelligence' is problematic. Intelligence is not a talent buried in the psyche, but a living relationship that alters and develops (see Vernon 1969). Even if one accepted the trivial definition that intelligence is what intelligence tests measure, there would still be questions about whether the same intelligence test measures the same characteristics in different individuals, especially individuals from different cultures and linguistic groups, and also whether it measures them with the same efficiency. More technically, tests like the modified Stanford-Binet tests have not been standardized on Caribbean and Asian populations in the UK (Verma and Mallick 1982), and tend to be culturally and linguistically biased to the detriment of such pupils. (On the cultural and ideological bias built into such tests, see, for instance, Karier 1976; and Kamin 1977.)

Structures, processes and inequality

It seems to me, then, that the overall situation of Caribbeans – and of many other Black minority ethnic pupils – in the British education system is very much one of inequality rather than simply of 'underachievement'. Thus, Caribbean – and other Black – pupils are overrepresented at the bottom end of the education system. They have been overrepresented in non-selective schools. They have been overrepresented in lower streams and in non-examination classes. Caribbean pupils in particular have also been overrepresented in ESN schools and, apparently, in disruptive units. (See, for example: ILEA 1967; Coard 1971; Townsend 1971: 56ff; Townsend and Brittan 1972; Figueroa 1984b and 1974, Tables 2.7–2.9 and 7.8; Fethney 1973; Tomlinson 1982; Taylor 1981: 107–11 and 125–31; and Taylor with Hegarty 1985: 294–7.)

However, there is still a dearth of substantial and sophisticated research into how the structures and processes of the education system and of individual schools might be failing to facilitate the full academic development of minority ethnic pupils and especially of Caribbean pupils. There is a need for more research information on overt and covert racism in schools and in the education system, and on how this relates to performance and wider educational issues. It could be argued that it is up to the school, and the education system as a whole, to adapt to the pupils. The school can hardly hope effectively to fulfil its task of enabling pupils to acquire the necessary skills, knowledge, attitudes and ways of behaving unless it is able to make contact with the pupils on their wavelength, and to start from where they are. Important as the classroom teacher is in the school process, the issue here is not just to do with the individual teacher. How do the policies – or lack of coherent, stated policies – of (among others) the DES, the LEAs, the professional associations, and the examination boards, fundamentally influence the opportunities of ethnic minority children, especially of Caribbeans? What of the practices of such bodies? What programmes and strategies – if any – do they have for implementing and evaluating the working of their policies? What of the policies, staffing, organization and ethos of the schools? What of the typical curriculum and its ethnocentrism? What of the teaching materials? What of the assessment and placement procedures? What educational opportunities, experiences and teaching do certain minority ethnic pupils and especially Caribbean pupils typically receive? What, also of the attitudes, stereotypes, expectations and ignorance of many of the teachers and White British pupils? And what of the (lack of) training of the teachers and of the teacher educators as indicated, for example by Craft 1981; DES 1981; Eggleston *et al.* 1981; and House of Commons 1981?

Although adequate research evidence is not available on most such questions, there are nevertheless some pointers. For instance, Craft and Craft (1983), discussed above, have found that although a large proportion of Caribbean pupils stay on in full-time education beyond the fifth form, more of these than of their peers transfer to further education rather than remaining in school. Could this reflect on the treatment or situation of Caribbeans in mainstream schools?

Again, there is some evidence that, compared with White British pupils, the reading scores of Caribbean pupils in British schools are more likely to become worse over the years of schooling (Payne 1974; Little 1975; Mabey 1981). Roberts (1988: 103) also shows that from about age 9 the reading scores of the Black pupils fell behind compared with those of the Whites. Clearly, at best, this does not signal a success on the part of the schools; and it may be directly related to various school processes.

First of all, the issues of language bias, and more widely of cultural bias, and in general the issue of the validity and reliability of the measures used, which have been touched on earlier, apply not only to research. More crucially, they also apply to the tests and assessment procedures used throughout a child's school career. The over-representation of Caribbean children in ESN schools seems to illustrate this. Coard (1971) was one of the first to suggest, on the basis of the early ILEA (1967) figures, that this overrepresentation could be the result of school processes, and in particular of the assessment procedures. These ILEA statistics in fact indicate a significant incidence of misplacement of Caribbean pupils into ESN schools. Coard also states that only a very small proportion of such children ever return to normal schools: once misplaced, their chances of a (relatively) high status education are, in practice, for the most part irrevocably – and unjustly – denied. It may not be insignificant that some White British researchers have apparently found it necessary to minimize Coard's work by labelling it as, for example, 'emotive', 'polemical', 'anecdotal', and 'not research' (see, for instance, Tomlinson 1980; Taylor 1981).

Furthermore, there is evidence to suggest that less dramatic misplacement, misplacement into lower and non-academic streams for instance, also occurs to a disproportionate extent among Caribbean pupils, and – especially when it occurs at a relatively early age – likewise tends to have a long-term and academically damaging outcome. Kysel, in the study referred to earlier, states that:

> there was some indication that when there was a mismatch between the VR [verbal reasoning] band in which a pupil had been placed by teachers and that based on test performance, Caribbean pupils were more likely to be placed in the lower VR band . . . while ESWI [English, Scottish, Welsh and Irish] pupils were more likely to be placed in a higher VR band than their test scores would suggest.
>
> (Kysel 1988: 88)

There is also the phenomenon of what has been referred to as 'channelling'. For instance, Carrington (1983: 61) concludes on the basis of a case study of an 11–16 inner-city comprehensive school in Yorkshire, 'that the overrepresentation of West Indian pupils in school sports teams is, in part, the outcome of channelling by teachers' of such pupils out of the academic mainstream and into sport.

The stereotyping of Caribbean and other pupils – and more widely racist and ethnicist frames of reference – would seem to play an important part in such misassessment, misplacement and channelling, as well as in other aspects of schooling. Thus, Tomlinson (1982), in a study concerning forty children passing into special education (only eighteen of whom, however, were of 'immigrant parentage' and only nine of whom were of West Indian origin) and including interviews with thirty head teachers and with various other professionals, found evidence which suggests that the misplacement of Caribbean pupils as educationally sub-normal (ESN) is at least partly the outcome of stereotyping. Head teachers had stereotypes of Caribbean pupils which corresponded to the criteria they use for ESN placement. They also tended to stereotype Asians, but in ways which did not have similar negative educational implications. For instance, head teachers considered that West Indian children were 'bound to be slower – it's their personalities' (Tomlinson 1982: 164); whereas, 'the functional problems' of Asian children 'were considered to be related to language' (Tomlinson 1982: 168). Tomlinson concludes that 'the actual referral and assessment procedures, based as they are on cultural and racial beliefs of professionals, would certainly seem to work against the children of West Indian origin' (Tomlinson 1982: 167). Carrington's study also indicated that the channelling was at least partly a consequence of teachers' stereotypes of West Indians as having skills of the body rather than skills of the mind, despite 'a substantial body of research suggesting that no credence can be given to naturalistic interpretations of black sports involvement' (Carrington 1983: 51).

Furthermore, Brittan (1976) in a national study of 510 teachers in twenty-five primary and secondary schools with between 18 and 84 per cent ethnic minority pupils discovered widespread academically unfavourable stereotyping of Caribbean pupils by teachers. Mabey (1981) found that teachers tend to rate 8-year-old Caribbean pupils negatively. For instance, they thought that most of the Caribbeans had negative attitudes towards school. Yet, as indicated earlier, others have found that Caribbeans are positively orientated towards education (see, for example: Hill 1968; Evans 1972; Figueroa 1974; Jelinek 1977 and Dawson 1978).

Edwards (1978, 1979) found in a study of twenty student teachers, in which she used tape-recordings, that they reacted negatively to Creole. The student teachers, purely on the basis of the dialect spoken, judged the West Indian speakers as having the least academic potential. Edwards (1979: 97–8) also argues that, 'the stereotyping process leads features of Creole to be stigmatized and to develop connotations of . . .

low academic ability.' The language issue is a separate and central issue, but a large and complex one (see, for example: Le Page 1981; Edwards 1984; and Linguistic Minorities Project 1985). It may be, however, that what matters most here is not the language Caribbean pupils speak, but the misconceptions and stereotypes held about it by teachers – and others.

It is, indeed, not only among teachers that stereotypes of Caribbeans seem common. Besides, the issue is not one merely of stereotyping, but, more generally, as I have argued, of thinking, perceiving, feeling, judging, evaluating, rationalizing, acting and interrelating in terms of a racist (and/or ethnicist) frame of reference. We have seen, for instance, evidence of such frames of reference among White British pupils; and this, too, could have adverse effects on the school careers of Caribbean pupils. Similarly, Edwards (1978, 1979) found negative attitudes towards West Indian Creole among White British pupils. The very ethos and curriculum of a school might have a covertly racist or culturally biased dimension, and as a result tend not to work in the best interests of Black pupils.

Another factor which might help to account for some of the apparent differences in the situation of Caribbean and other ethnic minority pupils, apart from the differences in stereotyping touched on earlier, might be a differential allocation of resources. For example, variables 857 and 853 in Bagley's (1982) re-analysis of data from the National Child Development Study indicate that Caribbean pupils are allocated fewer resources than many others. Also, much has been done about English as a second language for 'Asians', but very little about Standard British English where this might be helpful for Caribbean pupils (see Townsend 1971; Little and Willey 1981). Again, although some (limited) attention has been given to Asian mother tongue languages, even less has been given to Creole or British Black English. Referring to Nandy (1981), Monica Taylor (1981: 234) has reported that Black studies have not much affected practice. That Caribbean pupils have received comparatively little attention where issues of language and culture are concerned is perhaps not surprising, since differences in these respects from the majority in the UK are perhaps less clear cut, less simple and probably less well understood and more negatively stereotyped in their case than in that of other ethnic minority groups.

However, there is evidence which suggests not only failure to cater for Caribbean pupils but that they experience more direct forms of educational 'disadvantage'. Stone (1981) has suggested that often Caribbean pupils are not given fair educational opportunities and rigorous teaching. She, too, argues that stereotyping by teachers tends to direct

Caribbean pupils away from academic pursuits, and to rationalize a 'watered down' curriculum for them.

Wright (1986, 1987) has also produced evidence which suggests that Caribbean pupils are treated unequally in the process of allocation to bands and examination sets. Her findings and interpretations fit well with my own. She carried out 'an intensive ethnographic and statistical survey of two multiracial comprehensive schools between 1982 and 1984' (Wright 1987: 110) focusing on the fourth and fifth years. She found the classroom 'interaction between the teacher and the individual Afro-Caribbean student . . . frequently characterized by confrontation and conflict' (Wright 1987: 110). The teacher often expressed criticism, and frequently made 'remarks or jokes regarding the Afro-Caribbean student's ethnicity and physical characteristics' (Wright 1987: 111). This caused 'considerable distress' and also led to very negative perceptions of schooling. Wright's observations led her to the conclusion that behind this negative interaction lay 'the generally adverse attitudes and expectations which the teachers held regarding these students' (Wright 1987: 111). One teacher clearly did not think anything of telling a Black pupil that if she was not careful he would send her back to the 'chocolate factory' (Wright 1987: 112). Nor did he mind recounting this in another class with Black students and a Black researcher present. And yet he was insensitive enough, to put it mildly, to tell the Black researcher that his Black students had a 'chip on their shoulder about being black' (Wright 1987: 113).

Were these negative teacher attitudes and expectations, this teacher insensitivity and especially this frequent teacher criticism of and negative interaction with Afro-Caribbean pupils associated with depressed educational achievement by the Afro-Caribbeans? In fact Smith and Tomlinson (1989: 163–4, 177–8) found a relationship of low attainment and academic progress with their index of blame (being told that one has done poor work and, especially, being told off). They argued on the basis of their data (1989: 164) that this was much more likely to mean 'that children who are often criticized tend to progress slowly as a result' than that poor progress led to negative criticism. They also found (Smith and Tomlinson 1989: 177) that 'girls tend to receive much less criticism than boys, and south Asians much less than those originating from the UK or from other countries' – which included the West Indies. Could it be that the worse performance of Afro-Caribbean boys than Afro-Caribbean girls is related at least in part to this?

Wright (1987: 123) found that the Caribbeans were treated unequally and 'denied educational opportunities' in several ways, in addition to being more likely to be 'picked on' in the classroom than 'Asians',

Table 9.15 Third-year examination marks and allocation to CSE and GCE 'O' level examination sets in one Midlands school

Pupil	Subject marks (out of 100)				Set placement (GCE = GCE 'O' Level)			
	English	Maths	French	Physics	English	Maths	French	Physics
Caribbean								
A	73	44	58	–	CSE	CSE	CSE	–
B	62	63	60	59	CSE	CSE	CSE	CSE
C	64	45	56	72	CSE	CSE	–	CSE
D	68	37	82	–	CSE	CSE	CSE	–
Asian								
E	51	77	–	55	GCE	GCE	–	GCE
F	60	56	58	–	GCE	GCE	GCE	–
G	61	62	55.5	–	GCE	GCE	GCE	–
H	54	55	–	40	GCE	GCE	–	GCE
White								
I	61	62	–	62	GCE	GCE	–	GCE
J	52	57	55	–	GCE	GCE	GCE	–
K	75	82	77.5	72	GCE	GCE	GCE	GCE
L	54	75	64	72	GCE	GCE	GCE	GCE

Source: Wright 1987: 124.

'Whites' or others. They were disproportionately likely to be suspended or expelled, often not being offered alternative educational provision. Critically, teachers' assessment of Caribbean pupils seemed 'to be influenced more by behaviour criteria than cognitive ones' (Wright 1987: 123), with the result that Caribbean pupils were more likely than others 'to be placed in ability bands and examination sets well below their actual academic ability' (Wright 1987: 123). This is illustrated by comparing the allocation of four Caribbean, four Asian and four White pupils in one of the schools to CSE versus GCE 'O' Level examination sets (Table 9.15). This allocation was done on the basis of third-year internal examinations.

If the pattern shown in the table reflects a general one, it is not surprising that the Caribbeans were underrepresented among those entered for and obtaining 'O' Levels. Yet in one of the schools in the year group concerned the Caribbeans 'entered the school at eleven plus with an average reading age slightly above the whole intake for the year' (Wright 1987: 125).

Wright (1987: 126) thus concludes that 'the education experience of Black students, especially those of Afro-Caribbean origin, may be better understood in terms of "educational disadvantage" or "inequality" rather than in terms of "underachievement"'.

To conceptualize the situation of the Caribbeans – and of other minority ethnic pupils – as one of educational inequality is not to rule out individual characteristics and background – such as self-esteem, motivation and parental support – as unimportant. Rather, it is to place these in a wider context. It also highlights that many Caribbeans may do very well, despite the general situation in school and outside of school, which may often act as a handicap. Undoubtedly, the reality of the situation of ethnic minority pupils and in particular of the Caribbeans is a complex one, to which many factors contribute. But the concept of inequality places these factors in a wider perspective, and points one's attention also to the crucial realities of the structures, dominant frames of reference and processes within schools and outside schools. In other words, this conceptualization points one's attention, to the reality that, despite their great efforts and despite their many achievements, Caribbean people in Britain and some other ethnic minority groups are, on the whole, as already indicated, more likely than others in the population to be unemployed, to be in semi-skilled or unskilled employment, to be low paid, and to be living in below average accommodation (see especially Brown, 1984). Furthermore, the conceptualization of the situation of ethnic minority pupils and in particular Caribbean pupils, in terms of inequality, focuses one's attention on the reality that they are more likely than most to experience discrimination and probably to be seen in negative or narrow and stereotypical ways, as already indicated (see especially DES 1985a, Brown 1984, Brown and Gay 1985, and DES 1981).

Educational inequality is related both as cause and effect to inequality in the society at large, of which it is part and parcel. It cannot be accounted for simply in individual terms, and least of all simply in terms of real or supposed individual characteristics of Caribbean, or other ethnic minority, pupils. Rather, it must above all be understood in systemic and structural terms, and in terms of the characteristics, perceptions, frames of reference and behaviour of the majority population.

In the case of the Caribbeans in particular, the constant emphasis on their supposed educational 'underachievement' can itself be seen as part and parcel of the dominant negative and narrow frames of reference regarding them, and as part and parcel of their unequal location within the society. More generally, the unequal structural realities, and the processes and frames of reference integral to them, are fundamental in accounting for the situation and performance of Black ethnic minority pupils, as well as in understanding the dominant modes of perceiving, conceptualizing and relating to this situation and this performance. But if Black educational inequality and 'underachievement', and in general Black social inequality and White racist and ethnicist frames of reference, are 'constructed' through processes of social relations, social interaction and social interpretation, they can also be 'deconstructed' through similar processes. What is required is radical social and educational 'reconstructing'.

References

Abraham, A.S. (1977) 'Dispute over textbook "censorship"', *The Times Educational Supplement*, 9 September: 10.

Adeney, M. (1971) *Community Action: Four Examples*, London: Runnymede Trust.

All London Teachers Against Racism and Fascism (ALTARF) (1984) *Challenging Racism*, London: ALTARF.

Allen, S. and Smith, C. (1975) 'Minority group experience of the transition from education to work', in P. Brannen (ed.) *Entering the World of Work*, London: HMSO.

Alleyne, H.M.McD. (1962) 'The effect of bilingualism on performance in certain intelligence and attainment tests', unpublished MA thesis, University of London.

Althusser, L. (1971) *Lenin and Philosophy and other Essays*, London: Newleft Books.

Ardener, S. (ed.) (1978) *Defining Females: The Nature of Women in Society*, London: Croom Helm.

Aristotle, translated by E. Barker (1946) *The Politics of Aristotle: Translated with an Introduction, Notes and Appendices*, Oxford: Clarendon Press.

Badcock, C.R. (1975) *Lévi-Strauss: Structuralism and Sociological Theory*, New York: Holmes & Meier Publishers.

Bagley, C. (1968) 'The educational performance of immigrant children', *Race*, 10 (1).

—— (1970) *Social Structure and Prejudice in Five English Boroughs,* London: Institute of Race Relations.

—— (1971) 'A comparative study of social environment and intelligence in West Indian and English children in London', *Social and Economic Studies*, 20 (4) December: 420–30.

—— (1975) 'On the intellectual equality of races', in G. Verma and C. Bagley (eds) *Race and Education Across Cultures*, London: Heinemann.

—— (1982) 'Achievement, behaviour disorder and social circumstances in West Indian children and other ethnic groups', in G. Verma and C. Bagley (eds) *Self-concept, Achievement and Multicultural Education*, London: Macmillan.

——, Bart, M. and Wong, J. (1979) 'Antecedents of scholastic success in West Indian ten-year-olds in London', in G. Verma and C. Bagley (eds) *Race, Education and Identity*, London: Macmillan.

—— and Verma, G. (1972) 'Some effects of teaching designed to promote understanding of racial issues in adolescence', *Journal of Moral Education*, 1 (3): 231–8.

—— and Verma, G. (1975) 'Inter-ethnic attitudes and behaviour in British multi-racial schools', in G. Verma and C. Bagley (eds), *Race and Education Across Cultures*, London: Heinemann.

—— and Verma, G. (1978) *Racial Prejudice, the Individual and Society*, Farnborough: Saxon House.

Bailey, B.L. (1966) *A Transformational Grammar of Jamaican Creole*, London: Cambridge University Press.

Banks, J. (1981) *Multiethnic Education: Theory and Practice*, Boston: Allyn & Bacon.

—— (1984) 'Multicultural education and its critics: Britain and the United States', *The New Era*, 65: 3, 58–65.

—— and Lynch, J. (eds) (1986) *Multicultural Education in Western Societies*, London: Holt, Rinehart & Winston.

Banton, M. (1955) *The Coloured Quarter: Negro Immigrants in an English City*, London: Jonathan Cape.

—— (1959) *White and Coloured: The Behaviour of British People towards Coloured Immigrants*, London: Jonathan Cape.

—— (1967) *Race Relations*, London: Tavistock.

—— (1977) *The Idea of Race*, London: Tavistock.

—— (1979) 'The idea of race and the concept of "race"', in G. Verma and C. Bagley (eds) *Race, Education and Identity*, London: Macmillan.

—— (1983a) *Racial and Ethnic Competition*, Cambridge: Cambridge University Press.

—— (1983b) 'Race prejudice and education: changing approaches', in B. Whitaker (ed.) *Teaching about Prejudice*, London: Minority Rights Group.

—— (1985a) *Promoting Racial Harmony*, Cambridge: Cambridge University Press.

—— (1985b) 'Mixed motives and the processes of rationalization', in T.S. Chivers (ed.) *Rational Choice Revisited*, a special issue of *Ethnic and Racial Studies*, 8 (4): 534–47.

—— (1985c) 'Name and substance: a response to criticism', in T.S. Chivers (ed.) *Rational Choice Revisited*, a special issue of *Ethnic and Racial Studies*, 8 (4): 590–5.

—— (1987) *Racial Theories*, Cambridge: Cambridge University Press.

Barrow, J. (1988) 'The Brent Inquiry: findings and implications', in G. Verma and P. Pumfrey (eds) *Educational Attainments: Issues and Outcomes in Multicultural Education*, London: Falmer Press.

Barry, A. (1988) 'Black mythologies: the representation of Black people on British television', in J. Twitchin (ed.) *The Black and White Media Book: Handbook for the Study of Racism and Television*, Stoke-on-Trent: Trentham Books.

Baynes, R, (1983) 'Multicultural education as exemplified in the Stationers' Company's School', in Council for Cultural Co-operation, *Education of Migrants' Children – Compendium of Information on International Education Schemes in Europe*, Strasbourg: CCC, School Education Division, Council of Europe.

Becker, H.S. (1952) 'Social class variations in teacher–pupil relationships', *Journal of Educational Studies*, 25: 451–65.

Beltz, C. (1985) 'Review of migrant education in Australia', *Education News*, 19 (3) May, 19–25.

Bernstein, B. (1971) 'On the classification and framing of educational knowledge', in M.F.D. Young (ed.) *Knowledge and Control: New Directions for the Sociology of Education*, London: Collier-Macmillan.

Birley High School, Manchester, Working Party of Teachers (1980) *Multi-cultural Education in the 1980's*, (Chairman, A.G. Watkins, Deputy Head), Manchester: City of Manchester Education Committee.

Blumer, H. (1939) 'The nature of race prejudice', *Social Process in Hawaii*, 5: 11–20.

—— (1953) 'Psychological import of the human group', in M. Sherif and M.O. Wilson (eds) *Group Relations at the Crossroads*, New York: Harper.

—— (1955) 'Reflections on theory of race relations', in A.W. Lind (ed.) *Race Relations in World Perspective*, Honolulu: University of Hawaii Press.

—— (1958) 'Recent research into race relations: United States of America', *International Social Science Bulletin*, 10: 403–7.

—— (1961) 'Race prejudice as a sense of group position', in J. Masuoka and P. Valien (eds) *Race Relations: Problems and Theory*, Chapel Hill, NC: University of North Carolina Press.

—— (1969) *Symbolic Interactionism: Perspective and Method*, Englewood Cliffs, New Jersey: Prentice-Hall.

Bolt, C. (1971) *Victorian Attitudes to Race*, London: Routledge & Kegan Paul.

Brandt, G. (1986) *The Realization of Antiracist Teaching*, London: Falmer Press.

Brittan, E. (1976) 'Multicultural education 2. Teacher opinion on aspects of school life. Part 2: Pupils and teachers', *Educational Research* 18 (3): 182–91.

Brown. C. (1984) *Black and White Britain: The Third PSI Survey*, London: Heinemann Educational Books.

—— and Gay, P. (1985) *Racial Discrimination: 17 Years after the Act*, London: Policy Studies Institute.

Bullivant, B. (1981) *The Pluralist Dilemma in Education: Six Case Studies*, Sydney: Allen & Unwin.

Burns, E. (1976) *British Imperialism in Ireland*, Cork: Cork Workers Club.

Carlyle, T. (1853) *Occasional Discourse on the Nigger Question*, London: Thomas Bosworth.

Carrington, B. (1983) 'Sports as a side-track: an analysis of West Indian involvement in extra-curricular sport', in L. Barton and S. Walker (eds) *Race, Class and Education*, London: Croom Helm.

Carter, Bob and Williams, J. (1987) 'Attacking racism in education', in B. Troyna (ed.) *Racial Inequality in Education*, London: Tavistock.

Castles, S. and Kosack, J. (1973) *Immigrant Workers and Class Structure in Western Europe*, London: Oxford.

Cherrington, D. and Giles, R. (1981) 'Present provision in initial training', in M. Craft (ed.) *Teaching in a Multicultural Society: The Task for Teacher Education*, Lewes: Falmer Press.

Chivers, T.S. (1985) 'Introduction: rationalising racial and ethnic competition', in T.S. Chivers (ed.) *Rational Choice Revisited*, a special issue of *Ethnic and Racial Studies*, 8 (4): 465–70.

—— (ed.) (1987) *Race and Culture in Education: Issues Arising from the Swann Committee Report*, Windsor: NFER-Nelson.

Chubb, B. (1970) *The Government and Politics of Ireland*, London: Oxford University Press.

Coard, B. (1971) *How the West Indian Child Is Made Educationally Sub-Normal in the British School System*, London: New Beacon Books.

Cohen, L. and Manion, L. (1983) *Multicultural Classrooms*, London: Croom Helm.

Cole, W.O. (ed.) (1983) *Religion in the Multi-faith School: A Tool for Teachers*, Amersham: Hulton Educational.

Commission for Racial Equality (1978) *Ethnic Minorities in Britain: Statistical Background*, London: CRE.

—— (1985) *Swann: A Response from the Commission for Racial Equality*, London: CRE.

—— (1988) *Learning in Terror: A Survey of Racial Harassment in Schools and Colleges*, London: CRE.

Coogan, T.P. (1971) *The IRA*, London: Fontana.

Craft. M. (1981) 'Recognition of need', in M. Craft (ed.) *Teaching in a Multicultural Society: The Task for Teacher Education*, Lewes: Falmer Press.

—— and Craft, A. (1983) 'The participation of ethnic minority pupils in further and higher education', *Educational Research*, 25 (1), February: 10–19.

Cummins, J. (1981) *Schooling and Language Minority Students: A Theoretical Framework*, Los Angeles: Evaluation, Dissemination and Assessment Centre, California State University.

Curtis, L. (1984) *The Same Old Story: The Roots of Anti-Irish Racism*, London: Information on Ireland.

Daniel, W.W. (1968) *Racial Discrimination in England*, Harmondsworth: Penguin.

Davey, A. (1983) *Learning to Be Prejudiced: Growing up in Multiethnic Britain*, London: Arnold.

—— (1987) 'Inter-ethnic friendship patterns in British schools over three decades', *New Community*, XIV (1/2), Autumn: 202–9.

Davidson, B. (1978) *Discovering Africa's Past*, London: Longman.

Davie, R. *et al.* (1972) *From Birth to Seven*, London: Longman.

Dawson, A. (1978) 'The attitudes of Black and White adolescents in an urban area', in C. Murray (ed.) *Youth in Contemporary Society – Theoretical and Research Perspectives*, Slough: NFER.

Dawson, A. (1988) 'Inner city adolescents: unequal opportunities?' in G. Verma and P. Pumfrey (eds) *Educational Attainments: Issues and Outcomes in Multicultural Education*, London: Falmer Press.

Department of Education and Science (DES) (1971) *The Education of Immigrants*, (Education Survey 13), London: HMSO.

—— (1981) *West Indian Children in Our Schools*, (Rampton Report) London: HMSO.

—— (1985a), *Education for All* (Swann Report) London: HMSO.

—— (1985b) *General Certificate of Secondary Education, the National Criteria: General Criteria*, London: HMSO.

—— (1985c) *General Certificate of Secondary Education, the National Criteria: History*, London: HMSO.

—— (1990) *History for Ages 5 to 16 (National Curriculum History Working Group Final Report)*, London: DES.

Deutsch, M. (1968) 'Group behaviour', in *International Encyclopaedia of the Social Sciences*, vol. 6, 265–76.

—— and Collins, M.E. (1951) *Interracial Housing: A Psychological Evaluation of a Social Experiment*, Minneapolis: University of Minnesota Press.

Dex, S. (1985) 'The use of economists' models in sociology', in T.S. Chivers (ed.) *Rational Choice Revisited*, a special issue of *Ethnic and Racial Studies*, 8 (4): 516–33.

Dijk, T.A. van (1984) *Prejudice in Discourse: An Analysis of Ethnic Prejudice in Cognition and Conversation*, Amsterdam: John Benjamins.

Dillon, M.C. (1988) *Merleau-Ponty's Ontology*, Bloomington: Indiana University Press.

Driver, G. (1977) 'Cultural competence, social power and school achievement – West Indian secondary school pupils in the Midlands', *New Community*, 5 (4).

—— (1980) *Beyond Underachievement: Case Studies of English, West Indian and Asian School-Leavers at 16 Plus,* London: Commission for Racial Equality.

Durkheim, E. (1888) 'Introduction à la sociologie de la famille', in V. Karady (ed.) (1975) *Emile Durkheim: textes – 3. fonctions sociales et institutions*, Paris: Les Editions de Minuit.

—— (1910) 'A discussion on the notion of social equality', in W. Pickering (ed.) (1979) *Durkheim: Essays on Words and Education*, London: Routledge & Kegan Paul.

Edwards, A. (1967) *Marcus Garvey 1887–1940*, London: New Beacon.

Edwards, V.K. (1976) 'Effects of dialect on the comprehension of West Indian children', *Educational Research*, 18 (2).

—— (1978) 'Language, attitudes and underperformance in West Indian children', *Educational Review*, 30 (1): 51–8.

—— (1979) *The West Indian Language Issue in British Schools: Challenges and Responses*, London: Routledge & Kegan Paul.

—— (1984) 'Language issues in school', *Education and Cultural Pluralism*, London: Falmer Press.

Eggleston, S.J., Dunn, D.K. and Purewal, A. (1981) *In-Service Teacher Education in a Multi-racial Society,* Keele: University of Keele.

Ethnic Minorities Unit, Greater London Council (1986) *A History of the Black Presence in London*, London: GLC.

Evans, P. (1972) *Attitudes of Young Immigrants*, London: Runnymede Trust.

Farrell, M. (1976) *Northern Ireland: The Orange State*, London: Pluto Press.

Festinger, L. (1957) *A Theory of Cognitive Dissonance*, New York: Harper & Row.

—— and Carlsmith, J.M. (1959) 'Cognitive consequences of forced compliance', *Journal of Abnormal and Social Psychology*, 59: 177–81.

Festival of India Trust (1982) *Festival Review*, first edition (2), April.

Fethney, V. (1973) 'Our ESN children', *Race Today*, 5 (4) 109–15.

Figueroa, J.J. (1971) *Society, Schools and Progress*, Oxford: Pergamon.

—— (ed.) (1982) *An Anthology of African and Caribbean Writing in English*, London: Heinemann Educational Books.

Figueroa, P. (1968) 'Can West Indian school-leavers in London break the colour barrier?' unpublished report to the Institute of Race Relations, London.

—— (1974) 'West Indian school-leavers in London: a sociological study in ten schools in a London borough, 1966–1967', unpublished PhD thesis, London School of Economics and Political Science, University of London.

—— (1976) 'The employment prospects of West Indian school-leavers in London, England', *Social and Economic Studies*, 25 (3): 216–33.

—— (1982) 'The West Indian experience', in Open University, *Ethnic Minorities and Community Relations: Minority Experience*, Milton Keynes: Open University Press.

—— (1984a) 'Race relations and cultural differences: some ideas on a racial frame of reference', in G. Verma and C. Bagley (eds) *Race Relations and Cultural Differences: Educational and Intercultural Perspectives*, London: Croom Helm.

—— (1984b) 'Minority pupil progress', in M. Craft (ed.) *Education and Cultural Pluralism*, London: Falmer Press.

—— (1984c) 'Educational inequality of children of Caribbean background in Britain', in K. Watson (ed.) *Dependence and Interdependence in Education – International Perspectives*, London: Croom Helm.

—— (1985) 'Racist name-calling in a British school', paper given to the annual conference of the Sociological Association of Australia and New Zealand, University of Queensland, 30 August–2 September.

—— (1986) 'Cosa è L'educazione multietnica? – riflessioni filosofiche e sociologiche', paper given to an international conference on *Regioni d'Europa – Frontiere Educative*, University of Catania.

—— (1987) 'Beyond bargaining in British "race relations"', *Canberra Anthropology* 10 (1): 86–95.

—— (1989) 'Student-teachers' images of ethnic minorities: a British case study', in S. Tomlinson and A. Yogev (eds) *Affirmative Action and Positive Policies in the Education of Ethnic Minorities*, vol. 1 of *International Perspectives on Education and Society,* Greenwich, CT: JAI Press Inc.

—— and McNeal, J. (1969) 'The coloured school-leaver', in House of Commons Select Committee on Race Relations, *The Problems of Coloured School-leavers*, London: HMSO, 198–9 and 207–13.

—— and Swart, L.T. (1982) *Poor Achievers and High Achievers among Ethnic Minority Pupils,* Report to the Commission for Racial Equality.

—— and —— (1986) 'Teachers' and pupils' racist and ethnocentric frames of reference: a case study', *New Community*, XIII, Spring/Summer: 40–51.

—— and Vida, L. (1984) *Examinations in a Multi-cultural Society: SREB Mode 1 C.S.E. History* (report no. 2), unpublished final report, Centre for International Studies in Education, University of Southampton, 59 pp.

File, N. (1983) *Assessment in a Multicultural Society: History at 16+*, York: Longman.

Freire, P. (1969) *Pedagogy of the Oppressed*, New York: Herder & Herder.

Fryer, P. (1984) *Staying Power: The History of Black People in Britain*, London: Pluto Press.

Furnival, J.S. (1948) *Colonial Policy and Practice: A Comparative Study of Burma and Netherlands India*, Cambridge: Cambridge University Press.

Gaine, C. (1987) *No Problem Here: A Practical Approach to Education and 'Race' in White Schools*, London: Hutchinson.

Giddens, A. (1979) *Central Problems in Social Theory: Action, Structure and Contradiction in Social Analysis*, London: Macmillan.

Glass, R. (1964) 'Insiders and outsiders: the position of minorities', *Transactions of the Fifth World Congress of Sociology, Washington, September 1962*, vol. 3, Louvain: International Sociological Association.

—— and Pollins, H. (1960) *Newcomers: The West Indians In London*, London: Allen & Unwin.

Glazer, N. and Moynihan, D.P. (1963) *Beyond the Melting Pot,* Cambridge, Mass.: MIT Press.

Gordon, M. (1964) *Assimilation in American life: The Role of Race, Religion and National Origins,* New York: Oxford University Press.

Green, P.A. (1972) *Attitudes of Teachers of West Indian Immigrant Groups*, unpublished M.Phil. thesis, University of Nottingham.

Hall, S., Critcher, C., Jefferson, T., Clarke, J. and Roberts, B. (1978) *Policing the Crisis*, London: Macmillan.

Harris, R.McL. (1979) 'Fever of ethnicity: the sociological and educational significance of the concept', in P.R. de Lacey and M.E. Poole (eds) *Mosaic or Melting Pot? – Cultural Evolution in Australia*, Sydney: Harcourt Brace Jovanovich.

Hatcher, R. (1987) ' "Race" and education : two perspectives for change', in B. Troyna (ed.) *Racial Inequality in Education*, London: Tavistock.

Haydon, G. (ed.) (1987) *Education for a Pluralist Society: Philosophical Perspective on the Swann Report*, London: University of London Institute Education.

Hechter, M., Friedman, D. and Appelbaum, M. (1982) 'A theory of ethnic collective action', *International Migration Review*, 16: 412–34.

Hegarty, S. and Lucas, F. (1978) *Able to Learn – The Pursuit of Culture-Fair Assessment*, Slough: NFER.

Herdeck, D.E., Lubin, M., Figueroa, J., Figueroa, D. and Almanzar, J. (eds) (1979) *Caribbean Writers: A Bio-Bibliographical-Critical Encyclopedia* Washington, DC: Three Continents Press.

Hiernaux, J. (ed.) (1965) 'Biological aspects of race', *International Social Science Journal*, xvii (i): 71–161.

Hill, C. (1967) *How Colour Prejudiced Is Britain?* London: Panther.

Hill, D. (1968) *The Attitudes of West Indian and English Adolescents in Britain*, M.Ed. thesis, University of Manchester.

Hiro, D. (1971) *Black British, White British,* London: Eyre & Spottiswoode.

Holland, D. (1980) 'The ideology of childhood – a Marxist reappraisal of theories of the cultural and historical specificity of modern childhood', unpublished MA dissertation, Department of Education, University of Southampton.

Home Office (1981) *The Brixton Disorders, April 10–12, 1981: Report of an Inquiry* (Scarman Report), London: HMSO.

Houghton, V.P. (1970) 'The white Jamaican hypothesis', *Race*, XI (3): 342–6.

House of Commons Home Affairs Committee (1981) *Racial Disadvantage*, vol. 1, London: HMSO.

House of Commons Select Committee on Race Relations and Immigration (1977) *The West Indian Community*, London: Home Office.

Hudson, L. (1971) 'Intelligence, race and the selection of data', *Race*, XII (3).

Hunter, Elizabeth (1971) *Encounter in the Classroom: New Ways of Teaching*, New York: Holt, Rinehart & Winston.

Husband, C. (1979) 'Social identity and the languages of race relations', in H. Giles, and B. Saint-Jacques (eds) *Language and Ethnic Relations*, Oxford: Pergamon Press.

—— (ed.) (1982) *'Race' in Britain: Continuity and Change*, London: Hutchinson.

Inner London Education Authority (ILEA) (1967) *Immigrant Children in ESN Schools: Survey Report*, London: ILEA Research and Statistics Group, November.

—— (1968) *The Education of Immigrant Pupils in Primary Schools*, Report 959, London: ILEA, February.

—— Research and Statistics (1989) *1989 Language Census* (Report RS 1361/89 written by J. Sinnott), London: ILEA.

Institute of Race Relations (1982a) *Roots of Racism*, Book 1, London: IRR.

—— (1982b) *Patterns of Racism*, Book 2, London: IRR.

Jackson, T.A. (1976) *History of the Irish Struggle*, London: Lawrence & Wishart (first published by Cobbett Press, 1947).

Jeffcoate, R. (1976) 'Curriculum planning in multiracial education', *Educational Research*, 18(3): 192–200.

—— (1979a) 'A multi-cultural curriculum: beyond the orthodoxy', *Trends in Education*, 4: 8–12.

—— (1979b) Positive Image: Towards a Multiracial Curriculum, London: Chameleon.

Jelinek, M.M (1977), 'Multi-racial education 3: pupils' attitudes to the multi-racial school', *Educational Research*, 19 (2): 129–41.

Jenkins, R. (1966) Address given by the Home Secretary to a meeting of Voluntary Liaison Committees, London: National Council for Commonwealth Immigrants.

Jordan, D. (1984) 'The social construction of identity: the Aboriginal problem', *The Australian Journal of Education,* 28 (3): 274–90.

Kamin, L.J. (1977) *The Science and Politics of I.Q.,* Harmondsworth: Penguin.

Karier, C. (1976) 'Testing for order in the corporate liberal state', in R. Dale, G. Esland and M. MacDonald (eds) *Schooling and Capitalism*, London: Routledge & Kegan Paul.

Katz, J. (1978) *White Awareness: A Handbook for Anti-racism Training*, Oklahoma: University of Oklahoma Press.

Kee, R. (1972) *The Green Flag*, volume III: *Ourselves Alone*, London: Quartet.

—— (1980) *Ireland: A History,* London: Weidenfeld.

Kelly, E. and Cohn, T. (1988) *Racism in Schools – New Research Evidence*, Stoke-on-Trent: Trentham Books.

Kelly, G. A. (1955) *The Psychology of Personal Constructs* (vols. 1 and 2), New York: Norton.

Kelly, J.M. (1967) *Fundamental Rights in the Irish Law and Constitution*, 2nd edn, Dublin: Allen Figgis.

Kerr, Tony and Desforges, M. (1988) 'Developing bilingual children's English in school', in G. Verma and P. Pumfrey (eds) *Educational Attainments: Issues and Outcomes in Multicultural Education*, London: Falmer Press.

Killian, L.M. (1970) 'Herbert Blumer's contribution to race relations', in T. Shibutani (ed.) *Human Nature and Collective Behaviour: Papers in Honor of Herbert Blumer*, New Brunswick, NJ: Transaction Books.

Kirp, D.L. (1979) *Doing Good by Doing Little: Race and Schooling in Britain*, Berkeley: University of California Press.

Kluckhohn, F. and Strodtbeck, F. (1961) *Variations in Value Orientations*, Evanston: Row Peterson.

Kornhauser, R. (1978) *Social Sources of Delinquency: An Analytic Appraisal of Models*, Chicago: University of Chicago Press.

Kysel, F. (1988) 'Ethnic background and examination results', *Educational Research*, 30: (2) 83–9.

Lacey, C. (1970) *Hightown Grammar: The School as a Social System*, Manchester: Manchester University Press.

Lashley, H. (1979) 'Examinations and the multicultural society', *Secondary Education Journal*, 9: 2.

—— (1981) 'Culture, education and children of West Indian background', in J. Lynch (ed.) *Teaching in the Multi-cultural School*, London: Ward Lock Educational.

Le Page, R.B. (1981) *Caribbean Connections in the Classroom: Pamphlet of Guidance for Teachers Concerned with the Language Problems of Children of Afro-Caribbean Descent*, York: Mary Glasgow Trust.

Lévi-Strauss, C. (1966) *The Savage Mind*, London: George Weidenfeld & Nicolson Ltd.

Lewin, Kurt (1948) *Resolving Social Conflicts*, New York: Harper Bros.

Lewis, J.K. (1968) *The Growth of the Modern West Indies*, London: MacGibbon & Kee.

Leyden, W. von (1985) *Aristotle on Equality and Justice: His Political Argument*, London: Macmillan.

Linguistic Minorities Project (1985) *The Other Languages of England*, London: Routledge & Kegan Paul.

Little, A. (1975) 'The educational achievement of ethnic minority children in London schools', in G. Verma and C. Bagley (eds) *Race and Education Across Cultures*, London: Heinemann.

—— and Willey, R. (1981) *Multi-Ethnic Education: The Way Forward*, London: Schools Council.

Little, K.L. (1948) *Negroes in Britain: A Study of Racial Relations in English Society*, London: Routledge & Kegan Paul.

Lloyd, B. and Gay, J. (eds) (1981) *Universals of Human Thought: Some African Evidence*, Cambridge: Cambridge University Press.

Lynch, J. (1986) *Multicultural Education*, London: Routledge & Kegan Paul.

—— (1987) 'Changing attitudes: prejudice and the schools,' in T.S. Chivers (ed.) *Race and Culture in Education: Issues Arising from the Swann Committee Report*, Windsor: NFER-Nelson.

Mabey, C. (1981) 'Black British literacy: a study of reading attainment of London black children from 8 to 15 years', *Educational Research*, 23 (2): 83–95.

MacDonald, Barry and Walker, Rob (1976) *Changing the Curriculum*, London: Open Books.

McFie, J. and Thompson, J. (1970) 'Intellectual abilities of immigrant children', *British Journal of Educational Psychology*, 40: 348–51.

McIntosh, N. and Smith, D. (1974) *The Extent of Racial Discrimination*, London: Political and Economic Planning.

Mackintosh, N.J., and Mascie-Taylor, C.G. (1985) 'The IQ question', in Department of Education and Science, *Education for All* (Swann Report) London: HMSO, 126–63.

——, Mascie-Taylor C.G. and West, A.M. (1988) 'West Indian and Asian children's educational attainment', in G. Verma and P. Pumfrey (eds) *Educational Attainments: Issues and Outcomes in Multicultural Education*, London: Falmer Press.

Maguire, M. (1973) *To Take Arms: A Year in the Provisional IRA*, London: Macmillan.

Martin, J. (1978) *The Migrant Presence: Australian Responses 1947–1977*, Sydney: Allen & Unwin.

Maughan, B. and Dunn, G. (1988) 'Black pupils' progress in secondary school', in G. Verma and P. Pumfrey (eds) *Educational Attainments: Issues and Outcomes in Multicultural Education*, London: Falmer Press.

Mead, G.H. (1934) *Mind, Self and Society*, edited by C. Morris, Chicago: University of Chicago Press.

Meade, J.E. (1973) *Theory of Economic Externalities: The Control of Environmental Pollution and Similar Social Costs*, Geneva: Sijthoff.

Mebrahtu, T. (1987) *Swann and the Global Dimension: Education for World Citizenship*, Youth Education Service.

Merleau-Ponty, M. (1945) *Phénoménologie de la perception*, Paris: Gallimard *(Phenomenology of Perception*, trans. C. Smith, London: Routledge & Kegan Paul 1962).

—— (1960) *Signes*, Paris: Gallimard (*Signs*, trans. R.C. McCleary, Evanston: Northwestern University Press, 1964).

—— (1964) *Le visible et l'invisible*, Paris: Gallimard (*The Visible and the Invisible*, trans. A. Lingis, Evanston: Northwestern University Press, 1968).

Mill, J. (1858) *The History of the British India*, Volume IV (first edition 1818).

Milner, D, (1975) *Children and Race*, Harmondsworth: Penguin.

—— (1983) *Children and Race Ten Years On*, London: Ward Lock.

Mullard, C. (1982) 'Multiracial education in Britain: from assimilation to cultural pluralism', in J. Tierney (ed.) *Race, Migration and Schooling*, London: Holt, Rinehart & Winston.

Nandy, D. (1981) *A Review and Assessment of Black Studies in London Schools*, SSRC report lodged with the British Library Lending Division.

National Antiracist Movement in Education (1985) *NAME on Swann*, Nottingham: NAME.

Newcomb, T.M. (1943) *Personality and Social Change: Attitude Formation in a Student Community*, New York: Holt, Rinehart & Winston.

—— and Charters W.W. (1952) *Social Psychology*, London: Tavistock.

Newsam, P. (1988) 'Policies and promising practices in education', in G. Verma and P. Pumfrey (eds) *Educational Attainments: Issues and Outcomes in Multicultural Education*, London: Falmer Press.

Nuttin, J.M. (1975) *The Illusion of Attitude Change: Towards a Response Contagion Theory of Persuasion*, London: Academic Press and Leuven University Press.

Oldman, D. (1987) 'Plain speaking and pseudo-science: the "New Right" attack on antiracism', in B. Troyna (ed.) *Racial Inequality in Education*, London: Tavistock.

Palmer, F. (ed.) (1986) *Anti-racism: An Assault on Education and Value*, London: Sherwood Press.

Parekh, B. (1986) 'The concept of multicultural education', in S. Modgil, G. Verma, K. Mallick and C. Modgil (eds) *Multicultural Education: The Interminable Debate*, London: Falmer Press.

—— (1988) 'The Swann Report and ethnic minority attainment', in G. Verma and P. Pumfrey (eds) *Educational Attainments: Issues and Outcomes in Multicultural Education*, London: Falmer Press.

Payne, J. (1974) *Educational Priority: EPA Surveys and Statistics,* vol. 2, London: HMSO.

Pettigrew, T.F. (1969) 'Race relations: social-psychological aspects', in *International Encyclopedia of the Social Sciences*, 13: 277–82.

Pickering, W. (1979) *Durkheim: Essays on Words and Education*, London: Routledge & Kegan Paul.

Pidgeon, D. (1970) *Expectations and Pupil Performance*, Slough: NFER.

Polanyi, M. (1958) *Personal Knowledge*, London: Routledge & Kegan Paul.

Price, C. (1969) 'The study of assimilation', in J.A. Jackson (ed.) *Migration*, Cambridge: Cambridge University Press, 181–237.

Raven, B.H. (1968) 'Group performance', in *International Encyclopaedia of the Social Sciences*, vol. 6, 288–93.

Reeves, F. (1983) *British Racial Discourse : A Study of British Political Discourse about Race and Race-related Matters*, London: Cambridge University Press.

Rex, J. (1970) *Race Relations in Sociological Theory*, London: Routledge & Kegan Paul.

—— (1985) 'Kantianism, methodological individualism and Michael Banton', in T.S. Chivers (ed.) *Rational Choice Revisted*, a special issue of *Ethnic and Racial Studies*, 8 (4): 548–62.

—— (1987a) 'Multiculturalism, anti-racism and equality of opportunity in the Swann Report', in T.S. Chivers (ed.) *Race and Culture in Education : Issues Arising from the Swann Committee Report*, Windsor : NFER-Nelson.

—— (1987b) 'The concept of a multi-cultural society', *New Community*, XIV (1/2): 218–29.

—— and Moore, R. (1967) *Race, Community and Conflict*, London: Oxford University Press.

—— and Tomlinson, S. (with the assistance of D. Hearnden and P. Radcliffe), (1979) *Colonial Immigrants in a British City: A Class Analysis*, London: Routledge & Kegan Paul.

Richmond, A. (1954) *Colour Prejudice in Britain: A Study of West Indian Workers in Liverpool, 1941–1951*, London: Routledge and Kegan Paul.

Rist, R.C. (1970) 'Student social class and teacher expectations: the self-fulfilling prophecy in ghetto education', *Harvard Educational Review*, 40 (3): 411–51.

Roberts, J.R. (1988) 'Educational achievement of ethnic minority children in a Midlands town,' in G. Verma and P. Pumfrey (eds) *Educational Attainment: Issues and Outcomes in Multicultural Education*, London: Falmer Press.

Roberts, L. and Clifton, R. (1982) 'Exploring the ideology of Canadian multi-culturalism', *Canadian Public Policy*, VIII, (1): 88–94.

Rodney, W. (1972) *How Europe Underdeveloped Africa*, London: Bogle-L'Ouverture.

Rogers, C.R. (1981) *A Social Psychology of Schooling*, London: Routledge & Kegan Paul.

Rose, E.J.B., Deakin, N., Abrams, M., Jackson, V., Peston, M., Vanags, A.H., Cohen, B., Gaitskell, J. and Ward, P. (1969) *Colour and Citizenship: A Report on British Race Relations*, London: Oxford University Press.

Rosenthal, R. and Jacobson, L. (1968) *Pygmalion in the Classroom*, New York: Holt, Rinehart & Winston.

Rubovits, P.C. and Maehr, M. (1973) 'Pygmalion Black and White', *Journal of Personality and Social Psychology*, 25: 2.

Rutter, M. (1982) *Growing up in Inner London: Problems and Accomplishments* Inner City Lecture, London, IBM/North Westminster, 4 October.

—— Yule, W., Berger, B., Yule, B., Mortimer, J. and Bagley, C. (1974) 'Children of West Indian immigrants, 1: Rates of behavioural deviance and psychiatric disorder', *Journal of Child Development*, 54: 1–29.

Ryan, L. (1981) *The Aboriginal Tasmanians*, St Lucia: University of Queensland Press.

Saunders, G. (undated) *Bilingual Children: Guidance for the Family*, Clevedon: Multilingual Matters.

Scarr, S., Caparulo, B., Ferdman, B., Towers, B. and Caplan, J. (1983) 'Developmental status and school achievements of minority and non-minority children from birth to 18 years in a British Midlands town', *British Journal of Development Psychology*, 1 (1): 31–48.

Schon, D. (1973) *Beyond the Stable State: Public and Private Learning in a Changing Society*, Harmondsworth: Penguin.

Schools Council (1976) *A New Look at History*, (History 13–16 Project) London: Holmes McDougal.

—— (1981) *Examining in a Multi-cultural Society*, (report of a conference held on 25 September), London: Schools Council.

Sharp, R. and Green, A. (1975) *Education and Social Control*, London: Routledge & Kegan Paul.

Siegel, A.E. and Siegel, S. (1966) 'Reference groups, membership groups and attitude change', in M.Jahoda and N.Warren (eds) *Attitudes*, Harmondsworth: Penguin.

Sivanandan, A. (1974) *Race and Resistance: The IRR Story*, London: Race Today Publication.

—— (1982) *A Different Hunger: Writings on Black Resistence* London: Pluto Press.

—— (1985) 'RAT and the degradation of the Black struggle', *Race and Class*, XXVI (4): 1–33.

Smith, D.J. (1977) *Racial Disadvantage in Britain*, The PEP Report, Harmondsworth: Penguin.

—— and Tomlinson, S. (1989) *The School Effect: A Study of Multi-racial Comprehensives*, London: Policy Studies Institute.

Smith, M.G. (1965) *The Plural Society in the British West Indies,* Berkeley: University of California Press.

—— (1985) 'Race and ethnic relations as matters of rational choice', in T.S. Chivers (ed.) *Rational Choice Revisited*, a special issue of *Ethnic and Racial Studies*, 8 (4) 516–33.

Smolicz, J. (1981) 'Cultural pluralism and educational policy: in search of stable multiculturalism', *Australian Journal of Education*, 25(2): 121–45.

—— (1984) 'Ethnic identity in Australia: cohesive or divisive? Educational support for ethnic literacy', in D.J. Phillips and J. Houston (eds) *Australian Multicultural Society: Identity, Communications, Decision Making,* Blackburn, Vict.: Drummond.

Southern Examining Group (1986) *Syllabuses for the General Certificate of Secondary Education: 1988 Examinations*, Guildford: SEG.

Southern Regional Examinations Board (1976–80) *Regulations and Syllabuses for the Certificate of Secondary Education* (1978–82), Southampton: SREB.

—— (1978–82a) *Certificate of Secondary Education Examination papers: History Syllabus R.,* Southampton: SREB.

—— (1978–82b) *Regulations and Syllabuses for the Certificate of Secondary Education*, Southampton: SREB.

—— (1981 and 1982) *CSE 1981 and 1982, History Syllabus R. Marking Schemes*, Southampton: SREB.

Sperber, D. (1979) 'Claude Lévi-Strauss', in J. Sturrock (ed.) *Structuralism and Since: From Lévi-Strauss to Derrida*, Oxford: Oxford University Press.

Spolsky, B. (1978) *Educational Linguistics: An Introduction,* Rowley, Mass: Newbury House.

Stenhouse, L.A. (1975) 'Problems of research in teaching about race relations', in G. Verma and C. Bagley (eds) *Race and Education across Cultures*, London: Heinemann.

Stone, M. (1981) *The Education of the Black Child in Britain: The Myth of Multiracial Education*, Glasgow: Fontana.

Stones, E. (1979) 'The colour of conceptual learning', in G. Verma, and C. Bagley (eds) *Race, Education and Identity*, London: Macmillan.

Strauss, A.L. (1956) *The Social Psychology of George Herbert Mead*, Chicago: University of Chicago Press.

Swart, L.T. (1983) *The Educational Achievement of Ethnic Minority Pupils: A Case Study of an Inner-city Comprehensive School*, unpublished MA dissertation, Department of Education, University of Southampton.

Tattum, D.P. and Lane, D.A. (1989) *Bullying in School*, Stoke-on-Trent, Trentham.

Taylor, M.J. (1981) *Caught between: A Review of Research into the Education of Pupils of West Indian Origin*, Windsor: NFER-Nelson.

—— (1987) *Chinese Pupils in Britain: A Review of Research into the Education of Pupils of Chinese Origin*, Windsor: NFER-Nelson.

—— (1988) *Worlds Apart? – A Review of Research into the Education of Pupils of Cypriot, Italian, Ukranian and Vietnamese Origin, Liverpool Blacks and Gypsies*, Windsor: NFER-Nelson.

—— with Hegarty, S. (1985) *The Best of Both Worlds . . . ? A review of Research into the Education of Pupils of South Asian Origin*, Windsor: NFER-Nelson.

Tomlinson, S. (1980) 'The educational performance of ethnic minority children', *New Community*, 8 (3) Winter: 213–34.

—— (1981) 'The research context', in M. Craft (ed.) *Teaching in a Multicultural Society: The Task for Teacher Education*, Lewes: Falmer Press.

—— (1982) *A Sociology of Special Education*, London: Routledge & Kegan Paul.

—— (1983) *Ethnic Minorities in British Schools: A Review of the Literature, 1960–82*, London: Heinemann Educational Books.

Townsend, H.E.R. (1971) *Immigrant Pupils in England: The L.E.A. Response*, Slough: NFER.

—— and Brittan, E.M. (1972) *Organization in Multi-Racial Schools*, Slough: NFER.

Troyna, B. (1987) 'A conceptual overview of strategies to combat racial inequality in education: introductory essay', in B. Troyna (ed.) *Racial Inequality in Education*, London: Tavistock.

—— (1988) 'Paradigm regained: a critique of "cultural deficit" perspectives in contemporary educational research', *Comparative Education*, 24 (3): 273–83.

Twitchin, J. and Demuth, C. (1985) *Multi-cultural Education: Views from the Classroom*, London: BBC (second edition).

Verma, G. (1987) 'The Swann Report and ethnic achievement: what next?' in T.S. Chivers (ed.) *Race and Culture in Education: Issues Arising from the Swann Committee Report*, Windsor: NFER-Nelson.

—— (ed.) (1989) *Education for All: A Landmark in Pluralism*, London: Falmer Press.

—— and Bagley, C. (eds) (1975) *Race and Education across Cultures* London: Heinemann.

—— and —— (1979) 'Measured changes in racial attitudes following the use of three different teaching methods', in G. Verma and C. Bagley (eds) *Race, Education and Identity*, London: Macmillan.

—— and Mallick, K. (1982) 'Tests and testing in a multiethnic society', in G. Verma and C. Bagley, (eds) *Self-concept, Achievement and Multicultural Education*, London: Macmillan.

Vernon, P.E. (1969) *Intelligence and Cultural Environment*, London: Methuen.

Vida, L. (1982) *Cultural Bias in Examinations for a 'Multi-Cultural' Society: the Case of the History Examinations, CSE Mode 1'*, (unpublished report, Examinations in a Multi-Cultural Society Project), Centre for International Studies in Education and Department of Education, University of Southampton.

—— and Figueroa, P. (1983) *Examinations in a Multicultural Society: SREB Mode I CSE History* (unpublished report to the SREB), Centre for International Studies in Education and Department of Education, University of Southampton.

Visram, Rozina (1986) *Ayahs, Lascars and Princes: Indians in Britain 1700–1947,* London: Pluto Press.

Walvin, J. (1971) *The Black Presence: A Documentary History of the Negro in England, 1555–1860*, London: Orbach & Chambers.

—— (1973) *Black and White: The Negro in English Society*, 1555–1945 London: Allen Lane.

Warzee, L. (1980) *The Education of Migrant Workers' Children. Dossiers for the Inter-cultural Training of Teachers. Belgium: The Socio-cultural Situation of Migrants and their Families*, Strasbourg: Council for Cultural Co-operation, School of Education Division, Council of Europe.

Watson, P. (1973) 'Stability of IQ of immigrant and non-immigrant slow learning pupils', *British Journal of Educational Psychology*, 43: 80–2.

Whitehead, D.J. (1980) *The Dissemination of Educational Innovations in Britain*, London: Hodder & Stoughton.

Wiles, S. (1968) 'Children from overseas', *Institute of Race Relations News Letter*, February/June.

Williams, E. (1944) *Capitalism and Slavery*, North Carolina: North Carolina Press.

Wilson, A. (1987) *Mixed Race Children: A Study of Identity*, London: Allen & Unwin.

Wright, C. (1986) 'School processes – an ethnographic study', in J. Eggleston, D. Dunn and A. Mahdu, *Education for Some: The Educational and Vocational Experiences of 15–18 Year Old Members of Minority Ethnic Groups*, Stoke-on-Trent: Trentham Books.

—— (1987) 'Black students – White teachers', in B. Troyna (ed.) *Racial Inequality in Education*, London: Tavistock Publications.

Yarwood, A.T. and Knowling, M.J. (1982) *Race Relations in Australia*, Sydney: Methuen.

Young, M. (1971) *Knowledge and Control: New Directions for the Sociology of Education*, London: Collier Macmillan.

Yule, W., Berger, M., Rutter, M. and Yule, B. (1975) 'Children of West Indian immigrants – intellectual performance and reading attainment', *Journal of Child Psychology and Psychiatry,* 16 (1) 1–17.

Zimbardo, P. and Ebbesen, B. (1969) *Influencing Attitudes and Changing Behaviour: A Basic Introduction to Relevant Methodology, Theory and Applications*, Reading, Massachusetts: Addison-Wesley.

Index